Waiting for the Rest That Still Remains

Waiting for the Rest That Still Remains

A Biblical Theology of the Former Prophets

Arie C. Leder

PICKWICK *Publications* · Eugene, Oregon

WAITING FOR THE REST THAT STILL REMAINS
A Biblical Theology of the Former Prophets

Pickwick Publications
An Imprint of Wipf and Stock Publishers
199 W. 8th Ave., Suite 3
Eugene, OR 97401

www.wipfandstock.com

PAPERBACK ISBN: 978-1-5326-9549-0
HARDCOVER ISBN: 978-1-5326-9550-6
EBOOK ISBN: 978-1-5326-9551-3

Cataloguing-in-Publication data:

Names: Leder, Arie C., 1946-, author.

Title: Waiting for the rest that still remains : a biblical theology of the former prophets / Arie C. Leder.

Description: Eugene, OR: Pickwick Publications, 2021. | Includes bibliographical references and index.

Identifiers: ISBN 978-1-5326-9549-0 (paperback). | ISBN 978-1-5326-9550-6 (hardcover). | ISBN 978-1-5326-9551-3 (ebook).

Subjects: LCSH: Bible. Former Prophets—Criticism, interpretation, etc. | Bible—Theology.

Classification: BS1286.5 L43 2021 (print). | BS1286.5 (ebook).

In memory of my parents
John (1917–1992) and Nel (1920–2006) Leder

Requiescant en pace

Fecisti nos ad te
et inquietum est cor nostrum
donec requiescat in te.

—Augustine

Contents

Acknowledgments

WRITING A BOOK COMES not by bread alone, but by research and writing, sharp colleagues, and libraries. Hearty thanks to Calvin Theological Seminary for sabbaticals and study grants, to its theological library, and the Interlibrary Loan staff. I am grateful to Ruth Bolt, for reading through the drafts with a sympathetic but critical eye. *Todah* to colleagues at the weekly roundtable where no idea goes unexamined or unchallenged: John Bolt, John W. Cooper, Richard A. Muller, and Calvin P. Van Reken. For polishing the rough edges, thank you editors at Wipf and Stock Publishers. Finally, to my wife Olga, for putting up with the relentless ups and downs of writing, *¡abrazos infinitos!*

Introduction

THIS BOOK COMPLETES A study of the Primary History in two parts. In *Waiting for the Land: The Storyline of the Pentateuch*, I focused on the move from humanity's exile from God's garden presence to Israel's anticipated entry to the landed presence. In Genesis–Deuteronomy this entry remains a future reality for its intended audience who, like God's post-Egypt people, wander in the wilderness of the nations (Ezek 20:35) undergoing a purification to which Exodus, Leviticus, and Numbers contribute the consuming-fire presence of Sinai's covenant LORD. *Waiting for the Rest that Still Remains: A Biblical Theology of the Former Prophets* focuses on Israel's squandering of God's gift of rest from the enemy all around and its ultimate consequences: a second exile, this time from the landed presence of the Lord. Where land is the Pentateuch's promised future, the Former Prophets proffer a future tied to the LORD's dynastic covenant with David and Solomon's dedicatory prayer. Pleas that God hear in heaven the prayers his people direct toward the temple in Jerusalem express hope for the good life in the land, but the prayer's last petition pleads that upon repentance (*šwb*) their captors be compassionate in the land of their captivity. There is no plea for return (*šwb*) to the land from exile (the second petition focuses on defeat in war, not exile). With the diminished role of the land, Israel's future looks more like that of Noah's dove who could not find rest outside the ark (Gen 8:9), God's people cannot find a place to rest the soles of its feet (Deut 28:65) in the wilderness of the nations. Outside of God's promise to David Joshua–Kings do not identify an earthly place, like Noah's ark or the land filled with God's presence, to which they might return. The Gospels point to a scion of David as the hope of Israel, and they with Paul reveal an unexpected temple, the body of Christ, in which God's people may rest from its burden.

    Waiting for the Rest that Still Remains treats each of the books, including Ruth, but not as an academic introduction to this literature as do Satterthwaite and McConville. Rather, as the sub-title claims, it is a biblical theology of these prophets with two foci, the divine presence and the promised rest from the enemies of God's people, both beginning in Genesis. I do not develop this theology based on a reconstructed history of Israelite religion for which Rainer Albertz argues,[1] but on the claims of the canon as a theological text, Rolf Rendtorff's argument in *The Canonical Hebrew Bible*.

Influenced by Brevard Childs, Gerald Sheppard, and others, and without disregarding the contributions of historical-critical contributions to solving tensions in the text, Rendtorff proceeds from the canonical text to answer the question, "how [have] the authors of the extant texts understood them in their present form and how [have] they wanted their readers to understand them?" Rendtorff employs von Rad's "retelling" in order "to bring the theological intentions of the texts into discussion by going step by step into the texts themselves." This he does by retelling what these texts say in the Hebrew canonical order,[2] and then eliciting from that reading ten theological themes, eight from the Pentateuch (the founding document of Israel), and two from the Prophets.[3] *Waiting for the Rest that Still Remains* focuses on what I take to be two aspects within Rendtorff's first theme, creation: the restful placing of the man in the garden, (different from God's sabbath rest in Genesis but convergent in Hebrews 3–4), and the presence of God, specifically in the garden. I then draw those themes from Genesis through to Kings, touch on the post-exilic narratives Chronicles–Esther, and examine the individual books of the Former Prophets with a view to these aspects. To that end I examine the use of *nwḥ* in its verbal and nominal forms in Joshua–Kings, with a view to the presence of God, especially its association with the ark of the covenant. Chapters on the individual books of canonical Joshua–Kings seek to answer several questions. What is the book about? That is, what is the subject matter, what does it tell its exilic-diasporic audience? What is the book about today? That is, what is the text's enduring claim on subsequent audiences who receive it as normative for faith and conduct in the light of Hebrews 3–4's citation of Psalm 95's "today" and the theme of the rest that still remains. What are the book's challenges for contemporary readers? A look at violence in Joshua or the treatment of Jephthah's daughter. How do we hear the book in the light of the NT? These questions are then applied to a particular text, such as the conquest of

---

1. Albertz, "Religionsgeschichte Israels statt Theologie des Alten Testaments," 3–24.

2. Rendtorff, *The Canonical Hebrew Bible*, 2–3. I depart from this by reading the Christian canonical order as found in, for example, the ESV, NIV, and NRSV.

3. The world as God's creation, covenant and election, the fathers of Israel, the promised and entrusted land, the center of Israel's life: the torah, the cult, and Moses. The kingship of David, and Zion.

Jericho in Joshua and Ruth on the field of Boaz. Herewith I attempt to give the preacher an opportunity for one sermon on what I believe to be a text through which the entire book may be heard by God's people. Each chapter ends with a brief reflection on the book's contribution to the theme of waiting for the rest that still remains.

The indefinite article in the sub-title *A Biblical Theology of the Former Prophets* is important. I am not offering *the* theology of Joshua–Kings nor arguing that the presence of God is the center of its theology. The phrase "biblical theology" assumes that the OT is a theological book and that the object of OT theology is the OT and of NT theology their canonical form.[4] Although discontinuous is many ways, the continuity between the testaments, clear in the opening chapters of the four gospels, makes possible a *biblical* theology. Where possible the biblical theological connections are warranted by published studies of the OT and NT, even though sparse as in the case of John 17 and 1 Kgs 8:22–53. You are, of course, free to disagree.

You will not find a chapter on method, but chapters 5–9 illustrate what has been called rhetorical criticism, literary reading, close reading, or careful reading of the text; my preference is for the last two, the first is too narrow and the second easily confused with literary source criticism. I've learned much from Robert Alter's *The Art of Biblical Narrative*, used his translations of Genesis and Samuel in the classroom, and from Jan P. Fokkelman's *Narrative Art in Genesis*, his *Reading Biblical Narrative: A Guide*, and his four-volume study of Samuel–Kings. Samuel Terrien's *The Elusive Presence* began my interest in the theology of God's presence. Finally, during my time in Latin America I learned from Fernando Lázaro Carreter and Evarista Correa Calderón's *Cómo se comenta un texto literario* the basic steps of explaining a literary text. Their first step is *lectura atenta del texto*, a careful reading of the text. Students often found this to be most difficult; they thought they knew the narrative, what it said and how it said what it said. And we were reading the Hebrew text.

A little knowledge of Hebrew is a dangerous thing; translators are traitors. Translations are unavoidable, a little Hebrew and Greek helpful, otherwise you cannot truly compare translations (NIV, NKJ, NRSV, ESV, for example) or understand long-standing disputes centered on the noun often translated "virgin" in Isa 7:14 or whether Rom 5:1 should read "we have peace" or "let us have peace." Reading the OT Hebrew or NT Greek has the added benefit of learning, helpful though they are, that the titles separating sub-units in the translations are not part of the text. You actually have to do

---

4. Rendtorff, "Die Hermeneutik einer kanonischen Theologie des Alten Testaments," 62–63.

your own close reading to discover what the text is about. You'll find Hebrew and some Greek in *Waiting for the Rest that Still Remains*, always transliterated and in brackets before a Scripture reference, for example: "The dove could not find rest (*mnwḥ*, Gen 8:9) for the soles of its feet." If the Scripture reference is located at the end then the Hebrew corresponds to the italicized word: "and there shall be no *resting place* for the sole of your foot (*mnwḥ*, Deut 28:65). The nouns and verbs of the "rest" cluster appear often throughout the discussion of Joshua–Kings for several reasons. First, to uncover the importance of this theme's contribution to a reading strategy; second, to demonstrate the theological importance of its sparse appearances; and, third, a pedagogical intent: repetition reinforces the thesis that the theme of rest is a crucial word-thread in the weave of Joshua–Kings, especially the connection to the other gods and their altars.

The final chapter proposes a specific modern altar that tempts Christian believers: the contemporary culture's materialistic or naturalistic human body as a passive surface upon which desire inscribes what and how it wills. This naturalistic body is the self's playground as were the ancient altars of Canaan. The latter, however, sought fertility; the former seeks to thwart it. In short, the human body is sacrificed to an earthly desire, searching for rest in newly imagined bodily coherences, instead of seeking it in the God who sent Jesus Christ in the flesh to rescue it from sinful desires and set it on the way to the rest that still remains.

Abbreviations

AB	Anchor Bible
ANE	Ancient Near East
BDB	*Hebrew and English Lexicon of the Old Testament.* Francis Brown, S. R. Driver, and Charles A. Briggs. Oxford: Clarendon, 1907
BHS	Biblia Hebraica Stuttgartensia
CBQ	*Catholic Biblical Quarterly*
CTJ	*Calvin Theological Journal*
ESV	English Standard Version
GKC	*Gesenius' Hebrew Grammar.* 2nd ed. Edited by E. Kautsch and A. E. Cowley. Oxford: Clarendon, 1910
Heb.	Hebrew
HBT	*Horizons in Biblical Theology*
IDB	*The Interpreter's Dictionary of the Bible.* 4 vols. Edited by George Arthur Buttrick. Nashville: Abingdon, 1962
Int	*Interpretation*
JBL	*Journal of Biblical Literature*
JPS	Tanakh: Jewish Publication Society
JSOTSup	Journal for the Study of the Old Testament Supplements
NKJV	King James Version
LXX	Septuagint
MT	Masoretic Text

NIDOTT	*New International Dictionary of the Old Testament*
NIV	New International Version
NKJV	New King James Version
KJV	King James Version
NOAB	New Oxford Annotated Bible
NRSV	New Revised Standard Version
OTL	Old Testament Library
PH	Primary History (Genesis–Kings)
TDOT	*Theological Dictionary of the Old Testament.* 14 vols. Edited by G. Johannes Botterweck and Helmer Ringgren. Translated by Geoffrey W. Bromiley et al. Grand Rapids: Eerdmans, 1974–2004
TLOT	*Theological Lexicon of the Old Testament.* 3 vols. Edited by Ernst Jenni and Claus Westermann. Translated by Mark E. Biddle. Peabody, MA: Hendrickson, 1997
WBC	Word Biblical Commentary

1

Approaching the Former Prophets

THE FORMER PROPHETS, LIKE the Pentateuch, is a narrative; unlike the Pentateuch, they are not considered torah, "instruction." Rather, Joshua–Kings evaluate Israel's time in the land through the lens of its compliance with the "instruction" God revealed through Moses. When Scripture uses phrases such as "the Book of the Law of Moses" or "this law" in various translations, the term "law" too easily calls up a disembodied code, not God's redemptive Sinai voice. To remind us of that voice I use the term "instruction" or the phrase "divine instruction." The Former Prophets begin with such divine instruction to Joshua, the servant of God who leads Israel from the desert into the land.

Introduction: From the Desert into the Land

The people Moses led out of Egypt received divine instruction in the wilderness between Egypt and Canaan; there it learned that only the Word of God brings life; there it also experienced divine mercy and justice for its whining and rebellion at the waters of Marah, Massah and Meribah. Forty years later, when the second generation arrives on the plains of Moab opposite Jericho, Moses repeats the instructions their parents had received at Sinai (Deut 1–34; esp. 5:2–5) because the first generation had died in the desert for disobeying God's Word (Num 11–25). Waiting on the plains of Moab, the wilderness behind and the land lying before it, Moses' instructions catechize the LORD's army for entry into and life in the land. Unlike the barren desert, the promised land flows with milk and honey;[1] the

---

1. Because honey is a metaphor for wisdom and fear of the Lord, Israel does not escape dependence on God. Goering, "Honey and Wormwood," 23–41, studies Proverb's treatment of sweet foods in relation to the bodily sense of taste and the role of the mouth.

patient waiting for daily manna or the divinely transformed bitter waters to quench their thirst will only be a memory; the land's abundance will tempt God's people to believe it earns her daily bread by hard work (Deut 8:17). What will the reader find when the narrative shifts from Israel's hard-won daily dependence on the LORD in the desert to a life of relative ease in the land? Will the generation that saw its parents die for rebellion against the LORD live righteously in the land? Will their descendants be faithful to divine instruction from generation to generation?

The Pentateuch keeps the desert instructions alive for every generation of God's people. Close to its center, Lev 18:1–5 summarizes this teaching: neither Egypt, where Israel had lived, nor Canaan, the land which they would enter, has the resources for life in God's presence, only the Word declared at Sinai provides the bread and water of life. The Former Prophets examine Israel's stewardship of the land in the light of this ever-normative desert instruction rooted in the LORD's Sinai presence and transmitted to God's people by Moses. Even though Moses dies outside the land, his instruction will shape Joshua's leadership and direct Israel's conduct in the land (Josh 1:7–8; 16–18; 23:6–13). In this way Moses accompanies Israel into the Promised Land to keep Israel and its leaders (Deut 17:14–20, kings; 16:18–17:13, judges and priests; 18:14–22, prophets) faithful to the LORD's desert instruction.

The Former Prophets' review of Israel's stewardship of divine instruction in the land depicts Joshua's successful leadership (Joshua); the failure of Israel to imitate Joshua and his generation and the rise of the judges (Judges); the rise of the kingship culminating in David (Samuel); and the consolidation of the kingship under Solomon, its subsequent failings, ultimate ruin and the exile of David's dynasty from God's Jerusalem presence (2 Kgs 25:27–30). Ezekiel places the exiles in the "desert of the nations" (Ezek 20:35) where they continue to await the rest from their enemies God had promised Moses (*nwh*, Deut 12:10; 25:19), a rest enjoyed in the days of Joshua (*nwh*, 21:44), but which Israel's fascination with the other gods spoiled (Judg 2:11–13, cf. Josh 23:6–7; 1 Sam 12:10; 1 Kgs 11:5–6; 2 Kgs 16–17; 2 Kgs 23:26, cf. 21:3–6). Hearing the Former Prophets raises questions for its audience. Those in exile and diaspora ask, "When will we again enjoy the rest they received in his Jerusalem (1 Kgs 8:56)?"; God's people of every age ask, "What effort is needed to enjoy rest in God's presence (cf. Heb 4:9–11)?"; today the question is: "What is the relevance of this ancient literature about our ancestors in the faith?"[2] We begin our journey through Joshua–Kings with a brief sketch of how OT Scripture has been understood to provide meaning for its readers since the early Church.

---

2. For a recent discussion, see Moberly, *The Bible in a Disenchanted Age*.

Reading the Former Prophets

The following history of interpretation has four parts. First, a description of the OT's address of its own environment—as in heaven, so on creaturely earth—an address that includes interpretations of earlier texts;[3] second, the reading of Scripture shaped by the analogy of faith, the "pre-critical" exegesis thus named by the modern academy; third, the reading of Scripture as a classical religious text shaped by the analogy of human culture, the critical methodologies of the Enlightenment; and, fourth, the reading of Scripture as a non-privileged text in the shadow of suspicion.

OT as Scripture: As in Heaven so on Creaturely Earth

The ancient world understood heaven and earth, the deities and humanity, to share the same substance, to wear the same garment.[4] Because it shared this garment of "divine" nature it fell to humanity to discern the will of the gods in nature's orderliness, for good life on the earth was the product of harmony with heaven. Because discrepancies between heaven and earth would lead to disorder and dissolution as experienced by political or social chaos (invasion of an enemy; rebellious subjects) or unexpected and devastating natural phenomena (rainfall at harvest time; floods, plagues), it was crucial to uncover the authors of the disorder, expunge them and so to restore harmony. The reason for the irruption of chaos was difficult to discern in a pantheistic universe because the divine will, woven into the garment of nature, the substance humanity and other creatures shared. Thus, experts trained to read livers[5] or the entrails of sacrificial animals, sought to understand ominous signs and to interpret them as expressions of the divine will.[6]

The biblical narrative opposes pantheism; its God and the humanity he created do not share the same substance. By his word God brings into being a creaturely life totally distinct from the divine, but not separated

3. Fishbane, *Biblical Interpretation in Early Israel.*

4. For a helpful summary of the ancient world and Israel's putative distinctiveness, see, Fishbane, "Israel and the 'Mothers'," 49–58. He concludes: "I am inclined to suppose that the accommodation of the 'Mothers' within biblical monotheism reflects a distinct longing for direct and immediate contact with the primordial sources of divine power which pulse throughout the cosmos; that it reflects a longing to overcome a felt alienation from God's concrete presence—from a god, that is, whose very life might be experienced in the world, and not only his will" (Fishbane, "Israel and the 'Mothers'," 63).

5. For an illuminating description of the liver's function, beginning with the ancients, see Selzer, *Mortal Lessons,* 64–65.

6. Nemet-Nejat, *Daily Life in Ancient Mesopotamia,* 196–212.

from it; in fact, totally dependent on divine will. As heavenly speech brings the earth and its creatures into being, so divine speech on the earth, whether in the Garden before sin or from east-of-Eden Sinai, declares its will for humanity on the earth. What today we call "nature" declares the glory of God and his power, but its instruction, even if perceived, is insufficient to teach human creatures how to live harmoniously with heaven on the earth. Only compliance with divine speech articulated in Scripture produces a life pleasing to heaven.

Genesis through Kings depicts the conduct of earthly humanity and subsequently Abraham's[7] descendants—taken from Ur, moving towards the land, receiving the land, exiled from the presence in that land and returning to Ur—in terms of God's speech: in compliance with the Garden of Eden instruction or not; in compliance with Sinai instruction on the way to the land and in the land, or not. OT narrative realism assumes that all creaturely existence owes its being to God and can only fully enjoy it in God's presence; that heaven rules earth, that east-of-Eden humanity is by nature disobedient. It also assumes that God disclosed himself to the patriarchs, to Israel from Sinai and in Jerusalem for redemptive purposes, purposes linked to a special people with a view to dealing with all nations of the earth, to return them into his presence and so live in harmony with God.

This monotheistic literature was heard in a polytheistic, pantheistic world driven by its own conceptions of heaven's rule, but inescapably restless according to this literature because exiled from the true presence of God (Gen 4:12, 14). This literature also depicts how harmony with heaven returns to a rest (cf. *nwḥ*, Gen 2:15) all who comply with heaven's instructions: Abraham and his descendants, and Gentiles such as Rahab and Ruth.

Reading Scripture: The Analogy of Faith

The Church read Scripture realistically, understanding its words to refer to people and things that existed and events that happened: Abraham, David, Rahab, the exile; and it held that these things referred to other things: God, sin, and forgiveness. In short, this mode of interpretation assumed the existence of heaven and earth, and their complex interrelationship as depicted by Scripture. Heaven spoke to earth, and earth was responsible to heaven. Earthly human creatures, Moses, David and the prophets, authored Scripture, but its true author was the Lord God of heaven and earth. Thus Scripture spoke directly to God's OT and NT people. This pre-Enlightenment mode of interpretation was aware of the historical distance between readers

---

7. I will use Abraham and Sarah throughout, irrespective of the chapter references.

and Scripture—an increasingly older literature—but because heaven addresses earthly creatures, and earth is ineluctably responsible to heaven, the heavenly author of these earthly documents addresses his people through them. Historical distance does not create an unbridgeable distance between Scripture's depiction of the deity and humanity, for Scripture testifies to God's involvement in earthly humanity's response to heaven's instructions.[8] Although ancient, these writings distinguish themselves from other ancient texts as Scripture, apostolically normative for the faith and conduct of God's people in all places and all times. This confessional reading seeks to support the faith once for all delivered to the saints.

Over time this mode of interpretation developed the four-fold sense of Scripture. In the fourteenth century, Nicholas of Lyra cited a popular refrain that sets forth this reading as follows: "The letter teaches events, allegory what you should believe, morality teaches what you should do, anagogy what mark you should be aiming for."[9] Thus, for example, Jerusalem refers to the city of David where Solomon built the temple indwelt by the glory of God. This is the letter. Belief understands Jerusalem to be the earthly city of God—his true throne being in heaven—from which he rules his people and all the nations of the earth. This is the allegorical sense. God's rule has a certain shape: the torah goes forth and instructs all how to live under his sovereignty. This is the moral sense. Sometime in the future, all who oppose this city will bend the knee and acknowledge God's rule. All the earth will acknowledge heaven's sovereignty. This is the anagogical sense. Thus, the letter, what you believe, how you conduct your life, what you hope for. Letting Scripture interpret Scripture in terms of these four levels guided Christian reading of the received canon.

Reading Scripture: The Analogy of Human Formation

The pre-Enlightenment mode of hearing Scripture, understanding that God speaks directly to his redeemed subjects, continues to be favored by God's people who seek heavenly guidance for earthly faith and conduct. The Enlightenment, however, launched an attack on heaven that steadily

8. The Antiochene readings of Scripture were more literal-historical and typological than the allegorical reading proceeding from Alexandria, exemplified in Origen's interpretations. "We would not be exaggerating greatly if we described the progress of biblical exegesis as the gradual abandonment of allegorical interpretation . . . . As early as the fourth century, we find in Antiochene exegesis a fairly systematic program aimed at debunking the more objectionable features of Origen's approach." Silva, "Has the Church Misread the Bible?," 47.

9. Lubac, *Medieval Exegesis*, 1 and 15–74, for a discussion of the four senses.

diminished its intimacy with and authority over the earth. Reason's ascent to dogmatic authority led to a practical separation of earth from heaven; earth's garment of natural materiality increasingly came into its own. Classical theism was exchanged for a deism[10] in which universal reason and its values alone would discern the earth's significance; the heretofore intimate ties between the literal and the spiritual senses of Scripture disappeared, becoming an uneasy relationship between the letter as a human historical document and spirituality as a particular faith, like that of Israel, would deal with heaven's will. Israelite religion as recovered from ancient texts cannot directly address the culture of the Christian church;[11] it is but an ancient people's expression of its experience of the divine. Reason's historical and literary judgments guided the reading of Scripture, judging it as it would any other ancient classical text. As with classical antiquity, so too Scripture became more a source to recover universal values beneficial for the formation of humanity.[12] Furthermore, where biblical narrative made claims about divine involvement in human affairs and the church understood Scripture to be divine by inspiration and human by earthly production, enlightened scholarly reading stripped Scripture of divine authorship, leaving merely human documents in its wake. The diversity of biblical documents, as the product of many human authors with its conceptual unity in divine authorship, became a plurality of human literary productions with the conceptual unity located in the historical reconstruction of underlying fragmentary documents and their putative authors, each shaped by reconstructed particular times and cultures. None of these underlying documents—with their putative authors, times, and places—was familiar to the reader of the canonical text. This post-confessional historical reading of Scripture identified Elohistic and Yahwistic sources in Genesis, subsequently supplemented by priestly and Deuteronomistic sources/traditions.[13] Enlightenment interpretation approached Scripture as another human, albeit classical, religious

---

10. See Moore and Sherwood, "Biblical Studies 'after' Theory," 87–113, for a brief discussion of deism's influence in the transformation of Scripture into a classical text.

11. Russell, *Paradise Mislaid*, 43–68.

12. Legaspi, *The Death of Scripture*, 64–68. For critical evaluation and consequences of the higher critical methodology, see also Levenson, *The Hebrew Bible*, 1–32; and, Plantinga, "Two (or More) Kinds of Scripture Scholarship," 374–421.

13. Driver, *An Introduction to the Literature of the Old Testament*, 1–159.

text,[14] which may or may not refer to things,[15] and, in any case, has first of all to do with Israel's ancient religion.[16]

Orthodox Christianity accepted the biblical understanding of a substantial difference and distance between the Creator and the creature, bridged by divine instruction in the earthly sphere, and understood the historical distance of the ancient text to be overcome by divine authorship and the spiritual senses. Critical interpretation emphasized the historical distance between Israel's ancient religion and the Christian religion of the contemporary reader, a separation evident from the modern biblical theological distinction between what a text meant (not means), "a descriptive study of biblical thought."[17] In practice this divided post-Reformation topical biblical theology into the disciplines of biblical and systematic theology,[18] where the former described Israelite religion and theology and the latter the universal embedded in those ancient theological expressions. In North America the biblical theology movement sought to overcome this bifurcation with a focus on the mighty acts of God in history but foundered on the rocks of its inability to locate such acts in history, never mind rooting them realistically in the ancient biblical text.[19] The last quarter of the twentieth century heard calls for canonical readings, not of an ancient text, but of Scripture in which text and reality were not separated. Brevard Childs argued that renewed reflection on Scripture as revelation was crucial.[20]

14. Legaspi, *The Death of Scripture*, 1–26. For a recent discussion, see Stendahl, "The Bible as a Classic and the Bible as Holy Scripture," 3–10.

15. For the controversy on "early Israel," see Provan, "The Death of Biblical History?," 3–35.

16. Albertz, "Religionsgeschichte Israels," 14, for example, writes that research into Israel's history of religion is less subjective (than examining the theology of the OT) because the available data can be better controlled with a historical methodology.

17. Stendahl, "Biblical Theology, Contemporary," 418. For an extended discussion of this description, see also Klink and Lockett, *Understanding Biblical Theology*, 29–56.

18. For a discussion of Johann Philip Gabler's distinction between biblical and systematic theology, presented in 1787, see Knierim, "On Gabler," 495–556. In his 1894 inaugural lecture as Professor of Biblical Theology at Princeton Theological Seminary, then still considered an orthodox institution, Geerhardus Vos treats Biblical Theology as "that part of Exegetical Theology which deals with the revelation of God," thereby clearly distinguishing it from the Enlightenment view of the discipline. See Vos, "The Idea of Biblical Theology as a Science," 6. For a discussion of the impact of this separation of disciplines in the Roman Catholic tradition, see Blenkinsopp, "Biblical and Systematic Theology: The Present Situation," 70–85.

19. See Childs, *Biblical Theology in Crisis*, 61–87, for a discussion of the problems.

20. Childs, *Old Testament Theology in Canonical Context*, 25, writes: "the use of the term revelation within the context of the canon reflects the concern to be open to the theological dimensions of the biblical tradition which can never either be separated

WAITING FOR THE REST THAT REMAINS

The move from a confessional to a historical and critical reading of the biblical text was accompanied by a shift in hermeneutics from a theory of the rules of biblical and theological exegesis to a theory of understanding of any literary text, then about understanding itself, to a hermeneutics as the deciphering of latent or hidden meaning. More recent hermeneutics have exercised a hermeneutic of suspicion vis-à-vis the author or the role of the reader vis-à-vis the text.[21]

Reading Scripture: The Shadow of Suspicion

It is not a step too far to move from a biblical text that requires the re-construction of its underlying sources and/or redactions, to a biblical text whose authorship is dubious but rooted in an ancient patriarchal culture, and thence to suspicion about that text's and/or "author's" intentions. Aided by romanticism's appeal to the self's *Gefühl*, Marxism's materialist under-standing of the self in the class struggle, and Freudian suspicion of the superficial self, historicist textual analysis blossomed into a full-blown bal-kanization of the ecclesial textual community. By the late twentieth century, Scripture, once the privileged text of the Church, had been severed from that privilege by an academic analysis that understood it as a classic text fit for enlightened formation to become the object of a romantic assertion of the self in a plethora of "interested" reader-response readings of this "clas-sic" text, each rooted in attitudes of suspicion: of patriarchal agendas and a variety of socio-political and gender oppressions.

Traditional critical literary and historical tools, developed as objec-tive scientific instruments, found themselves subordinated to the subjective interests of the reader's identity group, each with its own mix of critical, comparative religious, literary, structural, and sociological methodolo-gies. Hence the appearance of liberation theological, materialist, feminist and womanist, post-colonial African, and gender and sexual reorientation studies of the biblical text. Katharine Doob Sakenfeld writes: "No longer, for example, are categories such as Asian voices or even Southeast Asian voices adequate, but groups and individuals from different subcultures of many regions are distinguishing themselves."[22] The location of the Bible as

---

from or identified with the life of empirical Israel."

21. See Palmer. *Hermeneutics*, 33–45, for six modern definitions of hermeneutics; and Thistleton, *New Horizons in Hermeneutics*, for descriptions of contemporary hermeneutics and of the reading process itself. See also, Oeming, *Contemporary Biblical Hermeneutics*.

22. Sugirtharajah, *Voices from the Margins*; Christ, *The Laughter of Aphrodite*;

the Church's Scripture and heaven's interests as such, have been abandoned in favor of a balkanized, horizontal, socio-cultural reading of the Bible as an aid for the self's redefinition.[23]

Reading the Former Prophets as Scripture Today

Reading the Former Prophets as Scripture requires an understanding and acceptance of its theistic depiction of reality in which heaven's will is authoritative[24] for the earth, but especially for humanity as the creature uniquely endowed with a vocation in the presence of God (Gen 2:15–17). Genesis–Kings has an abiding interest in human compliance with divine instruction from the Garden instruction (Gen 2:15–17) to the Sinai instruction as summarized in Lev 18:5, and Israel's failure to comply with the torah of Moses (2 Kgs 17:13–18; cf. Josh 1:7–8). Indeed, Gen 2:4—3:24 defines the fundamental narrative problem as the divine exile of Adam and Eve from God's Garden presence for failure to comply with divine instruction. Genesis–Kings also depicts the solution to this problem: God brings the descendants of Adam and Eve through Abraham and Sarah into his presence at Sinai where they swear allegiance to the covenant's polity. In ironic imitation of the first ancestral pair, these descendants promptly display their covenant disloyalty by worshiping another god. Thereafter Genesis–Kings depicts the highs and lows of the relationship between the LORD and his people framed by the instruction–compliance structure. Genesis–Kings ends as it begins, with exile from the presence of the LORD (2 Kgs 23:27; 24:20).

Scripture speaks to its committed readers today as it did to those of old because the intended audience is that divinely shaped community which accepts this Scripture as God's word and therefore authoritative and definitive for faith and conduct. That is, it speaks to that community indwelt by the divine presence, whether the glory-cloud of the OT or the Spirit in the NT. Indeed, it is a community formed by a consciously shaped canon,[25] whose composition history, along with many of its authors and sources, remains beyond definitive reconstruction. The canon's literary and historical character no more compromises its divine authority than does Jesus Christ's humanity his divinity. Insofar as it is a literary text with realistic claims about

---

Sakenfeld, "Whose Text Is It?" 9.

23. See for example, West, "Indigenous Exegesis," 147–62; West and Haddad, 137–56.

24. On exchanging the authority of the Bible for its function in contemporary culture, see Clines, *What Does Eve Do to Help?*, 45–48; Clines, *The Bible and the Modern World*, 81–101; Tolbert, "Protestant Feminists and the Bible," 11–12.

25. See Sheppard, "Canonization," 21–33.

people and events it is capable of being analyzed as such, with the caveat that both its literary and historical character are aspects of the time and place of its production, insofar as these too can be determined. Keeping this in mind, I read the canonical shape of the Former Prophets with a view to understanding what it says and how it says what it says to God's people. I offer a close reading of the text, informed by other readings with the same and other approaches to the text, knowledge of the ANE's manner of depicting past history,[26] and of the ancient religions of Canaan.

If Genesis–Kings is Scripture, then I am not merely looking to understand a curious historical artifact and what it meant, but what the text means for the reader of the community it continues to address authoritatively. Such a reading will begin with understanding what the text meant for the exilic audience (for more on this see below). It continues with the understanding that what the text meant then (i.e., its claim upon the ancient textual community), continues to have similar significance for the community that reads the OT along with the NT as authoritative for its faith and conduct today. Put in another way, I do not understand the biblical theology of the Former Prophets to be merely a curiosity of an ancient people's religion, but speech about the relationship of the God and the people depicted in that text, without which there is no Christian Scripture.[27]

What follows below is not a scientific reading based on objective methods; the role of the subject in reading any text is undeniable. Neither, however, is this reading merely subjective. I try to listen to what the text says and how it says it in the same way I try carefully to listen to my friend as a neighbor, even though the speech may at times be harsh and unwanted, as in Joshua and Judges, or Jesus' withering woes on the Pharisees in Matthew 23. My act of reading is one of hospitality, not hostility; I seek to be interrogated by Scripture's severe mercy; not it by my culturally acceptable suspicions. Readers of the text in its final shape can and have abused it; basic human nature is tempted time and again to listen to the question: "Did God really say?" I offer this reading, knowing full well that "the first to present his case seems right, until another comes forward and questions him" (Prov 18:17 NIV).

---

26. The literature is varied: it extends from the history of such depiction as reconstructed by source, tradition, and form criticism, to a comparison of the OT to Herodotus and Thucydides, to Assyrian royal propaganda and iconographic studies, to the notion that Genesis–Kings is a Persian production meant to authorize a particular form of the community (the minimalist position on "early" and subsequent Israel).

27. Thus, this is not a theology that depends on understanding the development of the history of Israel's religion, nor on the reconstruction of its literary traditions.

Reading the Former Prophets Canonically

Their Canonical Placement and Implications

The Hebrew canon locates all the prophets, Joshua through Malachi, after the Pentateuch. The name "Former Prophets" describes the first part of these prophets (Joshua, Judges, Samuel, Kings)[28] to distinguish them from the Latter Prophets (Isaiah, Jeremiah, Ezekiel) and the Book of the Twelve. The third part of the Hebrew canon, the Writings, contains the Psalms, Proverbs and Job, the *Megilloth* (Song of Songs, Ruth, Lamentations, Ecclesiastes, Esther), followed by Daniel, Ezra–Nehemiah and Chronicles, the last book in the Hebrew canon. The Former and Latter Prophets in the Hebrew canon form a lengthy evaluation of Israel's compliance with divine instruction in the land (Josh 1:7–8; Isa 1:21–26; Jer 3:6–10; 5:30–31; 6:16; Hos 4; Mal 4:4). The Christian tradition, availing itself of the Septuagint canon, distinguished the so-called writing prophets—Isaiah, Jeremiah, Ezekiel, and the Twelve—from the more narrative historical, Former Pprophets, and moved them as a block to the end of the canon, following Job, Psalms, Proverbs, Ecclesiastes and Song of Songs. Malachi then becomes the last book of the OT.[29] The Christian canon locates Chronicles, Ezra–Nehemiah, and Esther after Kings, Daniel follows Ezekiel, Lamentations after Jeremiah, and Ruth finds itself among the Former Prophets between Judges and Samuel.[30]

Genesis through Esther in the Christian canon form three groups. The Pentateuch and the Former Prophets together depict God's dealings with the nations from the creation of all things in the presence of God, the subsequent exile of humanity from the Garden presence of God to the scattering from Babel, and then from Abraham and Sarah's leaving Ur to their descendants' exile from the presence of God in the Jerusalem. That two exiles from the presence of God frame Genesis through Kings suggests that neither the Pentateuch nor the Former Prophets be read as self-standing units but that in their canonical order form one narrative. Nevertheless, a good reason argues for two sub-units. Genesis through Deuteronomy narrates the story from the creation of all things, the exile of humanity from God's garden presence, the divine creation of Israel, its desert journey towards the land of promise, and its awaiting entry into that land on the Plains of

---

28. The name reflects Zech 1:4: "Do not be like your forefathers, to whom *the earlier prophets* proclaimed."

29. For a discussion on the differences between the Jewish and Christian Old Testament, see Josipovici, *The Book of God*, 29–49.

30. Nelson, *The Historical Books*, discusses Chronicles and Ezra–Nehemiah, but not Ruth.

Moab opposite Jericho. Joshua through Kings, the second group, reflects on Israel's stewardship of the land beginning with the ark's leading her across the Jordan and ending with exile from God's Jerusalem presence. Because Chronicles and Ezra–Nehemiah address the returned exiles, and Esther the exile-become-diaspora,[31] these form a third group.

Three consequences follow from separating the Former Prophets from the Latter Prophets and juxtaposing them to the Pentateuch. First, it creates a long narrative with a general chronological sequence from the creation and exile from God's garden presence to the exile from God's Jerusalem presence. Second, this extended narrative displays two distinct geographic epochs: the large amount of narrative time dedicated to the desert in the Pentateuch signals its importance;[32] the Former Prophets depict Israel's life in the land from the time of its entry, led by the divine presence signaled by the ark of the covenant (Josh 3:1—4:24), to its expulsion from the divine presence (2 Kgs 23:27; 24:33, 20). Third, the Former Prophets frame Israel's life in the land and evaluates her conduct according to the law of Moses (Josh 1:7–9; 23:6–8; 2 Kgs 17:7–23); as in the desert, so in the land, Israel is measured by her compliance with divine instruction. Locating Ruth between Judges and Samuel retards the neat linkage between Judges and Samuel and disturbs the flow of the scholarly defined Deuteronomistic History.

Moving the Latter Prophets and the Twelve to their present position in the Christian canon has a two-fold canonical effect. First, in the Hebrew canon Isaiah 1—even though it begins with a time before Jerusalem's destruction in its own prophetic evaluation—continues the theme of judgment on Jerusalem because it immediately follows 2 Kgs 25; Isaiah also proclaims a new future for Jerusalem. Separating Isaiah from its location in the Hebrew canon ruptures this continuity and abandons the reader to the ruins of Jerusalem and the temple, the ending of Genesis–Kings. Without Isaiah God's people can only pray (1 Kgs 8:43–56) towards the ruins of Jerusalem's temple; and David's throne (2 Kgs 25:27–30)[33] is also separated from Isaiah's prophecies concerning David. The temple rubble and the imprisoned Davidic king together underscore the narrative's purpose: that Israel repent of the sin for which it was justly exiled and place its hope and rest from the enemy in a kingship rooted in the divine promise of 2 Sam 7. Second, the break in continuity of the theme of Jerusalem creates a narrative that begins

31. Levenson, *Esther*, 15.

32. The amount of narrative space dedicated to Israel's desert wanderings varies, depending on how one reads the text. Looking at it from the point of view of the itineraries, these begin in Exod 12:37 and end in Num 22:1. See also Leder, *Waiting for the Land*, 195–209, on the desert epoch in the Pentateuch.

33. Rad, "The Deuteronomic Theology of History," 205–21.

with an exile from the garden presence of God, partially addressed to Israel at Sinai, and concludes with an unresolved exile from his Jerusalem presence (2 Kgs 23:16; 24:3, 20; cf. 2 Kgs 17:20, 23), and raises the question of the location of the divine presence.

Summarizing, the narrative which began with God placing humanity restfully (*nwḥ*, Gen 2:15) in his Garden presence, a rest to which God brought his people again in Jerusalem (*mnwḥh*, 1 Kgs 8:56), ends with a Cain-like restless wandering (*nᵓ wnwd*, Gen 4:12, 14) among the nations from which God had called Abraham (*Ur of Chaldees*, Gen 12:1–3; *Chaldea*, 2 Kgs 25:4, 13). The Christian canon connects the Former Prophets, including Ruth, to Genesis' theme of the divine presence and the theme of rest in that presence, first enunciated in Gen 2:15, restated in God's instructions in Deuteronomy, and developed in Joshua through Kings.[34]

"Pre-critical" Reading of the Former Prophets

Before the Enlightenment's historical critical adjudication of the biblical narrative's claims and interest in the composition history by the original authors, scholars of the church generally approached the books of the Former Prophets as individual entities first and then together as longer histories. This churchly scholarship is "pre-critical" only in a chronological sense, that is, as a mode of exegesis that predates historical-critical analysis.[35] In evidence since the early church, this mode of exegesis continued to be practiced and recommended after the Enlightenment.[36] Matthew Henry (1662–1714) and C. F. Keil (1807–1888) and F. Delitzsch (1813–1890)[37] exemplify this reading.

Henry distinguishes the Pentateuch, as law, from Joshua through Kings; the latter is a dependable historical record whose goal it is to edify "the conduct of human life." Typological hermeneutics makes possible these histories' direct address to the gospel church because it is the antitype of the Jewish church. These histories teach "that we are not to expect the perfect purity and unity of the church in this world"; that "we are not to expect the

---

34. These themes are developed in chaps. 2 and 3.

35. See Steinmetz's "The Superiority of Pre-Critical Exegesis," 27–38. Treier, "The Superiority of Pre-Critical Exegesis? Sic et Non," 77–103, answers three questions: What does "pre-critical exegesis" designate? What is superior about this exegesis? How should that change American Evangelical exegetical practices?

36. Childs, *The Book of Exodus*; Steinmetz, "John Calvin on Isaiah 6," 156–70.

37. From these works: Henry, *Commentary on the Whole Bible*, vol. 2, iii–vi; Henry, *Commentary on the Whole Bible*, vol. 1, iii–iv; Keil and Delitzsch, *Joshua, Judges, Ruth*, 1–12.

constant tranquility and prosperity of the church"; that "yet we need not fear the extirpation of it"; that "we may see the evil we should avoid and be armed against it, and the good we should do and be quickened to it"; and, "what we may expect from [God's] providence, especially concerning states and kingdoms." In his introduction to Joshua, Henry states that although parts of these histories were probably written soon after the events depicted, "they were put into the form in which we now have them by some other hand, long afterwards . . . [and] . . . it is not unlikely that the historical books, to the end of the Kings, were put together by Jeremiah the prophet, a little before the captivity."[38] Historical distance between the text and the reader is acknowledged and bridged by direct divine address to the church.

By the end of the nineteenth century, criticism had placed the historical distance between the ancient text (what it meant) and the contemporary reader (what it means) on a firm basis. Theories about the nature of history and historiography had blossomed to the point that, for Keil and Delitzsch, history had become an aid to understanding what the text continues to mean for the contemporary reader. Under the influence of the Erlangen school, they write that the historical books (without Ruth) "trace, in the light of divine revelation, and of the gradual unfolding of the plan of salvation, the historical development of the kingdom of God." This unfolding depicts not a natural but a theocratic development of Israel "as the channel of salvation which was to be manifest to all nations in the fullness of time." Hence the historical narratives testify to a *Heilsgeschichte*, a history of salvation with its own internal, organic drive towards this history's fulfillment, Christ. Keil and Delitzsch do not deny the natural causes of events, but argue that "the subjective motives which determined the conduct of historical personages, are for the most part left unnoticed, or only briefly and cursorily alluded to, whilst the divine interpositions and influence are constantly brought into prominence, and, so far as they were manifested in an extraordinary manner, are carefully and circumstantially described." For this reason, Keil and Delitzsch also insist on continuity between the Pentateuch and the historical books, but not as the result of some editorial hand making wise choices in the selection of materials. Rather, this continuity "arose from the very nature of the historical facts themselves, i.e., from the fact that the history of Israel was not the result of a purely natural development, but was the fruit and result of the divine training of the covenant nation."[39]

38. This suggestion does not make Henry a precursor of critical exegesis or his Jeremiah an ancestor of Martin Noth's Deuteronomist. Rather, it suggests that pre-critical post-Reformation exegetes, well-trained in the humanist tradition, were aware of the problems posed by ancient documents.

39. Keil and Delitzsch, *Joshua, Judges, Ruth*, 7–9.

A convergence of history as a process and Israel's documented experience of divine revelation produced the notion that history itself was a means of divine revelation. Thus, even as historical criticism argued that the biblical text was inaccessible to the contemporary reader, *Heilsgeschichte*[40] used it to argue for Israel's unique salvation history. Because salvation history continues in some sense, this reading provides some contact between the reader and the ancient text.[41]

Modern Approaches to the Former Prophets

Critical exegesis' search for underlying sources and/or traditions dissolved the Pentateuch as a unit; for a time these sources were thought to reach into Joshua, thereby creating a Hexateuch composed of sources first discerned in Genesis.[42] Gerhard von Rad's tradition historical argument for the development of the earliest credo (Deut 26:5–9) drew more attention to this larger literary unit with its own structure and interests.[43] This credal expression of Israel's faith, beginning with the patriarchs and ending with life in the land, grew over time into the body of literature which begins with the Abraham story and ends with the conquest of the land. The attractive part of this thesis is that it presents the first six books of the OT in a promise-fulfillment format. But it created new problems: the Pentateuch as a unit with its unique interests disappeared, and it left a truncated historical narrative "with little movement."[44]

Martin Noth argued that a single author (Dtr) used an earlier form of Deuteronomy, to which he added his own material, with a view to it becoming the introduction to Joshua through Kings, without Ruth. This author (Dtr) also shaped earlier versions of these books and added his own

40. Smart, "Beyond Historical Interpretation," 12–43, argued that "biblical historians must be theologians too if they are to grasp the significance of God's redemptive action in history." Smart developed this argument in *The Strange Silence of the Bible in the Church*. See also, Gnuse, *Heilsgeschichte as a Model for Biblical Theology*, 23–30.

41. Vos, *Biblical Theology*; VanGemeren, *The Progress of Redemption*; VanGemeren, *Interpreting the Prophetic Word*, exemplify such readings.

42 For example, Driver, *An Introduction to the Literature of the Old Testament*, 105–116; on 116–159 he discusses the prophetical and priestly narrative of the Hexateuch. Studies of biblical personalities/authors included the Yahwist, see Kittel, *Great Men and Movements in Israel*, 175–199; and, on the Yahwist and Priestly writers, James, *Personalities of the Old Testament*, 196–209, 425–42.

43. Rad, "The Form-Critical Problem of the Hexateuch," 1–78. Similarly, VanGemeren, *The Progress of Redemption*, 70–97, who takes the fourth period of redemptive history to stretch from Exodus through Joshua.

44. VanGemeren, *The Progress of Redemption*, 184.

material. The clear echoes of Deuteronomy's language in the subsequent books made this an attractive argument for another literary block within Genesis–Kings, the Deuteronomistic History (DH). Noth also argued that Dtr's purpose in creating the DH was to justify divine judgment and Israel's exile. Subsequent revisions of Noth's thesis argued for two versions of DH, one pre–exilic and more positive focusing on Josiah, the other exilic with a more negative message.[45] Noth's thesis is attractive for its pointing to the language of Deuteronomy in Joshua through Kings, and the unique role of speeches (Josh 1, 23, 24; 1 Sam 12; 2 Sam 7; 1 Kgs 8;) and reflections (Judg 2:11–23; 2 Kgs 17:7–22), crucial for understanding the significance of this literature. It also posed a significant problem: it left a truncated Pentateuch and added Deuteronomy to the Former Prophets.

Both the Hexateuch and the Deuteronomistic History are products of modern research's focus on the history of the biblical literature's composition. Brevard S. Childs, Rolf Rendtorff, and Erich Zenger acknowledged the importance of and engaged in the history of composition, but they also argued in favor of the scholarly study of the received canonical shape, including larger units such as a Pentateuch and the Former Prophets, and the effect of the canonical (re)ordering, especially the Christian canon.[46] The insistence on the canonical shape coincided with the rise of a rhetorical and synchronic study of Scripture.[47] Feminist, womanist and post-colonial readings of the Former Prophets, characterized by an eclectic use of modern and post–modern methodologies, have challenged "the dominant androcentric or patriarchal readings of the establishment,"[48] not without recognizing, however, "that the biblical texts themselves neither oppress nor liberate, . . . [but] that it is those who use them and the way they are used that can become oppressive or liberating."[49] Recent historical studies examine the growth and relationships

---

45. Noth, *The Deuteronomistic History*; Nelson, *The Double Redaction*; Cross, "The Themes of the Book of Kings," 274–89. For a review of scholarship on DH, including the thesis of three versions, see Pury et al., *Israel Constructs Its History*, especially 24–141; see also Satterthwaite and McConville, "What Are the Histories? A Survey of Recent Scholarship," 1–28.

46. See footnote 19 above, and Zenger, et al., *Einleitung in das Alte Testament*, 151, studies Ruth in its Christian canonical location, as does Mann in *The Book of the Former Prophets*.

47. Often taken to be signaled Muilenburg, "Form Criticism and Beyond,"1–18; Alter, *The Art of Biblical Narrative*; Alter, *The Art of Hebrew Poetry*.

48. Tolbert, "Protestant Feminists and the Bible," 17; and see, Brenner, *Ruth and Esther*; Brenner-Idan, *A Feminist Companion to Samuel and Kings*; Brenner and Yee, *Joshua and Judges*.

49. Meyers, *Rediscovering Eve*, 201.

between the Pentateuch, Hexateuch, the DH, or even an Enneateuch,[50] and how such units may be discerned.

Conclusion

This study takes the Pentateuch and the Former Prophets (including Ruth) as two sub-units of a larger narrative depicting God's relationship to humanity, and subsequently Israel, from the creation of the world and God's exile of humanity from his garden presence, to Israel's exile from the presence of God in Jerusalem. Although parts of the Former Prophets emerge from Israel's earliest experiences, its canonical shape addresses Judah's exiles. Together these form a devastating explanation for Israel's exile from the presence of God, but they also depict responsible leadership in the tradition of David, even into the shadows of the exile, Josiah's reign, for example, and Jehoiachin's elevation evokes God's promise to David in 2 Sam 7. Finally, the exiles can only hear the repeated calls to repentance in Solomon's dedicatory prayer, especially the invocations directed to Jerusalem's ruins as signs of hope and invocations to trust the LORD, as did Hezekiah, as they await rest from the enemy that remains.

This literature then must be heard first of all from the exilic perspective whenever and wherever it is heard: by the exiles who returned—instructed by Malachi, Zechariah, Haggai, the Chronicler, and Ezra–Nehemiah—but also for the many who remained abroad. This is especially true for Joshua's "rest from the enemy all around" (Josh 21:44), for rest is closely associated with the land of promise. Chronicles treats this theme for the returned exiles.[51] But what of those who did not return, the diasporic community? Will they have to return to the land to enjoy rest from their enemies? Esther depicts the diaspora community as gaining rest from its enemies under the wise leadership of Esther and Mordecai (Esth 9:16–20). And what of the Christian readers of the Former Prophets, how can they hear this literature? James (1:1) and Peter (1 Pet 1:1; 2:11; 5:13) challenge those readers to consider themselves as scattered among the nations, a diasporic community waiting to return home. Or, as Hebrews reminds them, a community that is waiting for the rest that still remains (Heb 4:9).

---

50. Dozeman, *Pentateuch, Hexateuch, or Enneateuch?*; Gertz, *T&T Clark Handbook of the Old Testament*.

51. Von Rad, "There Remains Still a Rest for God's People," 99–100.

2

Trajectories in Genesis–Kings

Egypt and the Land of Promise

Introduction: Former Prophets and the Pentateuch

WHILE POSSIBLE, IT IS not recommended to begin reading a novel in chapter 6; you'd have no idea about the story line nor how chapter six fits in. Nevertheless, committed readers of the OT often think about and read Joshua this way. And then they encounter the violence: invading territory others have occupied for generations, destroying their altars and the men, women and children who worshiped there for generations. That a book with a reputation for violence speaks about a safe place in God's presence may seem counter-intuititive. Nevertheless, rest from Israel's enemies is a major theme of Joshua.

What makes a place safe? How do you find such a safe place? From what is that place safe? How do you keep that place safe? Joshua through Kings answers these questions for an audience that knows the story of Genesis through Deuteronomy. Like the threads of a tapestry, the word-threads (words or phrases repeated so often they call attention to themselves) of the Joshua text (from the Latin *texere*, "to weave") belong to a weave that begins in Genesis and ends in Kings. By artful intertwining these word-threads produce an intertext by which the entire narrative from Genesis to Kings highlights themes, but with nuances shaped by the different literary contexts in which they emerge.

Awareness of intertextual repetition shapes an audience's understanding because it uncovers the wider context within which a particular narrative is set. Without such an awareness an audience might think Joshua is only about violence and not at all about a safe place. Knowing that Joshua is the sixth chapter of ten, the careful reader would be aware of Joshua's links to the antecedent chapters. Deuteronomy describes the gift of land, the declaration of blessings and curses on Mt. Ebal and Gerizim, safety or rest from the enemy, and the death of Moses. Numbers reminds Israel of its disobedience to God's instructions, their death in the desert and the rise of a new generation. Leviticus depicts the regulations for sacrificial, clean, and righteous living in God's presence in the land, and the deadly consequences of failure to do so. Exodus reminds its audience of the consuming-fire-God's indwelling their midst at Sinai after Israel leaves Egypt. Genesis describes how Israel came to be in Egypt after a long pilgrimage from Ur of the Chaldees, the violence among the nations and the descendants of Abraham and Sarah, and the creation of the earth/land by God the Creator.

All these threads, and many more, connect Joshua to Gen 1, the beginning of the ten–chapter narrative we know as Genesis–Kings. Examining the Hebrew of word-threads such as "land" (ʾrṣ), "rest" (nwḥ, mnwḥḥ, mnwḥ), and "God's presence/face" (pny) and depictions of violence, will begin to answer the questions—What makes a place safe? How do you keep that place safe? How do you find such a safe place? From what is that place safe?—as follows: God's presence defines any place as safe: Eden, Noah's ark, or the land; God brings his people to that place; compliance with God's declared will keeps the place safe from adversaries and even his own people's failures. In short, the Promised Land as a safe place has everything to do with who God is, what he did, and what he requires, according to the narrative that begins in Genesis. Genesis begins by declaring that the God who instructs Joshua to dispossess the Canaanites is the Creator of the heavens and the earth, who restfully placed (nwḥ, Gen 2:15) humanity in his presence, who wills righteous human habitation in all territories under the sun, and who brings the descendants of Abraham to dwell safely, restfully in his presence (1 Kgs 8:56; cf. Gen 49:15).

This and the following chapter will follow two distinct word-threads or themes anchored in the Garden of Eden: violent conflict and the restlessness that characterizes that conflict. Genesis' depiction of the Garden is the narrative ground zero: it is the safe place that defines humanity's fundamental vocation to be a compliant steward of that safe place by heeding the instruction of the God who placed them in his garden presence. God's exile of humanity from this safe place initiates the theme of violence; both divine—the conflict between the seed of the woman and of the serpent—and human (Gen 3:15). Fratricide and the inevitable restless wandering east of Eden continue throughout Scripture. Not even the NT resolves this violence; it only indicates a future solution (Rev 18). Although this violence has its roots in banishment from God's garden presence, Exodus depicts both the pervasive and limited character of this violence. Pervasive because the nations never abandon their attempts to annihilate God's people; limited because the ancient adversary cannot avoid the major, and ultimately final, battle with the God of this people. This chapter will examine this theme.

Banishment from God's garden presence also begins the theme of restless wandering east of Eden. The NT does not resolve this restless wandering; it only points to the Sabbath rest that remains (Heb 4:9). Although humanity's restless wandering is rooted in the divine expulsion from the Garden, Gen 4:1–24 depicts its pervasive but limited character. Pervasive because fratricide, hatred of the closest neighbor, is never far from the human heart's deepest desires (Gen 37:20); limited because God places limits on it, beginning with Cain himself (Gen 4:15) and later with humanity (Gen 6:11–13, 14; 8:4, 9). Josh 21:44–45 and 1 Kgs 8:56 depict the beginning of rest from humanity's wandering. Chapter three is dedicated to this theme.

Violence, from the Beginning (Gen 4:1—11:26)

The nations in Israel's socio-religious environment sought harmony with the will of the gods; evidence of disharmony was discerned by examining suspicious tears in the fabric of reality: flooded fields out of season or a military invasion. Both generated a kind violence in return: military action against invaders and sacrifices of animals or humans. Such violence was understood within the theological categories of nature's revelation of the problem and redemption through wars and/or sacrifices. That is, disturbances in nature or society revealed the problem and the appropriate treatment, often violent, would assuage the deity and restore order. Securing the natural order of things against the intrusions of disorder was the task of the king. All-powerful on earth, he was nevertheless duty bound to submit to heaven's decrees on the earth.

Biblical documents view reality similarly: God declares his will clearly (Gen 1:1—2:3), all creatures on the earth have the simple task of compliance with that will. And all do, except for the divine image bearers. Genesis' depiction of earthly humanity's relationship with heaven (Gen 2:4—4:26) begins with the violence of humanity's non–compliance with heaven's will, to which God responds with the violence of exile from the Garden presence; fratricide among Cain and his descendants soon follows. Thereafter human violence does not abate (Gen 6:5–7), nor the violence of heavenly justice for earthly malfeasance. Humanity's violent (*ḥms*, Gen 6:11, 13) corruption of the earth (*šḥt*) receives heaven's response: "I will destroy (*šḥt*) the earth" (Gen 6:11–12, 13).[1] "The waters do not merely multiply greatly; they triumph," over the

---

1. Unless a version is indicated the citations are my translations.

earth.[2] God destroyed all living things,[3] except for those safe from earth–covering waters, the ark Noah built upon divine instruction and design. The violence the biblical documents depicts is rooted in humanity's destruction of the harmony between heaven had established between it and the earth. "The eyes of the Lord God keep watch over knowledge, but he brings to ruin the words of the treacherous" (Prov 22:12).

Scripture's expectation that women and men obey heaven's revealed will on the earth confronts twenty-first-century readers with a transcendent authority over all creatures, but especially men and women. Post-enlightenment modernity rejects divine authority and its violent response to human *lèse majesté*; muting the divine, it elevates human authority over earthly decisions. Because biblical documents speak with sincere belief in the intimacy of heaven and earth—whatever the deities involved—the contemporary reader may respond in several ways. First, you could hold that the biblical depiction of God and humanity reflects ancient Israel's unsophisticated way of thinking. Since biblical depictions of violence belong to this underdeveloped humanity, a well-informed critical neo-Marcionite reading can still have what remains of Scripture: love and justice through Jesus Christ, whose Father in any case cannot be the cruel God of the OT. Second, when with the best critical and sociological tools Joshua is carefully reconstructed, you may conclude that Israel's slaughter of innocent Canaanites is a self-serving account written by supporters of an oppressive kingship, and that the surviving canonical account covers up the truth: originally a few Joseph tribes joined poor Canaanites in their struggle to overcome an oppressive economic elite society to create an egalitarian community that lasted several hundred years. This reconstructed narrative depicts what really happened: the struggle of an indigenous people against the powerful ancient city–states who controlled all of society for the benefit of foreign rulers. Their violent struggle (economic, social, and, some have argued, military) is redemptive and liberating. A respectable reconstruction of this original "biblical" story would be a model for the liberation of all kinds of oppressed groups, however they may identify themselves today.[4]

2. *Genesis 1–15*, 182, referring to the verbs "to multiply" and "be strong" (*rbh*, 7:17, 18; *gbr*, 7:18, 19, 20, 24; cf. Exod 17:11).

3. The third m.s. of "to destroy" (*mḥh*) in 7:23a can only refer to God; in 23b the verb occurs in the passive.

4. Senior and Stuhlmueller, *The Biblical Foundations for Mission*, 40–4, define violence as follows: "Violence . . . is here understood as any strong initiative or forceful action that reaches beyond normal dialogue, infringes upon the freedom of the other(s), and imposes a solution or a situation upon others, at times against their desires" 40–41). They list the following kinds of violence: physical, psychological, ascetical, liturgical, and prophetical. They also write: "Violence ought to be considered a charism or gift

The problem, however, is that many readers only read the canonical narrative, not the scholarly reconstructed history of oppressed peoples.[5] Third, accepting the Christian faith's commitment to the OT and NT as the word of God come in human words, you accept its authority for the faith and conduct of men, women and children. You read Scripture carefully, being aware of the cultural, linguistic, social and general exegetical and hermeneutical problems that impinge upon such a reading. The goal of your reading is to hear what it says to the community that first heard Joshua because your reading of the NT has convinced you that the body of Christ is organically linked to that community by the power of the Holy Spirit, and that the essential message of the OT is still relevant through Jesus Christ, whose Father you understand to be the God of the OT. These spiritual connections enable you to engage the scandals of the biblical message, including the divine and human violence depicted in Joshua, Judges, Samuel and Kings. In a sense, it means you are willing to accept that God is good, but not safe (Exod 24:17; cf. Heb 12:29). Reading the Bible as Scripture for faith and conduct today is neither easy nor safe.

Abraham's Move from Ur towards the Land

God's redemptive response to human disorder and violence came in the form of a lengthy journey begun with Abraham and Sarah; its goal would not be reached without engaging Egypt and Amalek, violent opponents to that journey. Similar opposition would also arise from within: Esau against Jacob, the descendants of Abraham against Moses and God, never mind the inter-tribal violence depicted in Judges and Kings. The beginning of the journey itself constitutes an act of social violence for God required Abraham to abandon the three spheres of his social and cultural identity: his land, his clan, and his father's house. Abraham's immediate compliance anticipates the disciples' following Jesus immediately and redefines his identity: he no longer identifies with the scattered-from-Babel humanity in Ur of the Chaldees; all its resources for a good life cannot match the promised blessings. Even so, the geographic end of the journey, "the land which I will show (rʾh) you," is not realized in the Pentateuch; Abraham and his immediate family move about Canaan (12:9), their only possession/inheritance (ʾḥzh, Gen 23:9) a grave.

put to the service of God's people and God's providential plan, just as truly as any other quality, like pacifism or prayer" (43).

5. Thus, Warrior, "A Native American Perspective," 287–95. The reconstruction Warrior has in mind is that of Gottwald, *The Tribes of Yahweh*. See more on this below, in chapter 5.

His more distant descendants continue the journey, but many would die in Egypt or the desert, their separation from Ur not fully realized. This includes Moses, whom God allows to "see (*rʾh*) this land with his own eyes" (Deut 34:4), before he dies outside the land for his own disobedience.

The move from Ur towards the land also separated Abraham and Sarah from normal, divinely appointed blessing: growth of the descendants of Adam and Eve. From Adam to Terah the nations enjoyed unbounded fertility (*yld*, Gen 5:1–32; 11:10–27);[6] but Sarah "was barren; she had no child" (Gen 11:30). Sarah is a hinge-figure. Last mentioned in a series of statements about human fertility, but before the journey from Ur begins, Sarah's barrenness is ominous: normal human means of production and reproduction are threatened by the human condition. Death overcomes all, if not at the end of a long life,[7] it prevents life from taking root in the womb. At the beginning of the journey and future mother of the multitudes that fill the earth (*wtmlʾ hʾrṣ ʾtm*, Exod 1:7) Sarah stands for a new social reality: bereft of the resources typical of the nations' natural growth, Abraham and Sarah's future is completely dependent upon God's blessing.[8] The barrenness of daughters-in-law Rebekah and Rachel further reinforces this new social reality. A new "father house" (*byt ʾb*, cf. Gen 33:17, *wybn lw byt*) will arise out of a tear in the social fabric that unites God with humanity, but that house will not be built by human ingenuity.[9]

Even as it stalks the nations (Gen 5; 11:29, 31), death constantly shadows the patriarchal journey and threatens the promised "seed"; from without: famine in the land of promise (Gen 12:10; 43:1), Pharaoh's and Abimelech's attempts to take Sarah and Rebekah (Gen 12:10–20; 20:1–18; 26:7–11); and from within: Esau threatens Jacob, and the brothers Joseph. All members of Jacob's family die "natural" deaths in Egypt. Jacob's sons bury him in his inheritance, the cave of Machpelah, but Joseph awaits burial in the land. The promised seed's enormous growth and filling of the land of Egypt is death's counter-weight, for through them God's purposes for humanity (to fill the earth [*wtmlʾ hʾrṣ*] Gen 1:28) are beginning to be realized in Egypt, the promised seed's waiting room and unexpected womb. When the womb turns into a tomb, which threatens to swallow the divine gift to barren Sarah,

---

6. The verb "to father" occurs 54 times in these two chapters.

7. The verbs "to father," "to live," and "to die" occur nine times in Gen 5:1–31. Gen 11:10–26 only employ "to father" and "to live." The deaths of Haran and Terah frame Gen 11:27–32, placing Sarah's barrenness in the middle.

8. God's blessing (*brk*, in all forms) occurs five times in Gen 12:1–3, responding to the five-fold curse (*ʾrr*, in all forms, Gen 3:14, 17; 4:11; 5:29; 9:25).

9. Both Sarah and Rachel use the passive of "to build" in their attempts to have a family. See, Leder, "Who Builds the House of Israel?"

the threatened journey from Ur turns into the LORD's victory march out of
defeated Egypt, and Abraham's descendants leave as the Lord's army.[10]

Remembering the LORD's Victory over Egypt

Ancient annals' depictions of kings returning to the imperial center after
successful military engagements at the periphery of the empire[11] includes
descriptions of numerous obstacles and irruptions of violence (deserts, adversaries, bodies of water, even mutiny) which the king must overcome. The
LORD's victory march from Egypt—the periphery from the point of view of
the land of promise and Jerusalem as the center of the LORD's kingdom—
only comes to an end when the Ark enters the Holy of Holies on Zion (1
Kgs 8:6), after surviving deserts, adversaries, bodies of water, and rebellion
in the ranks. The Pentateuch depicts this march in two parts: from Egypt to
Sinai and from Sinai to the plains of Moab.

The Exodus Itinerary: From Egypt to Sinai[12]

Even before the plagues begin the Exodus describes Israel as an army ($ṣb^ʾ$,
6:26; 7:4). In the exodus event itself the divisions of the LORD (12:17, 41, 51),
her men of valor (12:37; see 10:11 and Num 24:3, 15) and armed men (13:18;
see Num 32:17; Josh 1:14; 4:12; Judg 7:11) march out of Egypt without engaging in battle, for the God of the patriarchs defeats the gods of Egypt in a ten
round cosmic battle (2:23–25; 12:12; 15:1–5). Israel fights her first and only
successful battle under Moses' leadership against Amalek (17:8–16). That the

---

10. Unlike Exodus and Numbers, where the verb "to set out" (ns^c) shapes movements between Egypt and Sinai, and Sinai and Moab, Genesis depicts no such itineraries. The verb "to set out" depicts movements (11:2; 12:9; 13:11; 33:12, 17; 35:5, 16, 21;
37:17; 46:1), but not the patriarchal family's moves to Egypt, nor those between Canaan
and Paddan-aram. And although Jacob and his family settled in Egypt because of a
famine, Genesis does not depict Egypt as a threat; Joseph is threatened by his brothers
(still in the land) and by Potiphar's wife. Within that general move from the initial entry
to Canaan to Egypt, the movements depicted with the verb $ns^ʾ$ occur only within the
land (i.e., Gen 12:9). Ns^c in Gen 11:2 depicts humanity moving towards an "imperial"
center God declines to use, Babel; the itinerary to Sinai, and ultimately Zion is the
recommended center for God's people.

11. Ironically, Ur also lies at the periphery, but Abraham's journey, though difficult
and threatened, is not a military expedition (except for Gen 14). Because humanity
resides east of Eden, it also resides at the periphery.

12. This section is dependent on Leder, *Waiting for the Land*, 43–8.

first itinerary notice describes Israel's men as men of valor (12:27) defines the journey begun on Passover night as a military expedition.[13]

The analogy with ancient royal military annals illuminates the military character of God's people. Upon leaving Egypt, Israel follows its master strategist and tactician (14:1–4; 15:3), who protects his inchoate army against Egypt (13:21–22; 14:19–20) and gives them victory over Amalek. When the LORD subsequently declares Amalek to be an eternal enemy (17:16) Israel understands that being the LORD's army is basic to her self-understanding.[14] Israel left Egypt to be free from its servitude but only to assume the service of another.[15]

A final element in the ancient annals depicting a king's victorious return to the center of his empire is the building of a monument, palace or temple to celebrate the king's victories and honor his god. In Exodus, the LORD's victory march from Egypt halts at Sinai, for the time being the center of his rule over Israel and the nations (15:11–17). There, at the foot of his imperial throne (19:4; 24:10),[16] Israel swears bloody oaths (24:3, 8) to be the LORD's vassals alone, to promote his imperial interests (20:1–5; cf. 1:11; 5:1–23) and to assume their military responsibilities (23:20–33); there also the LORD instructs her in the construction of his dwelling place, a monument to his victory over Egypt and Israel (29:43–46). The highest expression of Israel's sworn commitment is the construction of the LORD's dwelling place—not without mutinous rebellion (32–34)—based on the people's voluntary contributions (25:2; 35:5, 20–21), unlike the forced construction of Egypt's store cities.

The itinerary verb "to journey" (ns', Exod 12:37; 13:17,20; 14:10, 16, 19bis; 15:22; 16:1; 17:1; 19:1, 2) connects Rameses, Israel's place of departure on Passover night (12:37), with Sinai three months later (19:1–2), geographies which represent different experiences. Rameses, associated with the death of Israel's first-born (Exod 4:22) and Egypt's on Passover night (1:11–21; 12:29–36), is the geography of death. Sinai, the place of Israel's submission to a new sovereign (19:3–8; 24:3, 7) whose Word makes the bitter waters sweet (15:23–25a), is a geography of life in the presence of God. Sinai also carries the

13. For a detailed study of the desert itineraries and Assyrian annals, see Roskop, *The Wilderness Itineraries*.

14. Neglected by Saul (1 Sam 15:17–35), remembered by David (2 Sam 1:13–16) and Mordecai (Esth 3:1–2).

15. Azou, *De la servitude*; Croatto, *Exodus*, 21–23. For a discussion of the identity of the Israel who left Egypt, see Levenson, "Exodus and Liberation," 132–140. The issue in the canonical shape of Exodus is not whether the Israelites were poor, but whose slaves ('bdym) they would be, Pharaoh's or the LORD's.

16. Keel, *The Symbols of the Biblical World*, 113–19.

weight of cosmic symbolism which the ancient world attached to mountain tops as the meeting place between heaven and earth.[17] The military journey from Rameses to Sinai is one from a land reduced to shambles for failure to comply with the LORD's instructions, to a place of reorientation through the Sinai instruction. This linkage creates and maintains a tension between two geographies (Egypt and Sinai), and two events (the Passover and submission to the covenant), both definitive for Israel's self-understanding. The LORD's victory march resumes in Num 10:11–36 when the ark leaves the mountain of the LORD to seek rest for the people.

Numbers 10:11—36:13: A Military Itinerary from Sinai towards Rest (*mnwḥh*)

Numbers emphasizes Israel's military identity with a census of the men of fighting age (Num 1), the arrangement of the military camp at rest and in battle order, the responsibilities for managing the Tent of Meeting within the camp and when it moves (Num 2–4), the requirements for the camp's purity (Num 5:1–4), and Israel's departure from Sinai in battle order (Num 10:12, 14–28). This first of two itinerary narratives in Numbers does not depict any battles, only Moses' repeated invocation, "Arise, O LORD, let your enemies be scattered, and your foes flee before you" (Num 10:35), and his exhortation, "Rise up, O LORD." It also depicts the continuation of the LORD's victory march from Rameses (Num 10:11–12).

The Israel that follows the ark from Sinai in Num 10 is not, however, identical to the Israel who arrived at the mountain a year earlier. Sinai transformed the people in several ways. By swearing covenant loyalty to the LORD (Exod 19:8; 24:3–8) Israel publicly declared it was no longer Egypt's vassal (ᶜbd, 5:15, 16), that it had placed its future in the LORD's hands. Furthermore, the divinely designed and indwelt tabernacle (40:34) transforms Israel herself into a living monument of God's victory over Egypt (25:8; 29:43–46) by means of her compliance with the sacrificial, cleanliness and holiness instructions from the Tent of Meeting (Lev 1–27). This Sinai-transformed community follows its sovereign in battle forma-tion (Num 10:12–28), without complaints about food or water as it did on the way to Sinai, and the ark of the covenant of the LORD leads it into battle (10:33b). Finally, the purpose of this military march, in terms of the ark's and the cloud's guidance, is to scatter the LORD's enemies and to seek rest (*mnwḥh*) for God's people (10:33c). Numbers' first itinerary narrative

17. Keel, *The Symbols of the Biblical World,* 113–19.

depics the first generation in full compliance with Moses' instructions and on the way to the rest the ark seeks for it.

Numbers second itinerary narrative (20:22—22:1)[18] is separated from the first by long non-travel narrative characterized by Israel's complaints, non-compliance—whose consequence is a longer journey for and death of the first generation—and divine instruction. This journey describes the same generation that left Egypt, but with several differences. First, the guidance of the cloud appears only in contexts of judgment. Second, the description of the first generation as an army in Num 10 (ṣbʾ, seventeen times; which forms an inclusion with Num 1 [where ṣbʾ, sixteen times]), is absent from Num 11–25; they are no longer the battalions of the LORD. Third, where Num 10:12–24 depicts no halts in the journey, the second itinerary includes specific encampments during which time Aaron dies, the people complain, Israel defeats Sihon and Og, and they arrive in Moab where the LORD frustrates Balaam. Finally, where the first itinerary ends positively with the ark seeking rest for Israel, the second ends disappointingly on the plains of Moab where Israel commits apostasy with the Baal of Peor.

Both Numbers itineraries depict the generation that left Rameses and Sinai. The first describes it in an ideal mode: it is wholly compliant and guided by the ark to the goal of its journey, rest for God's people. The second itinerary depicts the same generation realistically: it is in non-compliant mode, not guided by the ark, and ends in Moab and Israel's fatal apostasy with the Baal of Peor. The two itineraries suggest that it is not two generations that are compared, but two journeys. The ideal journey begins with a departure from Sinai, where the first generation was fully instructed, indwelt by the divine presence, and guided by the cloud; its goal, defined by the ark's "exploration" (twr), is the rest ultimately received at Zion (mnwḥh, Num 10:33; 1 Kgs 8:56), after the ark is brought in to the Holy of Holies (1 Kgs 8:6). The second journey begins at Kadesh (20:22), where the first generation refused to enter the land after a spying (twr, 13:2, 16, 17, 21, 25, 32bis; 14:6, 7, 34, 36, 38; 15:39) mission discloses the strength of the inhabitants. Where in the first journey the ark seeks Israel's rest by means of exploration (twr), the second journey— departing from a location where Israel's own exploration (twr) of the land ended with its rejection of that land (14:3, 31), God's judgment of death in the wilderness, and the ark's refusal to lead them into the land (14:44)—ends on the plains of Moab, where God rescues Israel from Balak (Pharaoh redivivus) but Israel commits apostasy with the Baal of Peor. The second journey depicts military victories consequent upon divine approval (21:3, 24), but the ark is

---

18. For the argument for two distinct itinerary clusters in Numbers, see Leder, "From the Mountain of YHWH," 513–34.

absent. Where in the first journey the ark seeks Israel's rest, the second ends in death because of the first generation's apostasy.

By divine command the second generation continues its military mission (Num 31; 33:50–56); the trans-Jordan tribes will accompany the others into the land until they also have received their inheritance (*nḥlh*, 32:17–19). In the Pentateuch, however, this generation will not move into the land until it too has heard the Sinai instruction (Deut 5:3), including that God will provide rest from its enemies (*nwḥ*, Deut 3:20; 12:10; 25:19; cf. *mnwḥ*, 28:65). Obedience to this instruction (Josh 1:7–8) and the guidance of the ark (Josh 3–4) leads Numbers' second generation to rest from its enemies (*nwḥ*, Josh 21:43–45). In this manner the second generation's journey into the land conforms to the ideal journey of Num 10, thereby also linking the ark's journey from Sinai with entry into the land. A hexateuchal reading could argue that the journey from Egypt ends with the crossing of the Jordan (*nsᶜ*, Josh 3:1, 3, 14) and the LORD's granting Israel rest (*nwḥ*) from its enemies all around (Josh 21:44–45). But the ark also moves in Samuel and Kings. A deuteronomistic reading, aware of the theme of rest introduced in Deut 3:20; 10:12; 25:19 would include references to rest in 2 Sam 7:1, 12 and then move to 1 Kgs 8:65. Reading the Former Prophets in the context of the Pentateuch, or as part of Genesis–Kings, we find that the themes of rest and the ark's journey from Sinai converge at the crossing of the Jordan and later at Zion.

The LORD's Victory March Enters the Land of Rest

When "the ark of the covenant of the LORD of all the earth" (Josh 3:11, 13) moves from Abel-Shittim on the plains of Moab it leads Numbers' second generation into its first battle in Canaan, one that evokes the last battle in Egypt. At the Sea and the Jordan God piled up the obstructive waters into a heap (Josh 3:16; Exod 15:8) to allow his people to pass through them on dry ground. The reference to the Sea (Josh 4:23–25), the celebration of the Passover (Josh 5:10–12) and the travel verb (*nsᶜ*, Josh 3:1, 3, 14), suggest that passage through the Jordan completes the first part of Israel's journey: from Rameses and Sinai into the land. The violent battles which define Israel's exit from Egypt and entry into the land, are not with people but with water, a powerful symbol of the constant threat of disorder in Israel's world, but also of fertility and useful for defensive features.[19] Although safe

---

19. Keel, *The Symbolism of the Biblical World*, 47–56, 73–5. For the dual nature of water, see figure 42. In the new creation the sea is no more (Rev 21:3).

behind the overflowing waters of the Jordan, Canaan feared the approach of Israel (2:10; 5:1).

The Destruction of Jericho

The military significance of the ark's crossing the Jordan is clear from its splitting of the waters[20] which robbed Canaan of its "Maginot" line, doing so at the height of the Canaanite deities' power to bless (3:15), and stopping opposite Jericho (3:16), a city so fearful of Israel its gates were tightly shut (6:1). With the unsheathing of the sword of the LORD (5:13), the battle of Jericho is a completed action (6:2, "I have delivered it into your hands," *ntty*; cf. *ntn* in 6:16 and 1:3). As with the defeat of the Jordan, the ark destroys Jericho's defenses, this time by encircling (6:3, 4, 7, 11, 14, 15bis) the city and the priests blowing the ram's horns during these processions. The focused use of the verb "to encircle" (*sbb*) and the preposition "around" (*sbyb*) in Joshua,[21] suggests that the ark's encircling Jericho leads to Israel's "rest from their enemies *all around*" (21:44; 23:1; cf. Deut 12:10; 25:19; and see 2 Sam 7:1).[22] Similarly, the appearance of the ram's horn (*ywbl*) in Josh 6:4, 5, 6, 8, 13. Occurring eighteen times in Lev 25 and 27 (cf. Exod 19:13; Num 36:4), the blowing of this horn during the ark's circling of the city evokes the year of jubilee when, upon the blowing of the horn, all property is returned to the family who first received it (Lev 25:10) from the LORD (Lev 25:1–7, esp. vv. 2 and 55). By extended paronomasia the sounding of the ram's horn as the ark circles Jericho signals the returning of the land to its original owner, the LORD himself (Josh 3:11, 13), who is free to redistribute it, as he does through Joshua (13:1—21:42). The ark's taking of Jericho by circling the city and blowing the ram's horn signals, *pars pro toto*, a total conquest and returning of the land to the LORD of all the earth. For this reason, Jericho's ruins, like the other piles of stones in Joshua, remind the subsequent generations of the LORD's victory (Josh 4:3, 5–9, 20, 21; cf. 22:26, 27 and 24:27), judgment (6:24; 7:25, 26; 8:29; 10:27) and righteous redistribution of the land to his own vassals. Jericho's ruins, cursed by Joshua (6:26), memorialize the return of the Master to his vineyard (Isa 5:1–7).

20. Keel, *Symbolism of the Biblical World*, 51, figs. 45 and 46, on the slaying of the chaos monster, depicted as a dragon or snake.

21. In Joshua the verb *sbb* occurs in the active only in chapter 6; elsewhere it describes the boundaries of tribal inheritances. The preposition *sbyb* occurs only in Josh 21:42, 44 and 23:1.

22. A rest exemplified by the tribal lands whose boundaries are said to be "around" or "surrounding" a given area (Josh 15:12; 18:20; 19:8; 21:11, 42).

Centuries later Ahab, "did more to provoke the Lord, the God of Israel, to anger than all the kings of Israel before him" (1 Kgs 16:33) by marrying the Sidonian Jezebel and bringing her foreign gods Baal and Asherah to Israel. Evidence of Ahab's wicked rule are described in two instances. First, during his reign Hiel of Bethel rebuilt Jericho sacrificing his children to secure its foundation and gates. Hiel's family violence not only recalls Joshua's curse on Jericho, his rebuilding the ruins Jericho also deconstructs the public memorial to God's mighty acts. Ironically, the ruins of Jerusalem would serve Israel as a memorial of God's mighty acts, but of judgment on disobedient Israel (Jer 19:8). Second, Ahab himself, assisted by Jezebel, erased the gift of land to God's people by violently dispossessing Naboth of his vineyard, all for his vegetable garden (1 Kgs 21:2). For this the Lord of the vineyard administered justice to Ahab-the-tenant and his whole house (1 Kgs 21:17–24; cf. Matt 21:40–41).

The theme of rest for God's people (*nwḥ*, Josh 1:13, 15) emerges in the crossing narrative and the ark's conquest of Jericho. Before the ark crosses, Joshua instructs the people: "When the soles (*kp*) of the feet of the priests who bear the ark of the Lord, the Lord of all the earth, rest (*nwḥ*) in the waters of the Jordan, the waters of the Jordan flowing from above shall be cut off" (3:13NEB). The representatives of the people comply with divine instruction, removing the stones from the Jordan's dry riverbed and placing (*nwḥ*, 4:3, 8, 20) them at Gilgal. As memorials of the crossing, these piles of "rested" stones at Gilgal anticipate Israel's receiving rest, but the first to enjoy the benefit of the ark's conquest is the Canaanite Rahab, who with her family was "rested" outside the camp (6:23). Only later, after taking the land the ark had already conquered, did God's people receive rest from their enemies all around (21:44; 23:1).

The ark's journey to its ultimate destination, Jerusalem, begins well with Joshua and his contemporaries, despite the obstacles Achan's disobedience and the Gibeonite's successful deception drew up. The next generation (Judg 2:10), however, so fails in its covenant loyalty that, ironically, "the enemy all around" receives rest from *Israel*. The narrator tells us: "In order to test Israel . . . the Lord 'rested' (*nwḥ*) those nations . . . ; Now these are the nations the Lord 'rested' to test (*nsh*) those in Israel who had no experience with war" (Judg 2:23; 3:1). Judges depicts this "second generation" as increasingly disobedient. Rather than taking the land the ark had conquered at Jericho and conforming its conduct in the land of promise to God's will, they went after other gods time and again resulting in God's sending the nations to punish Israel, a violence more than matched by the pervasive chaos and inter-tribal violence described in Judg 17–21.

Judges depicts a divinely revoked "rest from the enemies all around" and an Israel bereft of rest at the mercy of its enemies, an Israel who repeatedly failed to acknowledge that the covenant loyalty sworn before the ark in Josh 8:30–35 was the secret of its "rest from the enemy all around." Tested by the nations all around Israel is found wanting, her waywardness so complete that, without divine warrant, she takes the ark into battle against the Philistines, from where it "is taken" back to "Egypt" (cf. Deut 28:68), "exiled" from the land, its previous successes apparently undone.

The Ark in Samuel and Kings: From Exile to Rest

After its conquest of Jericho, the ark does not move again until the military conflict with Philistia in 1 Sam 4:1b—7:1. How the ark got to Shilo, and before that to Ebal and Gerizim and Bethel (1 Sam 4:3; Josh 8:30–35; Judg 20:27) is not explained, a lack which may attributed to the narrator's selection of those movements that mark significant events. That is, after the conquest of Jericho, the Former Prophets depicts the ark's capture by the Philistines after defeating Israel, the ark's victories over the Philistine god Dagon and the pentapolis, its twenty-year exile at the periphery of Israel, and finally, its victorious entry into the city of David/Jerusalem after David's defeat of the Philistines. David's victory over the Philistines at the LORD's command (2 Sam 5:25), contrasts sharply with Saul's inability to defeat the Philistines (1 Sam 14:52) and also, at the beginning of the Israel-Philistine conflict, with the LORD's giving Israel into the hands of Philistia (1 Sam 4:3).

The ark does not initiate its journey into Philistia, it "was taken" and placed beside (*nlqḥ*, 1 Sam 4:11, 17; *ʾṣl*, 5:2) Dagon in his temple. There the intended humiliation of Israel's God turns into humiliation of Dagon and the Philistines, when the power ("hand," *yd*, 4:8) Israel feared so much is shorn from Dagon and their deity lies prostrate before the ark (5:4). After the power (*yd*, 4:8; 5:7) the Philistines feared so much wreaks havoc in Ashdod, they enable the ark's military victory journey throughout the rest of the pentapolis in a manner reminiscent of its conquest of Jericho and Egypt: where ever the Philistines bring the ark around (*sbb*, 5:8bis; 9, 10; cf. Josh 6:3, 4, 7, 11, 14, 15bis), the LORD strikes with a plague (*mgph*, 6:4, 6). Thus, the LORD forces them to return the ark to its place (*mqwm*, 5:11; 6:2), but it lingers in Kiriath-Jearim for twenty years. Not until David defeats the Philistines (2 Sam 5:17–25), will it resume its journey.

Unlike the Israelites in Eli's days, David engages the Philistines with divine permission (5:19, 23), defeats them and ironically captures *their* idols. For the second battle God instructs David not to engage them head on, but to attack them from the rear (*sbb*, 5:23). In the context of these victories David organizes his soldiers and the people to escort the ark to its place (*mqwm*, 6:17; cf. 1 Sam 5:11; 6:2). Although David is king, he abases himself before the LORD during the ark's triumphal entry into Jerusalem, for the LORD gave David all his victories (2 Sam 8:14b). The ark completes its victory march from Sinai (Num 10:33–36) during Solomon's reign when the priests bring it into the Holy of Holies on mount Zion (1 Kgs 8:6). In his prayer of dedication Solomon praises God for bestowing rest (*mnwḥ*, 8:56a) on his people and for not having failed in any of his promises (1 Kgs 8:56b; cf. Josh 21:45). The ark's passing through the Jordan and its entry into the Holy of Holies might frame the Former Prophets were it not for the fact that the rest of the story reads like the book of Judges: Judah and Israel's kings did what was right in their own eyes; like Jericho, Jerusalem meets a violent end.[23]

Summary Reflections

Understanding the word-threads that connect Joshua–Kings as described above may not solve any problem a contemporary reader may have with violence in Scripture; it can illuminate the biblical depiction of earthly human nature and heaven's response. Since the days of Cain violence against the nearest neighbor is normal: "The LORD saw that the wickedness of men was great in the earth, and that every intention of the thoughts of his heart was only evil continually" (Gen 6:5 ESV). Abraham's descendants too were wicked in the eyes of the LORD, and, as in the days of Noah, they too were justly destroyed by a divine messenger, Nebuchadnezzar (Jer 25:9; 51:34), for they had defiled the safe place to which the ark had led them, the intimate presence of God in Zion.

Little, if anything, can change this fundamental biblical truth about humanity, not even a reconstruction of the text that changes Israel's identity to a few tribes who joined Canaanite peasants in a bloody revolution against an oppressive city-state culture. And, while the putative egalitarian society (a safe space) arguably survived for 200 years, an oppressive Davidic monarchy destroyed it, according to the theory. The victor may write the history, but not all histories survive, at least according to Ozymandias. There is no escaping human violence on any level, *pace* Stuhlmueller and Senior; feminist, womanist, post-colonial and many other contemporary

---

23. What happened to the ark after the destruction of the temple is a matter of debate. For a review of the positions, see Day, "Whatever Happened to the Ark of the Covenant?" 251–70.

readings of Scripture through the eyes of an "other" agree with the pervasiveness of human violence.

A keen reader of OT Scripture observed that all have sinned and that the wages of sin is death, that death is the last obstacle towards rest in God's presence, the true safe space of which both Eden and Jerusalem (Ezek 40–48; Rev 21:2) are emblematic, and where violence will be no more.

3

Trajectories in Genesis–Kings

Restful Eden and Jerusalem

AFTER THE ARCHANGEL MICHAEL escorts Adam and Eve down the cliff to the "subjected Plaine" and disappears, John Milton portrays the couple's unhappy state and unattended future as follows:

> They looking back, all th'Eastern side beheld
> Of Paradise, so late thir happie seat,
> Wav'd over by that flaming Brand, the Gate
> With dreadful Faces throng'd and fierie Armes:
> Some natural tears they drop'd, but wip'd them soon;
> The World was all before them, where to choose
> Thir place of rest, and Providence thir guide:
> They hand in hand with wandring steps and slow,
> Through *Eden* took thir solitarie way.[1]

Alone and lonely in their quest for "thir place of rest," Adam and Eve assume their "solitarie way" under Providence's guidance. As they exit the Garden of Eden, Milton has Adam say:

> Greatly instructed I shall hence depart.
> Greatly in peace of thought, and have my fill
> Of knowledge, what this vessel can containe;
> Beyond which was my folly to aspire.
> Henceforth I learne, that to obey is best,
> And love with feare the onely God, to walk
> As in his presence, ever to observe
> His providence, and on him sole depend.

---

1. This, the following, and the quotation at the end of this chapter are from "Paradise Lost," Book XII, 641–45 and 557–64. Cited in John Milton, *English Minor Poems*.

Milton understands Adam and Eve to have enjoyed rest in Eden, to have been so instructed there that Adam acknowledges true life to consist of compliance with divine instruction in God's presence, and that, looking back, he knows that only such compliance will bring them back to "thir place of rest."

The Israel exiled from God's Jerusalem presence heard similar words when they heard Joshua–Kings by the rivers of Babylon, and when Ezra read the Law of Moses at the Water Gate. Combined with the instructions and narrative of the Pentateuch, Joshua–Kings reminded them of the folly to which they aspired, the instruction they had ignored, the divinely granted rest they had wasted, and of their consequent solitary way among the nations. Joshua–Kings reminds all generations of God's people of their covenant commitment to the "consuming fire" deity who spoke to them at Sinai (Exod 24:17; cf. Heb 12:29), of their oath to fear him alone, and now, to seek repentance with faces turned to the throne of God (1 Kgs 8:30, 34, 36, 39, 43, 45, 49). These books also urge Christians, Jew and Gentile, to depart from our reading of Scripture "greatly instructed," filled with that knowledge "beyond which [it is our customary] folly to aspire." If Christians cannot hear these Scriptures by the ancient waters of Babylon, they may hear it as those living far away from the Jerusalem that holds their identity (Ps 87; Rev 21–22), as the twelve tribes scattered among the nations (1 Pet 1:1; Jas 1:1). Like their ancestors in the faith, Christians too are encouraged to praise and petition the heavenly Jerusalem (Matt 6:6–7; Rev 6:9–10) that they may enjoy the rest in God's presence that still is waiting for them (Heb 4:9–11). This chapter will describe the theme of rest in the presence of God as it unfolds in the Pentateuch, into the Former Prophets, Chronicles and Esther.[2]

Rest in the Presence of God: the Pentateuch

Rest in the Garden Presence of God

The overture (Gen 1:1—2:3) to the Pentateuch, the Former Prophets, and the rest of Scripture, depicts the divine council's perspective on the creation of the heavens, the earth and all that is in them. Before God spoke there was only the place of his dwelling; after that there was also a firmament and an earth. Divine speech brought both into being: God spoke and it was so, without a violent struggle against chaotic elements. Because non-divine

---

2. The theme of rest is usually limited to the Deuteronomistic History, see Rad, "There Remains Still a Rest," 94–102, who suggests its echoes are heard in Genesis–Kings; Laansma, *"I Will Give you Rest,* 18–34. I include Chronicles and Esther to discuss their treatment of "rest" with a view to the returned exiles and the diasporic people of God.

being became a reality by divine will depicted in speech, creatures have their being in the will and ineluctable presence of God, without sharing at the same time in God's own being. The repeated divine declaration that God saw all creatures as good suggests not only that earthly, material reality is good, but also that this created reality is by nature compliant with the divine will. That is, it is the nature of created things to conform their being to God's will and so to manifest the good he saw. The man—already unique among all creatures as the divine image-bearer and a divinely in-breathed material being (Gen 2:7; 1:26–28)—receives detailed attention about conforming to God's will in the garden narrative (Gen 2:8–17). *Where* the Lord speaks is as important as *what* he says, thus, after the in-breathing of the man, the narrative shifts to other divine activities which develop the identity of the man in terms of location and instruction.

The LORD God *plants* (*nt*ᶜ, 2:8a) a garden, *places* (*śym*, 2:8b) the man in it, and then *causes to grow* (*ṣmḥ*, 2:9a) from the ground trees desirable for food, including the tree of life and of the knowledge of good and evil; and rivers flow from the garden. Then the LORD God *takes* (*lqḥ*, 2:15a) the man and *places* (*nwḥ*, 2:15b)[3] him in the garden, and *gives orders* (*ṣwh*, 2:16a) about what to eat. Three verbs precede and three (all with the deity as subject) resume the narrative after depicting the garden's fecundity. The resumption, however, introduces a change: where 2:8a employs the verb *śym*, 2:15b uses the verb *nwḥ*, both commonly translated as "to place" (NIV, JPS, NRSV, ESV). In cases of resumptive repetition, when a narrative picks up its thread after a break, as in Gen 2:8 and 15, one typically expects the same verb to signal continuity. The unexpected appearance of a verb with the root meaning of "rest," however, argues for a shift in meaning: taking seriously its root meaning of rest, God "restfully places" him there.[4] Two infinitives of purpose, "to till it and tend it" (JPS), further modify this placement.

This combination of infinitives depicts humanity's primordial restful vocation in the presence of God, as if God had said, "Secure the garden and protect it from ruin, but remain within the living space I have given you, maintain its boundaries!"[5] That normal human work in the garden presence of God is restful, without opposition or obstacles, becomes clear when failure to comply with their vocation brings "painful toil" (ᶜṣbwn, 3:16, 17) upon them. That the same verb and its nominal form occur in the east of Eden portrayal of Noah's giving relief[6] from "painful toil" (*ynḥmnw*

3. See the appendix for a detailed discussion of the theme of rest in Genesis.

4. Thus Ebach, "Arbeit und Ruhe," 93.

5. Ebach, "Arbeit und Ruhe," 96.

6. On the word play between Noah and *nwḥ*, see Wenham, *Genesis 1–15*, 128–129.

and ᶜṣbwn, 5:29, cf. 3:16, 17) lends credence to the "restful" meaning of the verb in 2:15b. But its reference to painful toil suggests that this is not a rest from fatigue, but from a restlessness associated with the ancestral pair's failure to embody that restful placement. In addition, the vehicle Noah built according to divine instruction for escape from universal destruction itself comes to rest (nwḥ, 8:4) on the mountains of Ararat as the waters recede. After the flood, Genesis only describes the land of promise as a "resting place" in Jacob's blessing of Issachar (mnwḥ, Gen 49:15). Genesis then, depicts three places where humanity may enjoy rest in God's presence: the garden of Eden, the east of Eden ark, and the promised land. The temple–like depiction of the garden gives further theological shape to restful life in the presence of God.

In light of the ancient world's iconographic depictions of mountain-like divine centers from which water streams and whose streams produce trees,[7] the four rivers of Eden suggest that the garden of Eden is such a center (cf. Ezek 47:1, 12; Ps 1:3; Rev 22:1–2). Because humanity is restfully placed in this divinely constructed sanctuary space, its compliant tilling and tending of the garden may be construed as priestly activity.[8] Failure to comply with divine instruction within this space results in the expulsion of this community of priests from its created, divinely assigned restful work in God's presence. Defiled priestly humanity continues to till (ᶜbd, Gen 3:23; 4:12; cf. 2:15) the soil, but Cain refuses to be his brother's keeper (šmr, 4:9). East of Eden the divinely given complimentary elements of humanity's created vocation, "to till," and "to keep" (ᶜbd and šmr) are torn apart,[9] and return to restful placement in God's presence is impossible, for the cherubim guard (šmr, 3:24) the way in. East of Eden, Abraham is the first depicted as "keeping" God's will (šmr, Gen 18:19). Not until Mount Sinai will priestly descendants of Adam and Eve be allowed to pass by the cherubim into God's presence (Exod 29:31; Lev 9:23; cf. Heb 10:19–22). At Sinai the defining elements of humanity's restful vocation, torn apart by the ancestral pair's failure to comply, come together in God's instructions that Israel obey his messenger (šmr, Exod 23:20–21) and serve him alone, not other gods (ᶜbd, Exod 23:24–25). Like their ancestral parents, Israel shreds her restful vocation with its worship at an altar the Lord did not command (Exod 32:5). It will ever be thus in the land.

7. For a relief so depicting a temple, see fig. 42, in Keel, *The Symbolism of the Biblical World*, 47. On the temple metaphor in the ANE and OT, see also, Hurowitz, *I Have Built You an Exalted House*; Levenson, *Sinai & Zion*.

8. Wenham, "Sanctuary Symbolism," 19–25. For a brief discussion of priestly humanity, Leder, "Presence, then the Covenants," 183–185.

9. Ebach, "Arbeit und Ruhe," 95.

Failure to comply with divine instruction and the consequent defilement of God's presence produced a "new" creature, one driven to till the earth without regard for that instruction which alone provides rest in God's presence. East of Eden this defiled priestly community cannot escape the Creator's questioning presence nor his curse (Gen 4:10, 14, 16, *pny*; 6:5; 11:5, *rʾh*), nor does its material culture (4:17, 20–22) ameliorate the restless wandering (*nʾ wnwd*, 4:12, 14) and murderous violence inherited from Cain. Human violence becomes so pervasive (6:6–7, 11, 13) that the Creator removes the boundaries he imposed on the waters above and below allowing them to overwhelm all things living. God mitigates his judgment by instructing Noah to build an ark; his compliance (6:22; 7:5) creates a safe place within which, by divine instruction, the future of the creation is secured (7:17). Divine instruction relieves restless humanity from its painful toil, but only within the divinely designed safe/redemptive space resting on the mountains of Ararat. Noah's dove not finding a resting place for the soles of their feet (*wlʾ mṣʾh mnwḥ lkp-rglh*, 8:9; "to place," NIV, NRSV; but JPS, "resting place") illustrates the indispensability of this redemptive space. For exiles from the land where its ancestors were granted rest (Josh 21:44–45), the curse of Deut 28:65 recalls this dove's restlessness: "Among those nations you shall find no ease, *no resting place for the sole of your feet*" (*wlʾ yhyh mnwḥ lkp–rglk*).

The narrative problem the Pentateuch defines and develops in Gen 2:4—11:26 is that human failure to comply with divine instruction for restful life in God's Garden presence begets exile from that presence and life in an unsafe place, managed by restless people. Those weeping by the rivers of Babylon understood that problem existentially, for they had been expelled from the land shaped by divine instruction where God had brought them to rest in his Jerusalem presence (1 Kgs 8:56). Genesis 11:27—12:9 begins to develop the solution to humanity's exile and restlessness by its depiction of what God does with Abraham, Sarah, and their descendant(s).

Moving towards Rest in the LORD's Presence: From Ur to Sinai and the Plains of Moab

Divine instruction reverses humanity's restless wandering *pars pro toto* when God instructs Abraham to abandon the dispersion of Babel (not unlike the aimless wandering humanity of Cain), in his wandering from Ur (Gen 11:4, 8, *pwṣ*; cf. Gen 10:18; 1 Kgs 22:17; Ezek 22:33): "Leave your land, your clan, and your father's home" (Gen 12:1; cf. 11:28). Compliance with this instruction separates Abraham from the humanity God scattered from

Babel, to begin a precisely shaped journey with a specific goal: "the land which I will cause you to see (*ʾrh*)." That is, not any place will do, only the land where the exilic audience used to live restfully in God's temple presence (1 Kgs 8:56). Chronologically that journey took centuries; in narrative time Abraham complies and arrives immediately (*lk* [v. 1] . . . *wylk* [v.4]). And, although he has no fixed place of his own in the land (Gen 12:9), he builds an altar to the LORD "who had revealed himself to him" (*rʾh*, Gen 12:7–8). The repetition of the verb "to see" in 12:3 and 7–8 signals a partial solution to the problem of exile from the divine presence: Abraham, the father of all believers, found himself in God's presence. From that narrative point on the divine presence shapes the patriarchal journey towards the promised future and secures the land as a safe space for restful living. Patriarchal altars (Gen 12:7–8; 26:25; 35:7) evoke this restful life in God's presence, for they anticipate nothing less than the temple of Jerusalem, where Solomon—to whom God had revealed himself (*rʾh*, 1 Kgs 3:5; 9:2)—praised God for the rest he gave to his people (1 Kgs 8:56).

Where humanity built its mountain-altar at Babel in a concerted attempt to gain access to the divine presence, the LORD freely disclosed himself to Abraham, who then built an altar to memorialize that place of revelation, as would Isaac and Jacob (Gen 26:23–25; 28:10–22; 35:1–14; cf. Deut 12:4, 8). The patriarchal journey from Ur, rooted in divine instruction and executed immediately by Abraham, has as its goal the fullness of divine presence in Jerusalem. But the exilic audience, aware of the temple's destruction, might ask: Will the place where the promise of God's instruction to Abraham had once been fulfilled, again be a place of rest for the soles of Israel's weary feet? Who will defeat the opponents of Israel's promised future (cf. Ezra 4:3; Neh 2:20)?

The patriarchal journey from Ur to the land of promised rest, almost immediately endangered by Pharaoh's and Abimelech's attempts to compromise the matriarchs Sarah and Rebekah, must also overcome Egypt and Amalek's attempts to prevent Israel from reaching Sinai. Once in the desert, Israel's disloyalties at Meribah and Massah threaten their entering the rest of the LORD (*mnwḥ*, Ps 95:11); at Sinai Israel threatens the patriarchal journey by violating the LORD's sabbath with worship at an altar to "the gods" who brought them out of Egypt (Exod 32:1, 4).[10] At this point the Lord threatens to abandon Israel, to continue the journey with Moses and give him rest (*nwḥ*, Exod 33:14–15). Moses refuses, pleading his and the people's status

---

10. The Golden Calf episode interrupts two sabbath episodes (Exod 31:12–17; 35:1–3). See Childs, *The Book of Exodus*, 541–42. Houtman, *Exodus*, 588, the sabbath pericopes form an inclusion, Exod 35:1–3 forming the execution of 32:12–17's instruction.

as favored in God's sight (ʾny wᶜmk, 33:16b); rest remains for God's people, if they do not harden their hearts, as at Meribah and Massah.[11] A year later, fully instructed for life in God's presence at the mountain, Israel leaves Sinai and resumes its journey guided by the ark, which seeks rest for the people (ltwr mnwḥh lhm, Num 10:33).[12]

Because the generation that left Egypt dies in the desert for its rebellion, the second generation continues the journey, but not without first hearing from Moses that in the land God will give them rest from their enemies all around (nwḥ, Deut 12:10; 25:19), a rest achieved only after Israel destroys the seven Canaanite nations and their altars (Deut 12:29–32). Thus instructed, God's people await entry into her promised rest on the plains of Moab.

Rest in the Presence of God across the River(s): The Former Prophets

Rest from the Enemy All Around: Joshua

Eden's rivers continue to water all the earth; their fertility gave rise to generations of people and material culture that enhanced life. Nevertheless, these cultural goods did not ameliorate the pervasive restless wandering and violence east of Eden (Gen 4:12, 14; 6:11, 13), for restfulness depended on compliance with God's instructions in his garden presence. Thus, Abraham and Sarah crossed the mighty Euphrates (Josh 24:2–4) and became the ancestors of a great nation only by divine will (Gen 12:7; 18:9–14). Centuries later, Israel would weep by the barren waters Abraham and Sarah had left behind, lamenting its exile from God's Jerusalem presence (Ps 137) and for failure to root itself in the life-giving waters of God's instructions (Ps 1:3; Exod 15:25).

The Former Prophets begin with the patriarchal descendants crossing another river. Potent with Baal and Asherah's blessing the Jordan overflows its banks, its life–giving water producing fields burgeoning with

---

11. The issue here is not Moses' anxiety ("I will give you a secure existence," Houtman, *Exodus*, 699), but his special status as favored by God, hence "I will give *you* rest," but Moses reminds God this status belongs to Israel as well. "To give rest in the Old Testament is often connected with the possession of the promised land (Deut. 3.20; 12.10, etc.). If this is the sense intended, then God is reiterating his promise of the land. Still the explicit use of the singular pronoun—give *thee* rest—may point in another direction. God's promise remains focused on Moses personally" (*The Book of Exodus*, 594 [emphasis original]). The contest of pronouns in Exod 32:7–14 (God's people, Moses' people) underscores the close relationship among all three, but especially the people's dependence on Moses.

12. Leder, "From the Mountain of YHWH," 526.

ripening grain (Josh 3:15; 4:18). Before crossing the Jordan Joshua mediates the covenant polity (Josh 1:7–9, 16–18; Deut 28:1–11; 31:7, 23–29). Compliance with that polity would bring the rains, abundant fertility at home and in the fields of the promised land, and rest from the enemy all around (Deut 12:10; 25:19).

In its camp on the plains of Moab Israel was safe, free from all threats against the human flourishing that flows only from the sweet instructions of their Sovereign (Exod 15:22–27); in that camp Israel enjoyed the beginning of rest from all enemies who oppose the journey from Ur to the land. But, because the LORD dwells in their midst (Num 5:3; Deut 23:14–15; cf. Gen 3:8), Israel had to keep the camp clean and undefiled, nothing was allowed to corrupt the safe place in the God's desert presence. The goal of the journey and the divine instructions was to make the land as safe for God's people as the camp in the desert, but the land was not empty. Across the Jordan Canaanites loyally followed the instructions of fertility gods similar to the deities Abraham and Sarah abandoned when they crossed the Euphrates; the Baals and Asherah had prospered the Canaanites for generations. Loyalty to these gods would be like Abraham and Sarah returning to Ur and resuming the old ways, one where there is no rest for the soles of the feet on the journey to God's promised rest (Deut 28:65).

The LORD of all the earth (Josh 3:11, 13) consecrates the land to his purposes when the ark crosses the Jordan; compliance with his covenant instructions makes it a safe place in God's presence. Thus, Moses teaches Israel to be careful to obey these instructions in the land as it did in the camp (Num 35:34) and not defile this divinely consecrated space for restful living. Unlike Egypt, Amalek, and Moab—who stood in the way of Israel's completing its journey towards the land—the Canaanite enemies "all around" Israel constitute a threat to restfulness by tempting Israel to serve (ᶜbd, Exod 23:24, 33) their gods and so to defile God's presence. Because these landed[13] enemies stand in the way of the promised rest Moses tells God's people to destroy them and their altars (Deut 7:2, 5). Once at rest from their enemies all around, Israel could acknowledge the LORD's gift of rest with the appropriate sacrifices, for only so would it go well in the land (Deut 12:10, 11–27, 28). Israel's desert enemy, Amalek, receives a special place in Israel's covenant loyalty: "Remember what Amalek did to you as you came out of Egypt . . . When the LORD your God has given you rest from all your enemies around you in the land . . . you shall blot out the memory of Amalek" (Deut 25:17–19). King Saul forgot, Esther and Mordecai remembered.

---

13. On the difference between "landed" and "landless" enemies, see Leder, "Celebrating Relief from the Enemy," 232–35.

The theme of rest first appears in the Former Prophets in Joshua's commanding the trans–Jordan tribes to help the others until all have received rest (*nwḥ*, 1:13, 15; cf. 22:4) in the land. Language depicting the ark's crossing of the Jordan—"When the soles (*kp*)[14] of the feet of the priests who bear the ark of the LORD, the LORD of all the earth, rest (*nwḥ*) in the waters of the Jordan, the waters of the Jordan flowing from above shall be cut off" (3:13 NRSV)—suggests that the realization of this rest begins with the LORD's entry into the land. Similarly, when representatives of the people comply with divine instruction to remove stones from the Jordan's dry riverbed and place (*nwḥ*, 4:3, 8, 20) them at Gilgal. As memorials of the crossing, these piles of stones, "rested" at Gilgal, memorialize the passing through the Jordan for the subsequent generations, and anticipate the LORD's gift of rest. Ironically, the first to apparently enjoy the benefit of the ark's conquest is the Canaanite Rahab, who with her family "rested" outside the camp (6:23).[15] Although the verb *nwḥ* in Josh 3, 4 and 6 can be correctly translated as "to place," as in Gen 2:15, recourse to its root meaning supports Joshua's central theme of rest from the enemy all around, and broadens it. That is, rest is now concretely associated with the ark of the covenant of the LORD of all the earth; upon its entry into the Holy of Holies Solomon praises God for giving his people rest (1 Kgs 8:56).

Hearing Joshua on the other side of the River reminds exiled Israel that the LORD had given her ancestors rest from its enemies all around (Josh 21:43), on both sides of the Jordan (1:13, 15; 22:4); that, having received this rest (23:1), they were told to follow divine instruction (23:6–8); and that they had vowed to serve the LORD alone (24:16–28). A rock near the holy place (24:26) witnesses Israel's commitment to future fidelity in God's presence (24:1). Hearing these words reminds the exiles why they now reside east of the Euphrates, without a resting place for the soles of their feet (Deut 28:65). Unlike Noah's dove, there was no ark to receive them safely.

Rest for the Enemy All Around: Judges

Whereas Joshua and his generation received rest from the enemy, the following generation chooses the gods of their enemy "all around"; and, the LORD sold them into the hands of the enemy "all around" (*msbyb*, Judg 2:12, 14). This inversion of Israel's relationship to the enemy is paired with a similar use of the verb "to rest": "The LORD had left those nations" (*nwḥ*, Judg 2:23,

14. Remember *kp* with *nwḥ* in Deut 28:65 and Gen 8:8. See also Leder, "Hearing Esther after Joshua," 267–79.

15. Hawk, *Every Promise Fulfilled*, 74, acknowledges the verb's root meaning here.

NRSV); and, "These are the nations the LORD left" (*nwḥ*, Judg 3:1, NRSV).[16] To translate these verbs in the sense of "rest" may be wooden, but doing so underscores the irony: the divine judgment meant for the nations now falls on Israel because she had joined the nations' religious practices. Because "Israel did evil in the eyes of the LORD" (*bᶜny yhwh*, Judg 2:11; 3:7; 3:12; 4:1; 6:1; 10:6; 13:1) God sold them into the hands of foreign kings/nations (Cushan-Rathatayim, *mkr*, 3:8; Moab, *ḥzq*, 3:12; Jabin, *mkr*, 4:2; Midian, *ntn*, 6:2; Philistines, *mkr*, 10:7; Philistines, *ntn*, 13:1; cf. Rom. 1:24, 26, 28). Furthermore, the ironic gift of rest to the nations who oppressed faithless Israel is construed as a test whether she would "keep the way of the LORD" (*šmr drk-yhwh*, Judg 2:22; 3:1, 3; cf. Gen 18:19) as did their ancestors, a reference to the generation that entered the land under Joshua's leadership (Josh 23:12–13).[17] The divine gift of rest to the nations "all around" also recalls its bestowal on the Canaanite Rahab and her family.

The internal chaos consequent upon Israel's disobedience—ascribed to a lack of kingship ("in those days there was no king in Israel and everyone did what was right in his own eyes" (*bᶜnyw*, Judg 17:6; 21:25)—in the context of the depicted failures of Benjamin and the successes of Judah, justifies the Davidic kingship, and is suggestive of the king who restored Israel's rest from the enemy all around (*wyhw hnyḥ–lw msbyb mkl-yᵇbyw*, 2 Sam 7:1). Because there was no resting place for the soles of Israel's feet (Deut 28:65) during the days of the judges, one family moved from the "breadless" city of David to Moab (Ruth 1:1–5). Like Rahab, the Gentile Ruth would also find rest in Israel.

Rest in the House of Boaz: Ruth

That Gentiles like Rahab and Ruth receive rest seems odd until one realizes that Israel herself was separated from the nations when God instructed Abraham to leave his land, place of birth and father's house (Gen 12:1). Divinely promised rest is achieved only by abandoning the restless wandering characteristic of the nations (Gen 4:12, 14), and joining the journey towards that rest in the promised land (Gen 49:15). Rahab received rest as the result of her loyalty to Israel instead of her own people (Josh 2), but she and her father's house remained outside the camp (6:23). Similarly, Ruth finds rest

---

16. The verb *šqṭ* in Judges depicts a time of inactivity. In Judges especially it cannot mean the same as rest from the enemy all around. For a brief discussion see Leder, "Hearing Esther after Joshua," 268.

17. The scarce occurrence of *nsh* suggests the testing in Judg 2:22; 3:1, 3 also evokes Marah (Exod 15:26 [cf. Massah, Exod 17:7]) and the sacrifice of Isaac (Gen 22:1).

by active abandonment of her past: she abandoned her mother and father and the land of her birth (2:11; cf. 1:16–17). Unlike Rahab, however, Ruth finds rest within the camp by joining the house of Boaz (4:11a, 12) and participating in the building of the house of Israel, as did other women who came from afar: Leah, Rachel and Tamar (4:11b, 12).[18]

Naomi drives the theme of rest: she wishes the LORD give Ruth and Orpah rest (*mnwḥh*, Ruth 1:9), each in the home (*byt*) of a husband in Moab. Having joined her mother-in-law in Bethlehem (*byt lḥm*) Ruth submits to Naomi's plan to find rest for her with Boaz (*mnwḥ*, 3:1), a distant kinsman-redeemer; he takes her into his house to keep alive the name of Mahlon. During the time of the judges, when Israel (Naomi) had no rest from the enemy "all around," a righteous Gentile from Moab finds rest in the house of Boaz in Bethlehem (*bbyt lḥm*, 4:11), to become the ancestress of David, who brings Israel rest from its enemy, the Philistines (2 Sam 7:1; 8:1). This intimate linking of rest with a particular royal house continues in the book of Samuel.

Rest in the House of David: Samuel

Like Ruth, Samuel begins during the time of the judges, a time of disobedient leadership in Israel when the nations enjoy so much "relief" from Israel that they defeat her, capture the ark of God and place it beside the god Dagon (1 Sam 4:1b—5:2), where it stays until David returns it. The description of the ark's triumphal entry into Jerusalem is followed by the declaration that the LORD had given David rest from the enemy all around and David's desire to build a house for the ark. An acknowledged high point in Samuel, 2 Sam 7 rejoins the theme of rest to that of the ark and of the conflict between the houses of Saul and David (2 Sam 3:1bis, 6, 8, 10, 19, 29bis; 6:20, 21; 9:1, 2, 3, 4, 5, 9, 12), and thus to the question of who would build a house for whom, David or the LORD (2 Sam 7:5, 6, 7, 11, 13, 16, 18, 19, 25, 26, 27, 29bis). David's construction of his palace postpones the building of a house for the ark, and the end of its journey of seeking rest for Israel (Num 10:33).

Rest from the enemy for David can only be understood in terms of the Philistine threat. Where Israel failed, the LORD of the ark defeated the enemy in his own house (*byt*, 1 Sam 5:5)[19] and contained the Philistine enemy during Samuel's judgeship (1 Sam 7:12–15). Although Saul had many military successes during his reign (1 Sam 14:47–48), his failure against the

---

18. Rahab receives a similar role in Matt 1:5.

19. The verb *sbb*, used to depict the ark's moving around the Philistine pentapolis, evokes the ark's movement around Jericho and the phrase "the enemy all around."

Philistines receives special note (1 Sam 14:52); David's defeat of the Philistines receives pride of place in the list of his military accomplishments (2 Sam 8:1). David's rest from the enemy is defined in two ways: First, God will plant his people in a place where the wicked cannot disturb them (2 Sam 7:10); second, the list of David's military accomplishments ends with the declaration that David did "justice and righteousness" for all his people (2 Sam 8:15), a fitting description of rest for the Israel, not the nations (Judg 2:23; 3:1), and relief from David's enemies.

The "conflict" about who would build a house for whom adds another aspect to the meaning of "rest from the enemy." As the jubilant prince who escorted his LORD's ark in its triumphant entry, it was only normal for David to build a memorial to celebrate his LORD's triumphs, something similar but more permanent than the tabernacle (Exod 29:43–46), and thereby mark the end of its journey. Divine disapproval of this plan turns into the building of a house that would secure forever what the LORD had given David in his time and build the house David had contemplated (*nwḥ*, 7:1, 11–16). David would not see the ark reach its intended goal nor the rest for God's people signaled by the house built for the Name; nor the rise of the inter–tribal warfare that would turn rest into the troubled times like that of the judges.

Rest for God's People in His Jerusalem Presence: Kings

The ark's entry into the house Solomon built for the Name signals the end of the military journey it began at Sinai: "And I have made (*śym*) a place there for the ark which contains the covenant the LORD made with our fathers when he brought them out of the land of Egypt" (1 Kgs 8:21). The use of *śym* to indicate the ark's placement, rather than the expected *nwḥ* (cf. "whenever it rested," Num 10:36), highlights the fact that the journey from Sinai is not about the ark's resting, but its seeking rest for the people (Num 10:33). Thus, when Solomon says "Blessed be the LORD who has given rest (*mnwḥh*) to his people Israel . . ." (8:56), it signals that the ark has also accomplished this purpose.

The words following this declaration, ". . . according to all he spoke. Not one word has failed of the good words he spoke through Moses his servant," recall the words of Josh 21:45: "Not one of all the good words that the LORD had spoken to the house of Israel failed; they all came true"; and in Josh 23:14: "not one word has failed of all the good words that the LORD has spoken concerning you." In the context of Solomon's declaration that God had given his people rest from their enemy on every side (21:44; 23:1), this evocation of Joshua suggests that the rest received in Joshua, not yet complete in view of Josh 23:5, has now been fully given. Furthermore, completing the rest received in the days of Joshua required a faithful keeping of the Mosaic instructions, especially those concerning the worship of other gods (Josh 23:6–13). Solomon hears similar words from the LORD: the house of David must be faithful to torah and not worship other gods or the LORD will deport Israel and let his house become a heap of ruins (1 Kgs 9:4–9). That is, the rest of God's people signaled by the ark's presence in the house (*byt*) Solomon built depends on the faithfulness of the house (*byt*) of David; the divinely permitted destruction of God's house and the exile of David's descendant Jehoiachin signals the end of rest from the enemy. In this way the book of Kings answers the question: Did the royal houses of Israel, that of David and of those who ruled in the footsteps of Jeroboam, treat the house of God according to divine instruction or the instruction of other gods?

When Solomon himself fractured the rest from the enemy all around by turning to the gods of his foreign wives (11:2–6), God sent adversaries (11:14, 23). After this, the remainder of Kings depicts how the north and south treat the house of God, presumably with the ark in the holy of holies (1 Kgs 8:8, "they [the poles for carrying the ark] are there to this day."). Ironically, Jeroboam's anti-David and anti-Jerusalem policy (12:16, 29, 31) is not original; Solomon built a high place "on a mountain opposite Jerusalem" (11:7) for his foreign wives. The description of Ahab's reign—"He built an altar to Baal in the temple of Baal which he built in Samaria" (16:32)—well describes the reason for Israel's expulsion; Manasseh's worse-than-Ahab's reign, especially his defilement of the Jerusalem temple with other gods (2 Kgs 21:4–5), led to Judah's expulsion. Not even Josiah's temple reforms assuaged God's wrath. Notably, the narrative insists that God himself removed both Israel and Judah from his presence (2 Kgs 17:20, 23; 23:27; 24:3, 20).[20]

Kings ends with the enemy cutting a devastating swath through all the houses of Judah (*byt* used nine times), beginning with the treasuries of the house of God and that of the king (2 Kgs 24:13), which were then burned along with all the houses of Jerusalem (2 Kgs 25:9). Adding to the humiliation, the columns of God's house and the bronze sea were broken up and taken to Babylon (25:13). This destruction of the foundational houses of God and of the king appears to leave Judah bereft of any hope of restoration of the rest it once enjoyed. The note that the scion of the house of David is freed from prison (*byt klʾ*, 25:27–28) and enthroned above all others at the king's banquet table, recalls God's word to David about his house and of the LORD's

---

20. The exception (2 Kgs 25:21) notes that Judah went into captivity, away from her land (*ʾdmh*, not *ʾrṣ*).

own house (2 Sam 7). Given the important role of "house" in Kings, Jehoi-achin's release from prison suggests something new: the warfare that brought destruction on the houses of Jerusalem is over (Isa 40:1–2).

The ruins of Jerusalem, though obviously a symbol of God's judgment, continue to mark the place where God made his name to dwell forever (*mqwm*, 1 Kgs 9:3). It is the place where Solomon gave thanks for the rest God gave his people, and the place toward which God's people is encouraged to pray and petition God in times of need (1 Kgs 8:27–30). That the rest once given remains for God's people is the concern of the Chronicler.

Rest for the Returned Exiles: Chronicles

Addressed to the returned of "all Israel" Chronicles provides a stark con-trast to Kings. Where Kings depicts the ark as entering the Most Holy Place under Solomon's supervision after which he gives thanks for the rest God gave his people, Chronicles attributes a state of rest to the ark when it lists the men David put in charge of songs "in the house of the LORD after the ark rested there" (1 Chr 6:31 [MT16]). Although the following verse states that this was "the tabernacle of the tent of meeting until Solomon built the house of the LORD in Jerusalem," identifying the ark's resting place as the house of the LORD and connecting it with David, resets the chronology of Samuel and Kings. Samuel states that God had given David rest (2 Sam 7:1) but not that the ark came to rest; Kings states that Solomon had received rest from his enemies (1 Kgs 5:4), but Chronicles depicts a *future* rest for Solomon (a man of *mnwḥh* whom God will give rest from all his enemies, (1 Chr 22:9). In Chronicles David says, "The LORD the God of Israel has given rest to his people and dwells in Jerusalem forever" (1 Chr 23:25) *before* Solomon brings the ark into the Holy of Holies, but in Kings Solomon says, "Blessed be the LORD who has given rest to his people Israel" *after* the ark's entry into the temple; a reversal of roles and royal epochs. Finally, and most distinc-tive, 2 Chronicles 6:41 has Solomon praying: "And now arise, O LORD, and go to your resting place, you and the ark of your might."

According to Chronicles, then, the ark itself achieved rest in the time of David, before Solomon built the house of God; the people enjoyed rest because God dwells in Jerusalem forever; and, the LORD himself has a rest-ing place. Via Psalms 132 and 95 Von Rad suggests that God's rest is "a gift which Israel will find only by a wholly personal *entering into its God*,"[21] and argues that this testimony is taken over in the New Testament, especially

21. A major difference from the deuteronomistic understanding of rest (from the enemy). Thus, Rad, "There Remains Still a Rest," 99.

by Hebrews. But Chronicles itself does not use the phrase God's rest in the sense of "entering into God." Rather, 2 Chronicles 7:1–4 depicts God's resting, prayed for by Solomon, with the fiery consumption of the sacrifices and the glory's indwelling of the house of God. Thus, not the people "entering into God['s rest]," but God and his ark resting among his people in a particular place. 1 Chronicles 23:25 connects this particular place with God's dwelling in Jerusalem: "The LORD, the God of Israel has given rest to his people, and he dwells in Jerusalem forever"; and, similarly, 2 Chronicles 6:1: "But I have built you an exalted house, a place for you to dwell in forever."[22] The audience of Chronicles hears that the ruins have not destroyed God's rule, nor the rest he has bestowed on them, because prayer towards Jerusalem will still be heard in heaven

This explains the depiction of the Davidic kings who received rest from the enemy: Asa (2 Chr 14:5, 7; 15:15) when he sought the LORD (14:4, 7; 15:2, 9, 13); and Jehoshaphat (2 Chr 20:30) when he sought the LORD (2 Chr 18:4; 20:3). God himself fought the battle (2 Chr 20:15; 18:31; 20:22). Not all such pious acts were performed in the temple. Notably, Hezekiah, solves the siege of Sennacherib by praying to God and the LORD rescued him "from the hand of all his enemies, and he provided for them on every side" (2 Chr 32:22).[23] The temple and the land move into the background, Jerusalem as the place (*mqwm*) of God's dwelling forever is foregrounded. Nehemiah calls it the holy city (Neh 11:1). Chronicles encourages the people and their leaders to seek the LORD who is committed to the place of his resting. Humility before the LORD (2 Chr 12:6, 12; 33:12–13) brings them into the LORD's resting. But what about rest for those who did not return to the ruins of Jerusalem?

Rest in the Diaspora: Esther[24]

In the exile-become-diaspora, Israel's paradigmatic enemy Amalek[25] in the person of Haman ("the enemy of the Jews," 8:1; 9:24), threatens destruction because Mordecai, Saul's distant relative, refused to bend the knee to Haman.

---

22. The only other use of *škn* in 1 Chr 17:9: "And I will appoint a place for my people Israel and I will plant them, that they may dwell in their own place."

23. A similar formula but for the verb *nḥl*. Referring to 2 Chr 22:18, BDB suggests the translation "give rest."

24. On *nwḥ* and the enemy in Esther, see Leder, "Hearing Esther after Joshua," 267–80; Leder, "Celebrating Relief from the Enemy," 230–46.

25. Noort, "Josua und Amalek," 155–56, writes that Amalek is a "contrastive image of the rest from the enemy that Yhwh will provide for Israel."

Esther and Mordecai's response to Haman's threats results in rest or relief[26] from this ancient enemy (*nwḥ*[27], 3:8[28]; 9:16, 17, 18, 22). In contrast to Joshua's divinely received rest, the gaining of rest from the enemy in Esther depends on human initiative: the ability to discern the enemy and to respond wisely to his threats. Regular celebration of Purim in the diaspora reminds God's people that the enemy is only awaiting another opportunity. Until "the eternal Haman"[29] is finally defeated, God's diasporic people awaits the rest that remains (Heb 4:8–10). In the words of Milton's Adam upon leaving restful Eden, however, they are no longer on a "solitarie way":

> Greatly instructed I shall hence depart.
> Greatly in peace of thought, and have my fill
> Of knowledge, what this vessel can containe;
> Beyond which was my folly to aspire.
> Henceforth I learne, that to obey is best,
> And love with feare the onely God, to walk
> As in his presence, ever to observe
> His providence, and on him sole depend.

26. Levenson, *Esther*, 118, 124; Clines, *Ezra, Nehemiah, Esther*, 16. Why translators prefer "rest" for Joshua and "relief" for Esther is not clear.

27. Translations of Esther 4:14 ("relief," NRSV, JPS, NIV), where *rwḥ* not *nwḥ* is used, creates confusion: readers might conclude that this crucial text participates in the meaning of the *nwḥ* cluster. That *nwḥ* is not used in 4:14, although one might expect it, suggests its absence is intentional. In the inter-column references, the NIV Study Bible specifically links the "relief" of 4:14 to 9:16, 22. Using "respite" instead of "relief" would avoid this confusion.

28 *Nwḥ* in Esther 3:8 is seldom translated as "rest" or "relief." Its use in the decree of destruction creates the irony of the king's second decree acknowledging the Jews' special status and allows them to achieve what Haman would deny them, rest or relief. A translation such as "It is not in your interest to give them relief," would exploit the irony intended by the repetition of *nwḥ*.

29. Horowitz, "Amalek," 107–46. On Purim and Easter, see Leder, "Celebrating Relief from the Enemy," 236–37.

4

Hearing the Former Prophets

Structure and Approach

IN RECOGNITION OF THE canonical shape of Scripture, recent studies of Joshua–Kings have returned to examining these books as the Former Prophets, including the book of Ruth, without at the same time abandoning the insights gained from exploring the Deuteronomistic History (DH).[1] This chapter will review the Former Prophets' literary structure, discuss the canonical effects of reading Ruth among these prophets, and then formulate an approach to reading the books of the Former Prophets.

The Former Prophets without Ruth[2]

Joshua–Kings narrates the history of God's people in the land from Joshua's destruction of Jericho to Nebuchadnezzar's desolation of Jerusalem; a tale of two cities whose literary ruins memorialize the LORD's mighty acts on behalf of and against Israel. Although each book in this general chronological sequence has its own viewpoint on Israel's stewardship of the Promised Land, viewing Joshua–Judges and Samuel–Kings as pairs—the first focusing on the conquest and its subsequent failures, the second on the rise of David's kingship, his and his descendants' failures—discloses contrasting thematic epochs.

Joshua and Judges

Joshua narrates the LORD's conquest and distribution of the land under the torah rule of Moses' servant Joshua. Having sworn loyalty to Joshua on

---

1. Mann, *The Book of the Former Prophets*, 9–10, 94–106; Zenger, *Einleitung in das Alte Testament*, 193–95, 222–29.

2. This chapter reworks material from Leder, "Paradise Lost," 9–27.

pain of death (1:16–18) the second generation of Numbers follows the ark through the Jordan into the land of promise. The LORD grants each tribe its inheritance (13:1–7), but not before Joshua takes Jericho and the tribes learn to take possession of the land in compliance with the Torah of Moses. All Israel then enjoys rest from its enemies all around (Josh 21:43, 44) and swears oaths to maintain that rest among the tribes (22:10–34) by serving the LORD alone, and no other gods (Josh 24:18, 22, 31).

Contrary to the second generation of Numbers, the second generation in the land "did not know the LORD nor the work he had done for them" (Judg 2:10), they did not honor the oaths of God's people, but did evil in the LORD's eyes by serving the Baals (2:11). When, according to the covenant stipulations, God brings Israel's enemies to disturb their rest, they cry to the LORD for help. God sends saviors to free them from the enemy time and again, but Israel resumes her ways after their judge-savior dies. The judge-saviors rescued Israel from its enemies but did not change her persistent disloyalty to God. Judges ends with sordid accounts of entrepreneurial religion, rape, dismemberment of a prostitute to incite Israel to fratricidal war, and the theft of brides for the leftovers of Benjamin's men. "In those days," the narrator concludes, "there was no king in Israel. Everyone did what was right in his own eyes" (Judg 21:25 ESV).

Hearing Joshua and Judges by the rivers of Babylon Israel cannot escape the conclusion that her Torah commitment was so shallow it took only one generation to forsake the LORD (Judg 2:10), that savior-judges in different locations did not hold the community together, and that the last two, Jephthah and Samson, were seriously flawed. Israel would need consistent national rule because she herself was incapable of living out of God's instructions; by nature, Israel sought blessing from the local fertility gods (cf. Jer 2:23–24).

Samuel and Kings

Samuel opens with an illustration of the pervasive corruption of the days when the judges ruled: loud and rude Peninnah, prodigiously fertile, verbally abuses a barren and distressed Hannah; the blind priest-judge Eli fails to recognize Hannah's distress and gazes blindly on his sons' abuse of the priesthood. Samuel then describes how the LORD fulfills his promised word to Hannah (1 Sam 1:17) through Samuel, Saul, and especially David, whose kingship the LORD promises to secure forever (2 Sam 7). Thus, the book of Samuel narrates how the LORD abases the proud among Israel, embodied first in Peninnah, then her judges and priests Eli, Hophni, Phinehas, and king

Saul; and how he exalts the lowly among Israel, embodied first in Hannah, and raises them to national rule: Samuel, Saul, and David. But even the righteous David fails: his adulterous affair with Bathsheba and his Eli-like ineffective dealing with abuse and injustice in his own household (Ammon's rape of his sister Tamar and Absalom's response) threatens the kingdom.

Kings opens with an aged, less than vigorous David and the battle for succession. After Solomon assumes the throne David reminds him that observing the LORD's instructions will secure the throne (1 Kgs 2:3; cf. 9:1–9). Solomon administers the kingdom wisely, builds his palace, and the temple of the LORD. After the glory of the LORD fills the temple, Solomon exhorts Israel: "Your hearts must be fully committed to the LORD your God, to live by his decrees and obey his commands as at this time" (1 Kgs 8:61). But the promise of faithful national rule by the kings ends in dismal failure. Beginning with Solomon's later years, the kings compromise God's instructions for such rule (Deut 17:14–20; 1 Kgs 11:1–8) by ruling according to the pagan practices of seeking blessing and fertility from the other gods in the land. In the northern kingdom Ahab introduces elements of contemporary Canaanite religions into Israel's covenant life thereby undermining the torah worship defined Moses (1 Kgs 17–18). In the south, Manasseh exemplifies such revisioning of national rule and Israel's conduct (2 Kgs 21:1–18); his rule alone, we are told, "led (Judah) astray to do more evil than the nations had done whom the LORD had destroyed before the Israelites" (2 Kgs 21:9; cf. v. 11). Manasseh's grandson Josiah "walked in all the ways of his father David, not turning aside to the right or to the left." He reformed Israel leading her in the ways of the Torah of Moses (2 Kgs 23).

Hearing Samuel and Kings by the rivers of Babylon, the exiles cannot avoid the conclusion that the kings' rule and conduct, like the people in the book of Judges, is only one generation away from torah-lessness; that they regularly dismiss the Torah's warnings delivered by the prophets (2 Kgs 17:13, 18, 23); that not even Josiah's massive reformation and submission to the torah of Moses turned the LORD from his decision to expel Judah from his presence (2 Kgs 23:27; 24:3, 20) as he had expelled Israel earlier. From the point of view of the larger Genesis–Kings narrative, neglect of torah begets a second exile from God's presence: Israel's failure to comply with God's instructions recall the failure of Adam and Eve to heed divine instruction. The exiles cannot avoid concluding that human rule of God's people is fundamentally flawed.

In addition to these contrasts between Joshua–Judges and Samuel–Kings there are similarities between Joshua and Samuel and Judges and Kings. As did Joshua's conquest of the land so David's defeat of Israel's enemies, especially the Philistines, gives her rest (2 Sam 7:1); and, both books provide a positive view of national rule in the persons of Joshua, Samuel and David. And, as the savior-judges gave Israel respite from enemy invasions but failed to change its corrupt ways, so the kings, like Jephthah and Samson, were flawed and corrupt like Israel herself. Summarizing, Joshua–Kings is thematically organized in in an ABA¹B¹ structure. follows:

Joshua	A	Israel commits itself to covenant polity	At rest from enemies
Judges	B	Israel violates covenant polity: other gods	Enemies sent by God
Samuel	A¹	David righteous	Rest from enemy
Kings	B¹	Kings violate covenant polity: other gods	Enemies sent by God

Beginning with Genesis and ending with Kings, the Primary History teaches the exiles in Babylon and those who've returned to the land, that they had been expelled from God's presence for the same reason he drove Adam and Eve from the Garden: refusal of divine instruction. More specifically, Joshua–Kings instruct its audience in the consequences of ignoring torah piety, a piety the Christian canon illustrates by placing Ruth at the center of the Former Prophets.

Ruth among the Prophets[3]

Like Abraham, Ruth abandons her own family and its security and clings[4] to a Naomi bereft of husband and sons. With the force of a self-maledictory oath Ruth forsakes her own identity—her people, her gods, a grave in her native soil—to share Naomi's unmistakably empty future. When Boaz tells Ruth, "I've been told . . . how you left your father and mother and your homeland and came to live with a people you did not know before" (2:11), his words evoke the LORD's instruction to Abraham: "Leave your country, your people and your father's household and go to the land I will show you" (Gen 12:1), and so identify the Moabitess as a daughter of Abraham. Ruth further demonstrates her new identity by gleaning in the harvest fields upon her arrival in Bethlehem, thereby behaving in accordance with the instruction of the LORD (". . . do not reap to the very edges of your field or gather the gleanings

3. Wolfenson, "Implications of the Place of the Book of Ruth," 153–167; Jobling, "Ruth Finds a Home," 130–31; Dearman and Pussman, "Putting Ruth in Her Place," 59–86.

4. The verb "to cling" (*dbq*) Gen 2:24: "For this reason a man will leave his father and mother and be united (*dbq*) to his wife, and they shall be one flesh." This verb evokes "firm loyalty and deep (even erotic) affection," according to Hubbard, *The Book of Ruth*, 115.

of your harvest . . . Leave them for the poor and the alien" (Lev 19:9–10; 23:22; Deut 24:19–22). In the middle of the larger Joshua–Kings narrative depicting the failure of Abraham's descendants, the Moabitess Ruth behaves as a true daughter of Abraham. Her compliance with divine instruction fills Naomi's emptiness (1:21), an emptiness emblematic of the consequences of Israel's careless ways with the LORD's instructions.

Boaz models compliance with divine instruction concerning the poor and the alien ("pull out some stalks for her from the bundles and leave them for her to pick up and don't rebuke her," Ruth 2:16). Furthermore, when Ruth asks Boaz to be Naomi's kinsman–redeemer, he gives evidence of his good faith by giving her six measures of barley so Ruth would not have to go back empty-handed (Ruth 3:17), and by maneuvering the nearer kinsman to abandon his claims. Boaz willingly assumes debt by redeeming Elimelech's fields. Boaz is an Israelite whose torah piety fills Naomi's emptiness: "[he] keeps his oath even when it hurts" (Ps 15:2, 4). What the savior-judges accomplished for Israel after Joshua and his generation had died, and David during national rule (2 Sam 8:15), Ruth and Boaz did in Bethlehem, David's city. Ruth and Boaz are the unexpected savior-judges whose torah piety rescued Naomi from a barren future. It's the kind of piety envisaged by Lev 26:3–13, Deut 28:1–14, and contemplated in Josh 1:7–9 and 23:6. Ruth's opening and closing historical references to the judges and David—whether Ruth is located in the Writings (MT) or among the Former Prophets (LXX)—contrasts their piety with Israel's disobedience to the torah of Moses during the time of the judges and during the monarchy.

Joshua and Samuel instruct God's people in torah piety; Judges and Kings in the consequences of disloyalty to divine instruction. Inserted between Judges and Samuel, Ruth illustrates the benefits of abandoning the other gods and clinging to the covenant LORD of Israel, for Gentiles and Israelites alike. Its location among the Former Prophets places Ruth in the center of Joshua–Kings:

Joshua	A	Israel commits itself to covenant piety	At rest from enemies
Judges	B	Israel violates covenant piety: other gods	Enemies sent by God
Ruth	C	Obedience to covenant piety	Righteous Gentile
Samuel	A¹	David: demonstrates covenant piety	Rest from enemy
Kings	B¹	Kings violate covenant piety: other gods	Enemies sent by God

This raises the question of its function in the Christian canon.

The Effect of Ruth between Judges and Samuel

There are good reasons for ignoring Ruth's place in the Christian canon, according to David Jobling: its MT place in the Writings of the Hebrew canon, scholarship's dependence on the DH thesis, and the opening of Ruth ("In the days when the judges judged."), because that refers to a time long ago. But then Jobling writes,

> Despite all this, we cannot ignore Ruth. It is as the canon that the Bible has been and is read; it is as the canon that it exercises its unique cultural power. The part played by canonical *sequence* in this exercise of cultural power needs further study, but it is hard to believe that it is not pivotal for the way a canon enters consciousness and habit. Sequence is likely to be of even greater significance for the Christian canons, which (including the New Testament) purport to tell *one* story from beginning to end, than for the Jewish canon. Canonically, any Bible that defines 1 Samuel as a book at all (i.e., the LXX and Christian Bibles) precedes it not with Judges but with Ruth.[5]

Ruth's placement in the Writings demonstrates the importance of sequence. In the MT Ruth follows Song of Songs and as such carries with it the overtones of love's commitments between a man and a woman. BHS, however, places Ruth after Proverbs, which ends with a description of a worthy woman ($^{3}\check{s}t\ hyl$, Prov 31:10–31). Because Boaz speaks of Ruth as a worthy woman ($^{3}\check{s}t\ hyl$, 3:11) the book of Ruth functions as a further meditation on this theme from wisdom. In the Christian canon, however, it follows Judges, which describes judges and soldiers as "a man/men of valor" ($^{3}y\check{s}\ hyl$, 3:29; 20:46; $gbwr\ hyl$, 6:12; 11:1;), because both Ruth and Boaz are described by these phrases ($gbwr\ hyl$, Ruth 2:1; 3:11 [$^{3}\check{s}t\ hylh$]). From that perspective Ruth and Boaz behave like the savior-judges who rescued Israel from her emptiness.

Ruth's location in the Christian canon also interrupts the inevitable sequence of utter chaos and corruption from Judg 17–21 to 1 Sam 1–2 with a contrastive miniature dramatization of true torah piety.[6] As such it evokes the torah piety illustrated by Joshua, Samuel and David who, though flawed like the savior-judges, did administer the LORD's rule righteously. Reading

---

5. Jobling, *1 Samuel*, 34–35. Emphasis in original. In his study Jobling offers Judg 2:11—1 Sam 12 as "The Extended Book of Judges" and 1 Sam 13—2 Sam 7 as "The Book of the Everlasting Covenant." This reading strategy "help[s] to defamiliarize for us the familiar biblical books. They also provide a worthy test of claims . . . that the canonizers made divisions at the most appropriate places" (Jobling, *1 Samuel*, 43–104).

6. For Jewish exegesis of Ruth, see Beattie, *Jewish Exegesis of the Book of Ruth*.

from Judg 21 into Sam 1 places the conflict between Peninnah and Hannah in the immediate context of the kidnapping of the daughters of Shiloh (Judg 21:16–24), and converts their story into one more example of the corruption so prevalent in the days when there was no king in Israel. In the Christian canon Ruth provides narrative surcease by distancing the story of Elkanah's household from the abuse of women in Judg 21, and it recontextualizes Hannah's story of barrenness in terms of Ruth and Boaz's filling Naomi's emptiness.[7] By depicting hope for one barren woman in Israel, Ruth extends this hope to all Israel through the birth Obed, the ancestor of Israel's great deliverer, David. Without Ruth, the highlighting Judah's successes and Benjamin's failures in conquest in Judg 1:1–21; 20:18–48, for example—taken by some as subtle references to David and Saul—and the repetition of "In those days there was no king in Israel and everyone did what was right in their own eyes" in Judg 17–21, leaves the reader bereft of a solution to the chaotic times after the conquest. Ruth's historical framework (1:1; 4:18–21) explicitly links those days to David, where Judges only mentions tribes.

Ruth and the Theological Themes of the Former Prophets

Although Ruth falls outside the various compositional theories of the DH (based on the MT), its location in the Christian canon illuminates themes identified by DH studies: that speak to Israel's judgment and consequent exile for failure to comply with torah; the emphasis on repentance, strongly underlined in Solomon's prayer of dedication of the temple (1 Kgs 8:22–53); and hope in the future promised to David, especially in the light of Jehoiachin's release from prison (2 Kgs 25:27–30).[8]

Righteous Gentiles: Boaz

Ruth amplifies the theme of judgment and hope in its telling of a Moabite (not allowed in the assembly of the LORD [Deut 23:3–6]) and an Israelite

---

7. The canonical placement of 2 Sam 21–24 has similar effects: it prevents a reading from 2 Sam 20 through 1 Kgs 1–2, and the references to a younger David in 2 Sam 21–24 contrast sharply with David in his dotage, thereby creating a new theme in 1 Kgs 1–2, the accession of Solomon.

8. Noth, *Deuteronomistic History*, 89–99; Wolff, "The Kerygma of the Deuteronomic Historical Work," 83–100; von Rad, "The Deuteronomic Theology," 205–21. Fretheim, *Deuteronomic History*, 21, suggests that the heart of the deuteronomistic historian's concern is the first two commandments of the Decalogue; Nelson, *The Historical Books*, 75, that the "warnings of Moses (Deuteronomy 31) and Joshua (Josh 23) set up the central plot" of the Deuteronomistic History.

who resolve Naomi's problems (famine, death, barren future) typical of the time of God's judgments on his people's torah faithlessness in the "days when there was no king in Israel." As a pair, Ruth and Boaz present a sharp contrast to two other Gentile–Israelite pairs: Rahab-Achan (Josh 2, 7) and Naaman-Gehazi 1 Kgs 5). Rahab of Canaan acknowledges the LORD's mighty works, complies with the spies' instructions, and so gains rest in Israel (Josh 2:8–12; esp. 6:22–25); Achan of Judah fails to comply with the LORD's instructions and dies, with his family (Josh 7:1, 24–26). When the Gentile Rahab acknowledges the LORD's acts, she subverts her Canaanite identity, affirms the LORD's power, exercises covenant kindness (ḥsd, Josh 2:12), and lives to tell about it. When Achan, an ascendant of David who received divine instruction about Jericho's future from the LORD's servant Joshua, sees and takes the forbidden (Josh 7:21; cf. Gen 3:6), he subverts his Israelite identity. Similarly, Naaman of Aram submits to Elisha's instructions and is cleansed; Gehazi of Israel craves what the kings of the nations' desire (2 Kgs 5:26) and becomes unclean. The Rahab-Achan and Naaman-Gehazi pairs illustrate the heart of the Former Prophets' message: Israel's failure to comply with divine instruction in the land begets exile from the presence of God, death and its attendant uncleanness. Rahab's inclusion in Israel after the conquest of Jericho and Naaman's healing by compliance with the prophetic word in the days of the kings' corruption confront the exilic audience with God's unexpected blessing on Gentiles, among whom they have been forced to dwell by divine judgment. The exaltation of Gentiles in these pairs, much like Elijah's blessing of the widow of Zarephath while Israel suffered the curse of famine, serves to move the exilic audience to jealousy, to confess its sin of abandoning God and provoking him to anger (Judg 2:10–23), and, to repent (šwb, 1 Kgs 8:46–51).

The book of Ruth removes the contrast between a righteous Gentile and an unrighteous Israelite to focus on an Israelite whose torah piety rescues Naomi and her Moabite daughter-in-law from a barren future. By so doing it illustrates the benefits of that piety and anticipates the righteous Israelite who concludes the epoch of chaos and corruption, David (Ruth 4:18–22; 2 Sam 8:15; 2 Kgs 25:27–30) and, in the wider Christian canon, of his descendant Jesus Christ, whose righteousness saves his people from their sin (Matt 1:1, 5–6, 16, 21).[9] Ruth teaches that all who are true descen-

9. "Righteousness raises a nation high, but sin is a stigma to any people" (Prov 14:34). Translation by Clifford, *Proverbs*, 142. This proverb uses ḥsd to mean "sin." Clifford writes, "The reader is meant to be momentarily puzzled in colon B. The word "righteousness" prepares one to understand *ḥesed* in its customary meaning of 'fidelity, steadfast love,' but the word 'sin' forces a rethinking and, finally, a recognition that the word must be the rarer word 'reproach, stigma'" (Clifford, *Proverbs*, 148). Read

dants of Abraham (i.e., who abandon their identity to join the journey of God's people to its divinely promised future [cf. Gal 3:29]), will not only enjoy the benefits of torah piety but may also be the LORD's instruments for responding to the needs created by unfaithfulness to Torah. Those who live in exile, in the rebuilt Jerusalem (Ezek 18; Ezra 10:2–4; Neh 8–9), or the diaspora (Esther), will only enjoy the promised rest by exercising the kindness (*ḥsd*) of torah piety Ruth illustrates.

Naomi's return from exile among the Gentiles evokes the theme of return from exile defined in Solomon's dedicatory prayer, where the Hebrew verb "to turn" (*šwb*) indicates return to the land (8:34), and turning to God, that is, repent (8:33, 35, 47bis, 48). The section that treats Israel's repentance in exile (1 Kgs 8:46–51) also mentions the compassion of their captors ("Cause their conquerors to show them mercy" [8:50]), no doubt a reference to Cyrus. Ruth does Cyrus one better by abandoning her home to accompany Naomi on her return (*šwb*, [12x in chapter 1]) from exile in Moab to Bethlehem.[10] Nowhere does the book of Ruth depict Naomi as a character in need of repentance or as repenting, the focus is on her return from exile to the city of David, accompanied by Ruth. Indeed, Naomi bitterly blames God for her descent into emptiness (1:13, 20–21), one filled by the LORD's redeemer who restores (*šwb*, 4:15) Naomi's life to fullness with the birth of her son (4:17). In this manner Ruth anticipates and reinforces the prophetic calls for Israel to return to God by showing how torah piety restores fullness to Israel's self-inflicted emptiness consequent upon disregarding the LORD's instructions.

Keeping your Vows in the Presence of God

Exile is the result of repeatedly violating the solemn oath that sealed the covenant made at Sinai and renewed at Mt. Ebal (Exod 24:3–8; Josh 8:30–35): "If you do not carefully follow all the words of this law, . . . [t]hen the LORD will scatter you among all the nations" (Deut 28:58, 64). Within the over-arching oath of the covenant God's people vow, for example, to praise the LORD for his

---

intertextually with the three Gentile-Israelite pairs, this upside-down meaning of *ḥsd* evokes the corrupt Achan and Gehazi, and Boaz's recognition of Ruth's fidelity (*ḥsd*, 3:10).

10. Similar moves by Rahab, who is moved close to the camp, and Naaman (faithful), who takes soil from the promised land to worship his Healer. The phrase "who returned" (*hšbh*, 1:21) modifying Ruth, has her returning to Bethlehem! On this problem, see Hubbard, *The Book of Ruth*, 128–29. Mann, *The Book of the Former Prophets*, 98, combining this verse with the beginning of the harvest, writes: "Naomi and Ruth have come *home* for Thanksgiving!" (emphasis added).

salvation (Jonah 2:9), to thank him for defeat of the enemy (Ps 76:11), or to dedicate themselves to the LORD as a Nazirite (Num 6:1–21).

The language of oaths and vows varies. Some are expressed in blood ceremonies (Gen 15:17; 17:9–14; Exod 24:3–8), others use the word "vow" (*ndr*, Deut 23:21–22) or the verb "to swear" (*šbᶜ*, Josh 2:13, 17, 20). Ruth uses the phrase "May the LORD deal with me, be it ever so severely" (1:17b) to vow her closeness to Naomi: "if anything but death separates you and me" (1:17c). Boaz tells Ruth "As surely as the LORD lives, I will do it," referring to what she asks of him (3:11, 13), and tells the elders they have witnessed (ᶜ*d*) his legal acquiring of Elimelech's property and Ruth (*qnh*, 4:9–10). About all such vows Moses instructs the covenant people: "If you make a vow to the LORD your God, do not be slow to pay it, for the LORD your God will certainly demand it of you and you will be guilty of sin. But if you refrain from making the vow you will not be guilty. Whatever your lips utter you must be sure to do, because you made your vow freely to the LORD" (Deut 23:21–23).

Without coercion and at great cost to themselves Ruth and Boaz make vows "to the LORD" that are essential to rescuing Naomi from her emptiness, vows characteristic of those who are worthy of dwelling in the LORD's sanctuary (Ps 15:1, 4b). The dramatic payment of these vows offers the exilic audience opportunities retroactively to evaluate vows made in Joshua–Judges and prepares it for such connections with vows in Samuel–Kings.

Retrospectively Joshua models vows in the service of divine instruction. All Israel promises to obey Joshua on pain of death (1:16–18). The spies swear (*šbᶜ*, 2:13, 17, 20; 6:22, 26) to save Rahab and her family from destruction; the altar at the Jordan stands as witness (ᶜ*d*, 22:27, 28, 34) of the trans–Jordan tribes' promise to worship only at the tabernacle; and, a stone serving as witness (ᶜ*d*, 24:27) of the people's covenant promise to serve the LORD alone. Nevertheless, Joshua makes and keeps a rash vow with the Gibeonites (*šbᶜ*, 9:15, 18, 19, 20), a vow that will later bring a famine because Saul killed the Gibeonites (2 Sam 21:1). Judges depicts Israel as breaking her covenant promises (2:11–22, echoing the language of Josh 24:16–28); Jephthah makes and keeps a rash vow (*ndr*, 11:30–36, 39; cf. Deut 23:21–23); Samson defiles his Nazarite identity (13:4–5, 7; acknowledged in 16:17); and, the men of Mizpah, swore an oath requiring the destruction of Jabesh-Gilead, the kidnapping of their women and later the virgins from Shiloh (*šbᶜ*, 21:1, 7, 18). Judges models vows in the context of willful rejection of divine instruction and of the moral corruption characteristic of the days when Israel had no king. In contrast to the savior-judges, who provided only temporary respite, the vows and torah piety of Ruth and Boaz not only fill Naomi's emptiness, but set the stage for vows associated with the development of the kingship.

Samuel begins with Hannah's vows to dedicate Samuel to the LORD. At the end of Samuel's ministry, the people agree that the "LORD is witness" (ᶜd, 1 Sam 12:5; cf. 7:13) to Samuel's successful ministry. Saul's oaths put him in negative light; David's vows with respect to the house of Saul paint a positive picture. Saul's oath (1 Sam 14:24–28) that any soldier who eats before victory over the enemy is cursed, recalls Jephthah's keeping of his rash vow: he is ready to execute Jonathan (14:43–44). In the long transition from Saul's to David's rule a series of oaths and vows, by Saul and between David and Jonathan (1 Sam 19:4; 20:2–3, 12, 17, 42; 24:21–22), keep all alive. Saul again swears foolishly to get the witch of Endor to summon Samuel from the dead (1 Sam 28:10). In the run-up to his kingship David makes covenants with the house of Saul and all Israel (2 Sam 3:12; 5:3). Vows in the aftermath of the Bathsheba affair paint a weak David; his self-condemnation (2 Sam 12:5–6) in response to Nathan's parable, elevates him somewhat. David also vows to protect the widow from Tekoa in Joab's plan to placate the king for Absalom's rebellion (14:11); Absalom then debases vows to cover his rebellion (15:7–8, 10–12). As David flees from Absalom, Shimei curses him saying this is the LORD's revenge for the blood of Saul's house (16:5–12). The Samuel narrative ends with the restoration of a broken oath: David avenges Saul's destruction of the Gibeonites, by which he violated Israel's oath to spare them (šbᶜ, 2 Sam 21:2).

Kings depicts vows and oaths in the rule of David's descendants and the prophetic ministries of Elijah, Elisha, and Micaiah. Oaths support Solomon as David's successor (1 Kgs 1:13, 17, 29), Solomon swears that Adonijah has forfeited his life for *lèse majesté* and Shemei breaks his vow (2:23–24; 37–38, 43–44). Jehoiada makes a covenant and an oath to protect Joash against Athaliah's threats (2 Kgs 11:4, 17). Kings uses the phrase "As the LORD lives" in Elijah's vow that the LORD will bring a drought on Israel, Jezebel that she will kill Elijah, Micaiah's prophecy against Ahab (1 Kgs 17:1; 19:2; 22:14), Elisha's in favor of Jehoshaphat (2 Kgs 3:14–20), and the king of Israel's vow to execute Elisha (6:31).

Vows and Covenant Theology

"The abiding truth of the covenant model," writes Mann, "is its insistence on absolute allegiance to God, over against any contenders, whether gods in the theistic sense or those powers which are socio-economic or political."[11]

---

11. Mann, *The Book of the Former Prophets*, 17–18.

The Israelite covenant, however, understands the socio-economic realities to be included in its monotheistic allegiance, as did the rest of the old world through its pantheistic commitments. The distinction between theistic and socio-politico-economic powers belongs to the disenchanted post-Enlightenment mind that reconceives transcendence as a horizontal project: overcoming obstacles to humanity's self-realization. Thus, for example, Marxist humanism's experiments of the twentieth century demanded absolute allegiance to the building of its egalitarian society. Similarly, contemporary interest groups insist on such allegiance and discipline in the various socio-political projects they embody, such as feminism-womanism, post-colonialism, sexual orientation, ecological interests, animal rights, and neo-socialisms. Although no formal covenants are made, the allegiances required in practice resemble the absolute character of old-world covenants, if only horizontally. A post-Enlightenment view of transcendence begets a ruthlessly egalitarian covenant theology, whose efficacy is limited to the power of the equals; a truly transcendent guarantor is excluded.

Scripture, however, reveals a Being who created all things out of nothing,[12] thereby making all created being, especially humanity, subservient and dependent on it for a full realization of its created identity (Gen 2:15–17). This same Being, the LORD God according to Scripture, responded to humanity's explicit rejection of its servant status with an oath-bound covenant not to destroy it along with the rest of creation (Gen 9:8–17). Beginning with Abraham, the LORD God made oath-bound covenants with him and his descendants to return all who swear allegiance to him their normal place in the divine presence, an oath supremely embodied in Jesus Christ (Heb 7:20–22, 28), begotten of the Father before all worlds. Biblical covenant theology is profoundly hierarchical: there is one LORD, all created things, especially human beings, are vassals. And, because covenant is itself emblematic of "oath" (Gen 15:17–20; 2 Kgs 11:4, 17; 1 Sam 20:16–17), a biblical vow has the force of the Guarantor who made a covenant with a blood oath (Heb 8:6; 9:12b). Covenant piety expresses itself in a covenant polity.

Approaching the Former Prophets Book by Book

Rather than presenting the structure of each book and surveying its contents, the following chapters will 1) provide a summary of the book and its central narrative interest; 2) discuss the connection of the book with the antecedent narrative; 3) discuss themes from the book that may challenge the

---

12. On the biblical basis of this doctrine, see Anderson, "Creation: *Creatio ex nihilo* and the Bible," 41–58.

contemporary reader; 4) discuss the books abiding claim; and, 5) examine
a text from that book to show how it illustrates that claim, this with a view
to enabling contemporary readers who are committed to this literature for
their faith and conduct to hear the claims of the book and the illustrative
text. That is, each chapter will state the claim of the text and what response
that text seeks from its audience "today."

Hearing and Preaching Today

Preaching Joshua, for example, will not take God's people on a historical
tour of the past: the configuration and power of the Jordan, a disputation
about the ruins of the "real" Jericho; nor of the present: the indigenous
peoples' loss of their land, Eurocentrism's imposition of western identity,
arguments for Israelis' rights to the West bank, or against contemporary
Israel because it invaded land belonging to the Palestinians. All of these are
crucial problems and Christians are involved in them as they engage in the
socio–political solutions of the day. As such they are relevant to the contemporary human community. However, preaching any part of Scripture,
OT and NT, is not primarily about "today" in the sense of contemporary
problems of human rights or the migration of peoples. Rather, preaching
the ancient text of Scripture provides an interface between the "today" of the
text and the "today" of God's people who live in a particular socio-cultural
environment "today."

The Today of Scripture and of the Church

When Psalm 95:7 declares, "Today, if you hear his voice, do not harden
your hearts as you did in Meribah," it refers to an event in Israel's past—its
rebellion in the desert and failure to enter the land of rest—but speaks of
this event to a much later audience. Although scholars differ on the original
occasion of Psalm 95's writing, any reading of Psalm 95 is heard by an audience no longer in the desert. That audience could be in the land of promise,
in Babylonian or Egyptian exile, or some other place in AD 1517 or 2020.
That is, the psalm's liturgical reading today no longer addresses the generation born after those who rebelled in the desert, but the descendants of
those people who live after the desert rebellion and after the time of the
psalm's composition. But its central claim, introduced by the word "today,"
does not change, no matter the culture, place, and time of its hearing. Psalm
95's central claim is: do not rebel against the LORD, today. This claim does
not change from one age to another, and, because it always makes that claim

in terms of Israel's desert experience, it requires the audience to know that those rebels did not enter the Promised Land. Hebrews cites this psalm (3:7–11; 4:3, 5, 7), including its "today," referring not to the past, but to its ever–new today. This is confirmed in the argument and exposition, which begins by encouraging the readers to exhort one another ('everyday, as long as it is called today,' 3:13)."[13] Later, Hebrews exhorts its audience: "Let us therefore make every effort to enter that rest, so that no one may fall through such disobedience as theirs" (Heb 4:11).

Luke uses "today" similarly, though not in terms of Psalm 95's use of the desert. After Jesus reads from Isaiah he declares, "Today this Scripture has been fulfilled in your hearing" (Luke 4:21). That is, Isaiah's central claim about the servant in his day is still valid centuries later for the audience on that particular sabbath in Nazareth's synagogue (in the form Luke cites), now extravagantly so in the person of the reader of the prophecy, Jesus Christ. Twenty-first-century readers of this passage hear the same central claim about Jesus. "Today" it is equally true that Jesus Christ is endowed by the Spirit of the LORD "to proclaim the year of the LORD's favor." He's not just Joseph's son (4:22). The phrase "today of the text," then, indicates the central claim the text places before its audience, the never-changing claim of that long-ago-written Scripture heard at another time, when God's people still struggle with the sincere obedience on its way to the promised rest.

Psalm 95 and Isaiah 61 place their claims on the primary audience: God's people, a people that lives by Scripture's abiding claims, but in different times and places. It is not these times and places, however, that hear the claim of Scripture, not even God's people as shaped by those times and places, but the Church of Christ (or Jewish community),[14] primarily defined by Scripture's re-presentation of what God has done and spoken in the past, a Scripture whose claim impacts the present of its audience for the sake of that audience's future. The church's self-understanding, its identity, no matter what the age or the culture within which it has its being, is shaped primarily by Old and New Testament Scripture, the history of interpretation, and the church's confessions. This self-understanding or identity constitutes the "today of the church." Of course, the church is not naïve about the challenges of hearing Scripture in particular times and places,[15] for there is no

---

13. Sturcke, *Encountering the Rest of God*, 269. The verb "to say" in the sentence "Therefore, the Holy Spirit says" (3:11) is durative, according to Sturcke. When the listener, therefore, hears "'today,' he feels directly addressed and does not immediately think of a day many years earlier when the psalm may first have been uttered."

14. Levenson, *The Death and Resurrection of the Beloved Son.*

15. The ecclesiologies may vary, the biblical claims that the church is the body of Christ and the temple of the Holy Spirit are clear.

reading or hearing of Scripture that is not shaped by time and location, but neither one of these defines the church's fundamental nature or identity. A disciplined listening to and careful hearing of the text defines the reading process in which the audience, in terms of its ecclesial "today," is interrogated by Scripture's "today" rather than the audience interrogating Scripture in terms of its environment's values. The "today" of any Scripture passage, its unchanging claim, always addresses a present audience, whose "today" is rooted in its unchangeable identity in Christ.

The Audience as an Exilic and Diasporic Community

In addition to its unchanging identity as the body of Christ, the Scripture defines the church as an exilic or diasporic people. Compositional arguments about the Pentateuch and the Former Prophets aside,[16] Genesis through Kings as a narrative unit in the Christian canon ends with a description of David's descendant Jehoiachin in exile. From the point of view of that ending the entire Genesis–Kings narrative, and each of its larger and smaller sub-units, is addressed to God's people in exile. And, all the reasons adduced for this exile in this narrative literature, especially the Former Prophets, add the following to the self-understanding of God's people: they are defilers of God's temple-presence and thus the implied destroyers of Jerusalem. Chronicles and Ezra–Nehemiah add another layer to this self-understanding: how can such defilers live in a newly constructed Jerusalem (Neh 7:1–5; 11:1–2)? Esther moves this self-understanding beyond the exile. Without referring to the reasons for the exile but accepting that the Jews are a special people now dwelling among the nations, Esther subtly depicts the Jews as a delivered people (Exodus) constantly threatened by the ancient (Amalekite) enemy in the diaspora. Without condemning the Jews' defilement of God's Jerusalem presence, Esther depicts them as a continually threatened community scattered among the nations.

The New Testament supports and develops the themes of exile, temple, and diaspora. Matthew depicts Jesus Christ as the divine solution to exile from God's presence: he is Immanuel, God with us, whose presence sustains his disciples among the nations "to the end of the age" (Matt 1:12, 17, 23; and 28:20). John depicts him as the builder of the temple of his body and as the sender of the Holy Spirit who will indwell his disciples and lead them into the truth (John 2:19–22, cf. 1:14; 14:15–16; 16:13). And, although Jerusalem remains an important center, Christ's instruction to be his witnesses

---

16. For a contemporary discussion of the compositional development of Genesis–Kings, see, Dozeman, *Pentateuch, Hexateuch, or Enneateuch*.

throughout the world, beginning with Jerusalem (Acts 1:8), underscores the diasporic character of communities formed by the apostles. James addresses "the twelve tribes in the dispersion" (Jas 1:1; 4:4) and Peter "the exiles of the dispersion" (1 Pet 1:1; 2:11; 5:13).

The newly founded church in diasporic Corinth learned from an exasperated Paul that they were the body of Christ and the temple of the Holy Spirit (1 Cor 3:16–17; 6:19–20); that their bodies, no longer their own, were not to be sacrificed to the culturally correct practices of human sexuality. Thus, the gospel, including the Former Prophets, continues to be scandalous: it requires a fundamental change in one's identity, simply because one's body is the temple of the Holy Spirit. Rather than diversity, it seeks the unity of all who are called in Christ (the eye ought not to lead the hand into temptation); nor does it seek to transform cultures, but to purify sinners for inclusion in the temple of the Holy Spirit and so be conformed to the image and will of Christ. By grace, tribes with a history of hatred will learn to love each other in the church, in the marketplace, and in the sharing of resources. By grace, those dedicated to "#whatever" will rejoice that there is no other name given under heaven whereby we must be saved (Acts 4:12; Isa 44:6–7). By grace, others will be free from the loneliness of a life centered on "my body," whether its mind or the womb, because the Spirit binds them to "Christ's body." "Today" if you hear his voice—no matter your tribe, ethnicity, politics, or culture—"do not harden your heart."

The Individual Texts for Today and the Rest That Remains

After discussing the abiding claim of the book each chapter will study a text selected to engage that claim in terms of 1) the wider and narrower canonical context of the text; 2) who does what: a discussion of the characters to determine who is the protagonist, including subsections on particular textual matters; and, 3) what the particular text means today. The selected texts: Josh 6, the ark's triumph over Jericho; Judg 10:4—12:7, the Jephthah episode; Ruth 2, the first encounter between Ruth and Boaz; 1 Sam 3:1b–41a, the LORD reveals himself to Samuel; and 1 Kgs 8:22–53, Solomon's dedicatory prayer. The discussion of each book will end with a brief discussion of how it contributes to the over-arching theme of waiting for the rest that still remains.

Summary, Central Narrative Interest, Opening Sentences of the Former Prophets

Because I do not discuss each of the Former Prophets as a whole, each of the following five chapters begins a with a summary of the book in question. The summary's paragraphs reflect what I take to be the macro-structure of the book. Thereafter, I provide a statement of what I take to be the central narrative interest of the book, then briefly discuss the opening title and the connection with the antecedent narrative.

There is a notable difference between the titles of the Pentateuchal books, the incipits, the opening words of the text ("In the beginning"; "These are the names"; "And [the LORD] called"; [And the LORD spoke to Moses] "In the desert"; "These are the words."),[17] and those of the Former Prophets, whose titles refer to the protagonists, whether individual or groups of persons (Joshua, Judges, Ruth, Samuel, Kings). Together with subtitles in modern translations of the Bible, titles of the individual books are paratexts that, because they are joined to the biblical text have "an influence on our interpretation of the text."[18] Thus, Gregory Goswell writes, the book titles of the Former Prophets, excluding Ruth, suggest an interest in leadership for in various ways they foreground crucial figures such as Joshua and the Judges; the limited role of Samuel and the entrance of prophets in Kings, raise questions with the received book titles,[19] but does not change the theme of leadership as such. Would using the incipits as titles make a difference? Would the Former Prophets still be about leadership? What is the commentary value of the incipits of the Former Prophets, including Ruth? Goswell makes only brief comments about opening words of Joshua and Kings: "after the death of Moses" contributes to the theme of leadership in Joshua; "Now king David was old" is a crucial division marker between 2 Sam 21–24 and 1 Kgs 1.[20]

Well-written opening sentences draw the reader into a narrative; others make it difficult to continue reading.[21] Well written or not, opening sentences provide a setting: "In the beginning God created the heavens and the earth": whatever the narrative that follows, all is subsumed under the aegis

17. Christian Bibles use latinized titles.

18. Goswell, "What's in a Name?" 262.

19. Goswell, "What's in a Name?" 271–76.

20. Goswell, 271, 275. Based on Genette's scholarship, Goswell discusses four functions of a title, and applies them to Joshua, Judges, Samuel and Kings. Goswell, "What's in a Name?" 263–64, 276–77.

21. For examples of both, see: http://americanbookreview.org/100BestLines.asp https://theamericanscholar.org/ten-worst-opening-lines/#.XaSoLUZKiM8

of God the creator. In a multi–chapter work, the opening line often functions retrospectively: "These are the names of the sons of Israel who came to Egypt with Jacob": the narrative does not begin with an exodus from slavery but an entry into Joseph's benevolent Egypt. Each of the following chapters will examine the opening sentences of the book in question, not as a paratext (the traditional title), but as the narrator's first hint of what is to come in the light of the antecedent narrative.

5

Joshua

*Israel's Vowed Loyalty in the Land at Rest
from the Enemy All Around*

Summary: After God's servant Moses dies, God instructs
Joshua to take the land according to the Torah of Moses, so
that Israel may receive rest. The people swear to follow Joshua.
From Rahab of Jericho Joshua's spies learn that all Canaan fears
Israel's approach. The ark of the LORD leads Israel through the
Jordan into the land. All Israel is circumcised (Josh 1:1—5:12).

According to the LORD's instructions Joshua and the
people follow the ark encirclement of Jericho for seven days.
When the walls fall in their place Joshua instructs Israel to
destroy all inhabitants except Rahab and her family, and to
place the spoils of the city into the LORD's treasury. Achan's
disobedience begets Israel's defeat at Ai; he and his family die
for his disloyalty. After Israel conquers Ai, the Gibeonites trick
Israel into making a peace treaty; they are condemned to being Israel's servants. After this Joshua leads campaigns in the
south and the north; Israel puts all the inhabitants to death,
according to the word of the LORD to Moses. The land enjoys
respite from war (Josh 5:13—12:24).

With land left to conquer, the LORD instructs Joshua to
distribute Israel's inheritance by lot. The LORD assigns cities of
refuge for unintentional murders. Levites receive special towns
as their inheritance. Israel rests from its enemies all around
because God has fulfilled his promises (Josh 13:1—21:45).

Intertribal war is avoided when the eastern tribes swear
an oath at the altar not to rebel against the LORD. Joshua instructs Israel to continue to live in the land according to the
Torah of Moses. After Joshua charges Israel to serve the LORD
always, a stone witnesses Israel's oath to serve the LORD alone.
Joshua, the servant of the LORD, dies (Josh 22:1—24:33).

> **Central Narrative Interest:** All Israel swears to serve the LORD
> their God alone, according to the torah of Moses, in the land
> where he gave them rest from their enemies all around.

Opening Sentence and Connection with Antecedent Narrative

THE OPENING SENTENCE, "AFTER the death of Moses, servant of the LORD,
the LORD spoke to Joshua the son of Nun, Moses' assistant," informs the audience of two important matters. First, the mention of Moses' death recalls the
reason for his death: like the rest of the generation that left Egypt, Moses did
not enter the promised land because of disobedience. Second, Moses' death
and the geographic shift from desert to land is accompanied with a change
in leadership. As Moses led Israel in the desert according to divine instruction, Joshua, commissioned in Num 27:12–23, receives divine instruction to
guide Israel in the promised land. The LORD instructs Joshua to obey "the
law my servant Moses gave you," and "do not let this Book of the Law depart
from your mouth" (Josh 1:7, 8). Moses died at the conclusion of the desert
epoch, but his voice—as depicted in Deuteronomy's "this book of the Law"
(Deut 28:61; 30:10; 31:26)—is the norm by which Joshua will guide Israel
and the LORD judges the faith and conduct of all generations of God's people
in the promised land (2 Kgs 17:13, 16; 21:7–9).

Before he dies Joshua instructs Israel to "obey all that is written in the
Book of the Law of Moses" (Josh 23:6). Obediently following the torah of
Moses will bring Israel rest from its enemies all around (*nwḥ*, Josh 1:15; 21:44;
22:4; 23:1; cf. Deut 3:20; 12:10; 25:19). "After these things," says Josh 24:29,
"Joshua the son of Nun . . . died," but not as Moses' assistant. Having complied
with divine instruction he receives the title of "the servant of the LORD."

The land Israel is about to enter is not empty. Because Canaan's nations will be a snare to Israel, Deuteronomy teaches all generations of God's
people to worship the LORD alone and not to follow other gods (Deut
6:1—11:32, esp. 6:4–9); to worship the LORD only at the place he chooses
to let his name dwell (12:11; 15:20; 16:2); not to intermarry with the Canaanites but to exterminate them; and to destroy the altars at which they
worshiped their gods (7:1–7; 12:1–7). Submission to the normative voice of
Moses in the land will bring blessing; disloyalty the curse (28:1–14, 15–68).
Judges illustrates Israel's and her saviors' disloyalty in these terms; prophetic
denunciations in Kings remind Israel's and Judah's kings of their failure to
heed the torah of Moses, a failure that would end with Israel's and Judah's
expulsion from the land (2 Kgs 17:7–23; 21:1–15; 23:26–27).

The Challenge to Reading Joshua: Violence

Taking land where others have lived for generations and destroying them and their religious culture to achieve that goal, keep the most committed readers from engaging Joshua as the Word of God. Scholarship seeks to ameliorate the scandal of canonical Joshua by arguing that it reflects ancient Near Eastern hyperbolic royal propaganda. This view explains the extremes of the destruction but cannot avoid the problem of violent disruption of an established society. The argument that Joshua describes the religious beliefs and practices of a primitive people ignores the horrors of post-Enlightenment warfare among more sophisticated people, and demonstrates the truth that "every intention of the thoughts of [man's] heart was only evil continually" (Gen 6:5 ESV). Reconstructions of what actually happened argue that there was no *Blitzkrieg* conquest, only a slow nomadic infiltration of Canaan, or that the Joseph tribes joined a peasant rebellion against foreign masters who controlled the Canaanite means of production. These explanations argue that the history behind the canonical Joshua explains the violence; the last one justifies violence.

Narrative and History

Liberation theologies of the last half of the twentieth century, argue that the conquest of Canaan is the conclusion to a narrative begun with Israel's exodus from Egypt; a triumphalist thesis that emphasizes freedom from oppression. Native American Robert Allen Warrior, however, points out that "Yhwh the Liberator" of the Exodus narrative then "becomes Yhwh the Conqueror" in Joshua. Worse, no matter how much Bible teachers intentionally empower local communities to interpret the conquest narrative through their own experience of oppression, "the danger is that these communities will read the narratives, and not the history *behind* them."[1] Norman Gottwald's reconstruction of that history depicts the Joseph tribes, having escaped Egypt, as joining a peasant rebellion of Canaanite craftsmen against their city-dwelling overseers who, supported by foreign investors, control the means of economic and social production with methods imported from abroad. Having overthrown this oppressive superstructure, the local peasantry along with the Joseph tribes established an egalitarian society that lasted about 200 years. When threatened by the Philistines this society formed a military for defensive purposes. Reorganizing itself as a monarchy this institution became oppressive, especially in its rewriting the history of the peasant

---

1. Warrior, "A Native American Perspective," 289–90, 292. Emphasis added.

rebellion to produce the book which depicts Joshua as the archetypal king.[2] Reconstructing the history behind the narrative, Warrior continues, enables the reader to side with the indigenous peoples of Canaan in their struggle for freedom—control of the means of production—not the foreign conquerors of the canonical narrative.

The peasant rebellion was violent, but its opposition to an unjust system imposed by foreigners was not a wanton slaughter of innocents nor an invasion. Rather, this reconstruction depicts oppressed peoples assuming socio-economic control of the means of production, of their own future in their own land; as such violence is justifiable. The establishment of this egalitarian society is the "biblical" paradigm of liberation for people or interest groups who consider themselves oppressed by an "other."[3] But "people who read the narratives read them as they are, not as scholars and experts *like* them to be read and interpreted. History is no longer with us. The narrative remains."[4]

Thomas Dozeman argues that historical reconstructions are unhelpful because they avoid "the ethical problems of genocide in Joshua by identifying the book as simply ideology or fictional theology, rather than as history."[5] He writes that

> the message of the book of Joshua is one of opposition to foreign rule in the promised land, represented by city-states; over against this the author idealizes a more primitive and rural life in the promised land. The origin story in Joshua contrasts with the competing myth of the empty land in Ezra and Nehemiah, where the promised land has lain fallow during the exile with the absence of cities . . . (Joshua is) a reactionary phantasy about the extermination of a superior people, whose technologically advanced city-states threaten the tribes who reject the dominant culture while living in a camp. The central plot of the book is to secure a pure form of religion and culture by destroying the infrastructure of the more superior city-states, executing all of the kings and undertaking genocide on the urban citizens, who have become irreversibly contaminated through assimilation into the more advanced society. The sense of threat from the

---

2. Gottwald, *The Tribes of Yahweh.*

3. See above chapter 1, for references to these hermeneutics of suspicion in the service of liberation.

4. Warrior, "A Native American Perspective," 290 (emphasis original).

5. Dozeman, *Joshua 1–12*, 91. For various discussions on this difficult topic, see Rutledge, *The Crucifixion*; Fretheim, "'I was only a little angry,'" 365–375; McEntire, "Recent Books on Violence and the Bible," 319–324.

dominant culture, the desire to reverse technological advance-
ment, the need to avoid contamination, and the permanent role
of conflict are central features in the rise of religious fundamentalism in the modern period.[6]

Fusing the horizons of Joshua's post-exilic Israel and modern fundamentalism is the key to Dozeman's interpretation of the violence, for "the
author (of Joshua) shares many of the same anxieties that drive contemporary fundamentalism." Viewed this way, the book of Joshua's canonical
function is negative, i.e., it exemplifies how not to live with the "other" and
how not to respond to superior technological knowledge. In short, Dozeman's Joshua depicts a society whose anxieties about social change places
them on the "wrong side of history." Modern fundamentalist resistance of
the dominant culture is facilitated by its most powerful weapon, "the selective retrieval of a religious tradition," similar to Joshua's selective retrieval
of the Torah of Moses.[7]

God and Violence

Placing the blame for Joshua's violence at the feet of fundamentalist "anxieties" may satisfy "non-fundamentalist" Christians; it could also (although
Dozeman does not touch on this) explain divine authorization of violence
as fundamentalism's desire for pure religion. Underlying Dozeman's reading, however, is the belief that Joshua is human speech about human affairs,
not depictive of divine irruption into human reality and, as such, revelation. Avoiding a discussion of Joshua as divine speech or revelation[8] fits
post–Gabler biblical theology and allows one to read Joshua as an ancient
religious document that expresses unacceptable views. But that approach is
as unacceptable as reading Joshua as fictional theology in order to sidestep
the problem of violence, or a fundamentalist psychologizing of cultural
changes. Fundamental questions remain. Is the God of the OT by nature
violent? What, if any, is the relationship between the Christian God and
violence? How do these questions shape the reader whose own personal or
communal history has been affected by violence and abuse? Moreover, if it

---

6. Dozeman, *Joshua 1–12*, 31, 92. Dozeman takes his description of modern fundamentalism from the studies of M. Marty and R. S. Appleby (*Joshua 1–12*, 134–35), but
fails to provide examples, nor does he engage Marsden, *Understanding Fundamentalism
and Evangelicalism*.

7. Dozeman, *Joshua 1–12*, 93–4.

8. In the light of modernity's attacks on it, Childs (*Old Testament Theology in Canonical Context*, 20–27) argues for renewed reflection on the nature of revelation.

is the unreconstructed, canonical narrative of Joshua that is before the contemporary reader, and if, like all Scripture, it is given by divine inspiration
and useful for teaching, reproof, correction and instruction in righteousness (2 Tim 3:16), this raises serious challenges for the committed reader,
although not for the first time in the history of interpretation.[9] Does the
violence of canonical Joshua belong to the same category as the crucifixion
of Jesus Christ, for that too is a scandal in the eyes of the world (1 Cor
1:18–31)? What should a committed reader do?

Thomas Mann counsels his readers not to avoid the horrors of the Rahab story (Josh 2–6) for three reasons. First, "the Bible generally does not
hide the questionable—even the damnable—traits of its characters, including
God." It's healthy to engage the questionable because our own history is filled
with the horrors of the genocide and the resettlement of native Americans,
the disappeared in Guatemala, the "killing fields" of Cambodia, and the
tragedy of Mi Lai, Vietnam. Understood this way, the text confronts us with
our own ugliness. Second, the invasion as described in Joshua is more than
likely a fiction, the reality was more like the peasant rebellion, a more palatable reading, but "it would not remove the theological problem of a God who
commands genocide." Third, Rahab herself represents "an *alternative* to the
merciless orthodoxy of extermination," an aspect of the narrative inserted
by the Deuteronomist, an ironic turn in the narrative "that forces a reinterpretation and loosening of the law and a developing of a 'situational ethic.'"[10]
Rahab's merciful survival makes Josh 6 more palatable, especially if biblical
speech about God is no longer referential to transcendent Being, but human
speech responding to the vicissitudes of physico-materialist processes.

Violence in Joshua, and elsewhere in Scripture, is fundamentally
nothing else than the scandalous problem of a God unacceptable to contemporary disciples of Marcion, and modern opponents of so-called fundamentalism. In Paul's day the claim of monotheism in polite polytheistic
society was scandalous, even more the claim that Paul's one God associated
with an unimportant Semitic offspring for the sake of the whole world.
How can one God alone manage the problems of order and disorder for
the whole world? Today the question is: How can the God of Joshua be
important for the whole world? There are no easy answers to this age-old
question, especially when it comes to the notion of divine holiness and
purity (Lev 18:24–30; 20:22–26). A contemporary engagement of Joshua,
according to Stephen Williams,

9. Early church interpreters of Scriptures recognized the problem of violence. See
Thompson, "Sacrificing Jephthah's Daughter," 33–47 and Thompson, "Reading Sex and
Violence," 185–214.

10. Mann, *The Book of the Former Prophets*, 22–25.

means reading it against a background of centuries of intellectual history during which the question of language about God has become an explicit theme of conscious reflection in parts of the world. Against the background of these intellectual habits, our consideration of holiness, divine being, and divine mystery in Joshua will lead us to qualify carefully, though not analyze definitively, our thinking and speaking about God as "good," "merciful," or "jealous."[11]

Such an engagement must not avoid contemporary discussions of the atonement, especially that of the so-called non-violent atonement.[12] The violence of Joshua is unavoidable, but is Joshua really about violence?

Violence or Compliance with Divine Instruction?

Joshua develops its storyline in four sections. Joshua 1:1—5:12 begins with the LORD's instructions to Joshua east of the Jordan and ends with the circumcision of Israel after crossing the river. In between, the people swear to follow Joshua as they did Moses, Rahab provides intelligence, and the ark leads Israel through the Jordan opposite Jericho. Throughout the emphasis is on Joshua's submission to the LORD and the people's submission to Joshua (1:17–18; 4:8; 5:2, 7). Joshua 5:13—12:24 begins with Joshua kneeling before the commander of the army of the LORD (as did Moses in the presence of the LORD at the beginning of his campaign against Pharaoh), the conquest and destruction of Jericho, Achan's stealing from the treasury of the LORD and his punishment, the conquest of Ai, the deception of the Gibeonites, the northern and southern campaigns, and summaries of Joshua's and Moses' conquests. Again, the emphasis falls on following the LORD's will as spoken through Joshua (6:8; 7:10, 16; 8:1, 3, 10, 18–19, 35; 10:8–9, 40; 11:9, 15, 23; failing to do so in 9:15). Only this section describes the conquest. Joshua 13:1—21:45 details the LORD's distribution of the land to the tribes beginning with the trans–Jordan tribes who had already received rest from their enemies (13:1–7; 14:1–5), and ending with the notice that the LORD had given his people rest from its enemies (21:44). Joshua 22:1—24:33 describes Israel's vowed commitments to inter–tribal peace based on worshiping only

11. McConville and Williams, *Joshua*, 226. This volume is valuable for its introduction and textual commentary, but especially for its theological treatment of conquest, genocide, and God.

12. Weaver, *God Without Violence*; Peacore, "An Evangelical Feminist Perspective on Traditional Atonement Models," 45–163; Van Dyk, "Vision and Imagination in Atonement Doctrine," 4–12.

at the place of God's choosing, and not serving the other gods, but the LORD alone (22:32–34; 24:19–27).

References to the torah of Moses (1:1:7–8, 17; 23:6–8) and Israel's commitments to follow Joshua (1:16–18; 22:28; 24:24–28) also frame the narrative further emphasizing that compliance with the torah of Moses and Israel's vowed commitments are Joshua's fundamental concerns. Reading Joshua within this narrative framework and retrospectively through the lens of Israel's vows in Josh 22:1—24:33, the audience Nebuchadnezzar forced into exile beyond the River (24:3) cannot avoid the conclusion that their exile is the result of breaking their vows to loyally maintain the gift of land according to the torah of Moses. Neither compliance with divine instruction—whether the torah of Moses or Joshua's mediating divine speech—nor Israel's vows to serve the LORD alone at the place he will choose, can erase the challenge of the violent of conquest. Rather, it more firmly places the authority to conquer Canaan in the divine will.

Violence and death in Joshua are not merely the result of Israel's conquest, however. The narrative begins with Israel's leaders promising to obey Joshua as they did Moses, and that "whoever rebels against your commandment and disobeys your words, whatever you command him, shall be put to death" (1:18 ESV). Achan and his family die for such disobedience. Once in the land, Joshua instructs Israel to remember the crossing of the Jordan in terms of their escaping death in the Sea of Reeds, after which Israel submits to the little death of circumcision by the sword of the LORD (4:19–24; 5:2–9).[13] Death is an inescapable reality for east of Eden humanity in punishment for failure to comply with divine instruction in God's Garden presence (Gen 2:15–17). From Abel to Terah death reigns unchecked until Abraham abandons Ur and, upon divine instruction, journeys toward the land God would show him. Only God's blessing Abraham, his descendants, and the other families of the earth, begins to check the curse of death. God seals the promised blessing with a self-maledictory curse and the little death of circumcision marks Abraham and his descendants as committed vassals (Gen 15; 17). Paul depicts this shift from curse to blessing as death reigning from Adam to Moses (Rom 5:14), the servant of God through whom God graced Israel with the Sinai covenant, divine instruction for life in God's presence. The death of about three thousand Israelites at the foot of Sinai illustrates the consequence of failure to comply with covenant instruction by worshiping other gods. The wages of sin, for all the descendants of Adam and Eve, is death (Rom 6:23); the manner of their deaths (old age, disease, famine, war, homicide, drowning) is secondary to death as the inescapable

---

13. More on this below in "The Context of Joshua 6."

punishment for sin. But, writes Paul, as sin reigned from Adam, so now the grace of God is revealed in Jesus Christ, and, he asks his audience, "Do you not know that all of us who have been baptized in Christ Jesus were baptized into his death. We were buried therefore with him by baptism into death, in order that, just as Christ was raised from the dead by the glory of God the Father, we too might walk in newness of life" (Rom 6:3–4). Engaging Joshua's depiction of violent death without considering Scripture's revelation about the reason for death abandons the reader to physico-materialist speculation about death. With Scripture's view of death in mind I will now describe what Joshua is about "today"[14] and read through Josh 6, the "paradigm for the entire conquest,"[15] in which "the essential relationship between God, Israel, Canaanites, and land is portrayed."[16]

What Is Joshua about Today?

By framing its account of Israel's entry into the land with references to the Torah of Moses, and throughout pointing to Joshua's compliance with divine instruction (Josh 3:7–9; 4:1–8a, 15–17; 5:2–3; 6:2–8; 7:10–16; 8:1–10, 18; 10:8–14; 11:6–9; summarized in 11:23), Joshua urges its exilic audience to meditate on the rest which compliance with divine instruction brought (21:44), and on the vows to maintain intertribal peace and serve only the LORD. In this manner Joshua teaches every generation of God's people, in exile or the diaspora, that compliance with canonical divine instruction mediated by Joshua, the servant of the LORD, brought them rest from their enemies. It also reminds God's people of its vowed obedience to maintain and bring to completion the rest from their enemies all around, a rest that remains, in part because of their failure to keep those vows.[17]

In the light of Israel's failure to keep its covenant vows (Deut 23:21–22), God's people who returned to the land under Cyrus' decree and those remaining in the diaspora await the rest that remains, specifically the divine glory that will revive the ruins of Jerusalem and build a new temple

14. This assumes the discussion about "today" in the previous chapter.

15. Nelson, *Joshua*, 91.

16. McConville and Williams, *Joshua*, 32.

17. Josh 4:19–24 signals Israel's corporate identity and corresponding responsibility, when it unites the children of the conquest generation to the generation that left Egypt by means of plural pronouns in vv. 23–24. A similar use of the plural pronouns to include subsequent generations is employed in Deut 6:20–25. Belonging to another generation does not invalidate the inherent corporate identity. Thus, the vows of Josh 22 and 24, and the instruction of 23, devolve also onto the exilic and subsequent generations.

(Ezek 40–48; John 2:20). But the land Joshua conquered is no longer the focus, it recedes into the background before Nehemiah's holy city (Neh 11:1, 18), and, along with the Spirit's driving the disciples to the end of the earth (Acts 1:8), Paul extends the landed inheritance of God's people to the cosmos (Rom 4:13).[18] In its wider canonical context, then, Joshua is no more a prescription for revolution or military conquest than Ezra 9 is for the dissolution of contemporary marriages with foreigners, or Galatians 3:29 for erasing the differences between women and men. Rather, Joshua places its representation of past events—the LORD's gift to his people of rest from their enemies in the land and the people's vows of loyalty to maintain the gift and its accompanying rest—into the present of the exilic audience with a view to eliciting a response to those events, especially the people's vows of loyalty to the LORD's Servant and his instructions. Reminded by Joshua to uphold its identity in the diaspora, all Israel (Rom 11:25–32) awaits the rest that remains.

The LORD's instruction to Joshua (Josh 1:1–9) and its transmission to Israel (Josh 23), along with the vows to maintain intertribal peace and serve the LORD alone together define Joshua's enduring claim, its "today": the gift of rest from the enemy all around, received by following Joshua servant of the LORD, is maintained by complying with the servant's instructions to complete the reception of that rest, that the whole land/earth (ʾrṣ, Num 14:20) may be filled with the LORD's glory. The servant who leads God's people today is not Joshua, neither David nor Peter, but Jesus Christ, son of David, son of Abraham, son of Adam (Luke 4). The mount of Transfiguration epiphany instructs those who would follow God's Servant today to "hear him!" "Follow me," says Jesus Christ. Where those who disobeyed God's servant Joshua would suffer death (Josh 1:16–18), following the instructions of God's Servant Jesus Christ includes taking up one's cross (Matt 10:38; Luke 9:23), and wielding the word of God which is the sword of the Spirit (Eph 6:17). This brings us to Josh 6.

Reading and Hearing Joshua 6 Today

The Context of Joshua 6

Near and distant contexts anchor our reading of Josh 6. In its nearer context, Joshua 6 continues the word–thread initiated in 5:2–9: the circumcision of Israel, effected with a *ḥrbwt ṣwrym* (5:2, 3), usually translated "flint knife" (ESV, NIV [both refer to Exod 4:25], JPS, RSV, NRSV). Apparently,

18. On this see Holwerda, "Jesus and the Land," 85–112.

circumcision with a sword is as unthinkable as shaving with one (cf. Ezek 5:1, 2). LXX has it both ways by expanding "flint knives" (ṣwrym) to "rock knives out of hard (or sharp) rock" (maxairas petrinas ek petras akrotomou kai kathisas). Why do the versions above take the last part of the expansion but ignore the word "sword,"[19] especially when Hebrew has a perfectly good word for knife, mᵃklh, almost used in the "circumcision" of Isaac (Gen 22:10)? Furthermore, if the instrument of circumcision is made of flint to indicate sharpness, why not use the same translation when "sword" (ḥrb) appears in 5:13 and 6:21 (ḥrbw šlwph; lpy ḥrb) and sixteen times in the rest of Joshua?[20]

Dozeman connects the drawn sword of the LORD's commander with circumcision as part of a transition which "signals a change in theme from the ritual of the identity of the Israelites to the execution of war against the 'other.' The sword as a symbol of executing the ban is prominent in the book from this point onward."[21] Following the word–thread from Israel's circumcision by "flint swords" (ḥrbwt ṣwrym) to the drawn sword (ḥrb) the commander of the LORD's armies wields, to the single time it is used in Josh 6, one may at least conclude to an intimate connection among the mentions of "sword." Perhaps all the inhabitants were completely "circumcised" by means of the ban (wyḥrymw, 6:21a)[22] as a permanent consecration,[23] that is, a complete removal from self-determination.

The pre-patriarchal nations' Babel and the patriarchal nation's Jerusalem provide a wider context for the Jericho episode. Each of the three cities has epochal significance: unfinished Babel of the hubris of pre-patriarchal nations,[24] banned Jericho of "the essential relationship between God, Israel, [and the] Canaanites,"[25] and Jerusalem's ruins of Israel/Judah's failed administration of the covenant in the land (2 Kgs 17:19–20; 23:26–27). Genesis-Kings ironically closes with Judah's deportation to Babel/Babylon, the place Abraham left (Ur of Chaldees, 2 Kgs 25; Gen 11:31). The prophets and the apostle John announce judgment on Babel/Babylon—built up despite the

19. Butler, Joshua 1–12, 318, points to the expansion, but he employs "flint knives" (333, 334).

20. Also, 8:24bis; 10:11, 28, 30, 32, 35, 37, 39; 11:10, 11, 12, 14; 13:33; 19:47; 24:12.

21. Dozeman, Joshua 1–12, 328.

22. According to Earl (Reading Old Testament Narrative as Christian Scripture, 88–92) the ḥrm narrative of Josh 6 symbolically depicts a liminal world that describes the proper response to the LORD "in the most demanding circumstance": Rahab, then, is taken to be a true Israelite, and Achan not.

23. Lohfink, "ḥrm," 188; McConville and Williams, Joshua, 34.

24. Fokkelman, Narrative Art in Genesis, 41.

25. Nelson, Joshua, 91; McConville and Williams, Joshua, 32.

divine scattering from Shinar—for its plundering of Israel and the temple (Isa 13; Jer 50–51; Rev 18). The destruction of Jericho and Jerusalem frames the Former Prophets with two ruins: one emblematic of the earthly kingdoms of the nations (i.e., a particularization of Babel), the other of the earthly kingdom of God. Joshua's curse over Jericho underscores its theological role: like the other piles of stone in Joshua, it reminds the generations of God's people of their LORD's enduring claim of sovereignty. Although rebuilt after 70 years (Jer 25:1–14; Ezra/Nehemiah; Haggai; Zechariah), earthly Jerusalem's canonical ruins in 2 Kgs 25 remind God's people of his punishing their disloyalty. Jerusalem's ruins serve as the place toward which diasporic/exilic Israel will pray (Dan 6:10), but their prayers will be heard in the heavenly and uncorruptible Jerusalem (1 Kgs 8:30b, 34, 39, 43, 45, 49; Rev 21–22; Ezek 40–48).[26]

Who Does What in Joshua 6?

Because biblical historical narrative depicts characters doing or saying something it's helpful to ask "Who does what?" This is true for Joshua as a whole and for narrative sub-units such as Josh 6. "Who" asks about the main, not all characters; "does" asks for a verb, the central action of the narrative; the answer to "what" tells us the result of the verbal action. Answering these questions provides us with the theme of the narrative, that is, the most important character and what that character did.

The LORD speaks first (6:1–5), instructing Joshua how to march around Jericho and so defeat it; Joshua speaks last, placing an oath on Israel not to rebuild the ruins of Jericho (6:26). In between there is an instruction-compliance pattern anchored in Josh 1: The LORD instructs Joshua (1:1–9), Joshua transmits these to the people (1:10–15), and the people swear an oath to follow Joshua (1:16–18). Joshua transmits the LORD's instructions about the order of the march around Jericho, thus complying with divine instruction (6:6–11); the people, following Joshua's instructions, devote Jericho to destruction (6:12–21), but the spies exempt Rahab and her family, again according to Joshua's instruction (6:22–25). From this it follows that, although the people execute Joshua's instructions, the main characters are the LORD and Joshua, the latter having been exalted to Moses' role of the LORD's mouthpiece (6:27; cf. Exod 4:15–16). A closer reading of the divine instruction (6:1–5) suggests that "The LORD has given Jericho into Joshua's hands" (6:2) is a fair answer to the

---

26. On the NT's fulfilment of the OT promise of a new temple, see Holwerda, *Jesus & Israel*, 59–83.

questions, "Who does what?" The verb "to give" in 6:2 is significant, for it signals completed action (echoing 1:3), meaning that Joshua and the people's compliance express the manner in which they are instructed to receive the gift already given. As this gift of Jericho is *pars pro toto* paradigmatic of the land, and Joshua's exaltation ends in his being "the servant of the LORD" (24:29), we could reformulate the theme as follows: "The LORD has given Jericho into the hands of his servant Joshua."

That Joshua is the servant of the LORD has immediate implications for a Christian understanding of this chapter. Christians follow the greater than Joshua, the Servant to whom God has given all authority over the nations, and who instructs his disciples that these should die the death of baptism and live under the ban of the Holy Spirit (Matt 28:18–20; John 16:8–11; 17:8–9). But questions remain.

To Whom Does Jericho Belong?

What right does God have to give Jericho into Joshua's hands? Or, for that matter, who has the right to give Jesus Christ all authority in heaven and on earth? These questions go to the marrow of Joshua, indeed, of Scripture, for they can only be answered from Scripture's depiction of God as Creator, his relationship to the creation and humanity as those responsible to the Creator, and specifically to the people of God as reinstructed by the servants of the Creator–Redeemer on righteous living in his presence. Aspects of these matters have been presented above; a summary will suffice.

In the light of Scripture, humanity's God-problem is the ancient one of human autonomy, depicted in the Edenic refusal to comply with divine instruction, of rejecting God's claims as the legitimate master-owner of what he brought into being. Thus, God rightly punished a violent world by letting the stored up waters break their barriers (Gen 7:11), scattering from Shinar the builders of Babel who rejoiced in their autonomy ("let us make . . ." 11:3, 4), and, finding not even ten righteous persons in the cities condemned by the Judge of all the earth (18:26). Scripture does not argue for divine ownership of the earth, it assumes the authority of heaven's Judge, Warrior, and King.[27] And this is the OT's scandal, no less than that of Jesus' parable of the land-owner who, upon returning to his vineyard, administers justice to all (Isa 5:1–7; Matt 21:33–46; 25:14–30).

Viewing God as the Master-Owner who expects his servants to promote their master's interests, the LORD's taking Jericho and giving it into Joshua's hands is not an abuse of the rights of Jericho's inhabitants, but a

27. Miller, "Cosmology and World Order," 53–78.

calling to account and an administration of the consequences for failure to respect the Owner's land. Furthermore, giving the city to his servant Joshua who curses its ruins anticipates Jesus' denunciation of the cities who refused to acknowledge his works (Matt 11:20–24; cf. Deut 13:12–18). Indeed, the Owner tells Joshua that the priests who lead the ark of the *Lord of all the earth* (Josh 3:11, 13) will announce the Owner's return with trumpets and ram's horns (*ywbl, šwpr*, 6:4, 5, 6, 8, 9, 13, 16, 20), an evocation of the Jubilee celebration of returning indebted land to its original inheritor (*ywbl hwʾ*, Lev 25:10, 11).[28] In this case, however, the jubilee is meant to last forever for Jericho may not be returned to its "original" owners after a year. Jericho's cursed ruins memorialize the true Owner's response to disloyal servants (as does Jerusalem's destruction); its disobedient rebuilding by Ahab also results in the complete devotion/destruction of Ahab's house (1 Kgs 21:20–24; 2 Kgs 9:7–10), and the capture of Samaria (2 Kgs 17:6).

Ahab's failure to comply with Naboth's divinely received inheritance illustrates in miniature Jericho's "stewardship" of the Owner's land. Viewed in the wider context of Genesis–Kings, Jericho's destruction teaches that earthly cities' promotion of human autonomy, from Babel to earthly Jerusalem (Jer 7:1–15; 18:11), has no future; they are built on sand.

Why Comply with Instructions to Destroy?

Why did God's servant Joshua tell the people to destroy all the inhabitants, animals, and place Jericho's riches in the God's treasury? And why did the people comply (6:16–17, 21)? Should good soldiers not refuse these the kind of instructions? These questions typically arise when Scripture's loyal readers meet difficult texts such as Josh 6.[29] An ancient answer to these difficult questions is to view the OT and its depiction of God as unchristian and focus entirely on the NT and the gospel of love. Although Marcion's teaching was decisively rejected by the church (he was excommunicated in A.D. 144), his views attract followers in every age.[30] Christian belief in the OT and the NT as equally the Word of God also recognizes important

---

28. Dozeman, *Exodus*, 336; Earl, *Reading Joshua as Christian Scripture*, 142–43.

29. Patristic and medieval exegetes already worried about these problems. See Thompson, *Reading the Bible with the Dead*.

30. For an older but still helpful discussion of Marcionite theological tendencies in readings of the OT, see Bright, *The Authority of the Old Testament*, 58–79, and 95–106, where Bright presents classical liberalism's narrowing biblical authority to its human aspect in the wake of Wellhausen's critique and thence to a narrow definition of Jesus Christ. Classic dispensational reading of Scripture, popularly defined in Scofield's Study Bible, distinguishes between Jesus' ministry to Israel and Paul's ministry to the Gentiles.

differences. The OT people of God, unlike the church of Jesus Christ, was a nation like any other, largely the descendants of Abraham and Sarah, that had its being in the interplay of those nations, friendly or not. Israel's Over-lord determined the status of those nations: the divinely declared enemies Amalek and the nations of Canaan merited destruction; enemies outside the land were handled differently (Exod 17:8–16; Deut 7:1–5; 20:10–15; cf. Josh 9:1–14). Israel fought its wars defensively and in support of treaty partners (Exod 17:8–16; Num 21:21–24; Josh 10:5–8; 11:1–9), but also offensively, against divinely approved targets such Jericho and Ai, and those not approved, such as Benjamin's war against Israel and the slaughter of women and little ones at Jabesh-Gilead to provide marriage partners for Benjamin (Judg 20:1—21:15). That war and its violence was part of OT Israel's experience, and that even Israel herself suffered offensive wars when God employed Ammon, Moab, Babylon and Assyria to punish her for disloyalty, does not explain Israel's participation in Jericho's destruction. In the light of Scripture, two things merit consideration.

First, Josh 6, like the rest of Genesis–Kings, is a narrative structured by divine instruction and subsequent compliance by Joshua and then Israel. This instruction-compliance begins in Gen 1:1—2:3: God spoke and there was light. Divine speech by its nature yields the willed response; the result of that speech is that all creatures by nature obey their Creator. Humanity, however, uniquely instructed according to 2:15–17, failed to comply. With the exception of righteous Noah who complied with the instructions to build the ark, humanity defies its creator, a *hubris* depicted in the Babel account. The journey to the promised land, begun with Abraham and Sarah, opens with divine instruction and subsequent compliance: unlike Adam, God spoke to Abraham and he complied (Gen 12:1, 4) by abandoning the scattered-from-Babel culture to begin a journey to the land God would show him. Failure to comply with God's instructions on this journey not only recalls Adam and Eve's disobedience, it compromises the journey to the promised future. Thus, Abraham circumcised all the males of his household according to God's instructions; his descendants wandered the desert for their failure to heed the instructions of Moses. Achan and his family died for disobeying Joshua's command not to take any plunder from Jericho.

Although the word is not used in the OT, "disciple" or "discipleship" describes well what it means to comply with divine instruction. When Jesus said, "Come, follow me," (Mark 1:16–20) the disciples did so, leaving all behind, just like Abraham and Sarah. In addition to leaving all behind, Jesus taught that "if you do not hate [your] own father and mother . . . and indeed [your] own life . . . he cannot be my discipleship. Whoever does not bear his own cross . . . cannot be my disciple" (Luke 14:26–27). When Israel put Jericho to the ban and destroyed it completely by the sword, they were following divine instruction, the essence of discipleship; and they demonstrated the cost of disobeying the LORD of all the earth.

The violence of Joshua cannot be explained away for the simple reason that death is the cost of *hubris*, a price determined by God in the instruction of Gen 2:15–17. No matter how or when it occurs, death robs humanity of its primary purpose: "the dead do not praise the LORD" (Ps 115:17). That God's people obediently administered the penalty to Jericho and Achan's family underscores the depth of sin; that Rahab and her family survived, the unmerited character of God's favor. To the natural objection that a loving God would not permit such violence, Scripture answers that God's love for the world is such "that he gave his only Son, that whoever believes in him should not perish but have eternal life. For God did not send his Son into the world to condemn this world, but in order that the world might be saved through him" (John 3:16–17). The gospel of John, like Lev 1–7 and 16, declares that God's love is inextricably linked to a sacrifice, in the case of Jesus Christ, of the innocent Son of God, "the Lamb of God, who takes away the sin of the world" (1:29). Sin has its wages, death (Rom 6:23); Jesus Christ's atoning death suffices to forgive all sin; it is efficacious for those who confess he is the Son of God. This takes us to the second consideration: the role of Rahab[31] in Josh 6.

Joshua qualified the destruction of Jericho: Rahab and her family were not to be placed under the ban but any Israelite who took plunder would be (6:17, 18). How did a Canaanite and her family, the people Moses placed under the ban (Deut 7:1–5), escape destruction with the rest of Jericho? Simply put, Rahab became a traitor to her own people and religion by hiding the Israelite spies. Before hiding them she made a confession of faith: "I know that the LORD has given you the land . . . ; for we have heard how the LORD dried up the water of the Sea, . . . and what you did to Sihon and Og . . . ; our hearts melted . . . for the LORD your God, he is God in heavens above and on the earth beneath" (2:9–11). Having abandoned her Canaanite gods in favor of the God of Abraham, Isaac, and Jacob, Rahab became a disciple. As a convert to the God of Israel she asked the spies to treat her like a member of the covenant community: I showed you covenant friendship, now be my friend (*ḥsd*, 2:12). Rahab believed, acted on her confession (Jas 1:18), and was saved from destruction with her household (unlike Achan, who was destroyed with his household for disobedience).

---

31. Stek, "Rahab of Canaan," 28–48, esp. 36–48. Stek argues that the prostitute's name subtly recalls the ancient monster Rahab (Ps 89:10; Isa 51:9). "As [at the Reed Sea] he overpowered Rahab, the monster that was Egypt, so here he had overcome Rahab the Canaanite" (Stek, "Rahab of Canaan," 40).

Choosing sides, the God of Abraham, Isaac, Jacob, and Jesus Christ, instead of the gods of the nations has real life consequences: believing the Gospel, OT and NT, rescues the sinner from death and gives birth to life in God's presence (Rom 6:5–11). Non-Israelites had joined Israel on their exodus from Egypt, but Rahab's declaration and consequent salvation from destruction is unique: she received the gift of rest[32] from her enemies all around *before* Israel did (21:44–45). As Jericho is the first fruit of the Canaanites to experience divine destruction so Rahab is the first fruit of those same nations to find rest in God's presence.

Christian scholarship has always recognized the continuity and discontinuity between the OT and NT. As mentioned above, where the OT depicts God's people organized as a theocratic state, the NT portrays God's people as the body of Christ that respects the state and the power of the sword it wields, but is itself not a state and therefore no longer has the power of the sword as did the OT theocratic state. NT discipleship, therefore, differs from its OT form in one crucial respect: devoting men and women, old and young to *physical* destruction as portrayed in Joshua, ended with the death of Jesus Christ, his death suffices for all who believe. Nevertheless, disciples continue to wield the Word (Eph 6:10–18; Heb 4:12) which cuts to the heart of people's natural rejection of the Creator and Redeemer (Rom 1:18–27). United to Christ's death in baptism the Spirit gives life to all who believe so they may comply with Paul's instruction: "Present your bodies as a living sacrifice, holy and acceptable to God, which is your spiritual worship. Do not be conformed to this world but be transformed by the renewal of your mind" (Rom 12:1–2). Making disciples of the nations is not physically destructive as was putting Jericho to the ban, but leaving behind your religious identity and dying to your former gods and their instructions, can create social violence, even death for converting to Christianity.[33] Thus Rahab the Canaanite prostitute died to her former way of life, Ruth the Moabite clung to Naomi's bitterness under the wings of the Almighty (Ruth 2:12; 3:9; Ps 91:4), and Naaman the Aramean vowed no longer to worship "other gods," but to worship on the soil he took from the Promised Land (2 Kgs 5:17).

---

32. Most translations have "placed," or "put" for the Hebrew *nwḥ* 6:23. See above chapter 3.

33. Christianity's missioning may even be understood to be violent or culturally offensive. Senior and Stuhlmueller (*The Biblical Foundations for Mission*, 40–41) define violence as follows: "Violence . . . is here understood as any strong initiative or forceful action that reaches beyond normal dialogue, *infringes* upon the freedom of the other(s), and *imposes* a solution or a situation upon others, at times against their desires." (Emphasis added)

Abandoning religious values may seem insignificant compared to the destruction of Jericho, but consider the changes involved: your body is no longer your own but a temple of the Holy Spirit (thus a different view of human sexuality, marriage and family); you may no longer have a restricted diet, but now assume the discipline of watching what comes out of your heart: evil thoughts, immorality, pride, envy (Mark 7:14–23); you're into a life-long ban. You no longer determine the shape of your life, the LORD does; you have died to two of the most powerful religious forces: the self and its desires, and the worldly culture that shapes them.[34]

Joshua 6 Today

In line with the enduring claim of Joshua, Josh 6 asks its audience to follow the instructions of God's servant Jesus Christ to receive and maintain the restful inheritance the Landlord gives to all, Jew and Gentile, who abandon what the culture most values—autonomy of body and soul—and to swear loyalty day by day to the God of Abraham, Isaac and Jacob, who is the Father of Jesus Christ. Divinely authorized, Jesus Christ sends his vassals/disciples, the body of Christ, to announce his sovereignty "to the uttermost ends of the earth" and add to the covenant community all who are slain by the sword of the Spirit. Furthermore, the curse over Jericho binds with an oath all covenant vassals not to rebuild the former way of life, a constant threat in the promised land then and in the church today: "Now this I affirm and insist on in the LORD: You must no longer live as the Gentiles live, in the futility of their minds" (Eph 4:17 NRSV). Because those who are loyal to the powers and principalities dispute this claim, Christ's loyal vassals put on the armor of God to withstand the wiles of the ancient enemy (Eph 6:10–17). This is the essence of covenant theology in its NT form: absolute allegiance to the greater than Joshua and his claim to universal authority over body and soul.

Waiting for the Rest That Still Remains: Vowed Commitment to the Gift of Rest

The conquest of Canaan according to divine instruction brought Israel the promised rest from her enemies all around. No longer on a desert journey, God's people lived in his landed presence without opposition from enemies such as Amalek (Deut 25:19). This rest, however, was not yet complete.

---

34. On the effects of contemporary culture, see Van Reken, "Christians in this World," 234–56.

Although Israel had received a secure deposit guaranteeing her full inheritance (Josh 21:44; cf. Deut 12:10; Eph 1:14), the claims of Canaan's gods in territory not yet fully possessed (Josh 13:1) would tempt her. Like the servants of Matthew 25, charged with administering the talents bestowed on them by their master, the LORD's gift of rest requires the diligent stewardship of complying with the LORD's instruction in a place still permeated by gospels of Canaan's deities. Centuries before Joshua's conquest of Canaan, Abraham had abandoned his native land beyond the Euphrates River and the gods who ruled Ur (24:2). Now, beyond the River Jordan, his descendants, having already received the blessing of land only promised to Abraham, vowed to work out the fullness of their rest by not surrendering to the values of Canaan's gods who remain to challenge their rest. Concretely, this meant destroying the visible symbols of those values (Baal's altars and the Asherah poles) and not worshiping there, as some Israelites already did (24:23). Fundamentally, completing the conquest was not a territorial matter but a profoundly spiritual battle against the powers and principalities that ruled Canaan.

Waiting for the rest that remains after Joshua's death asks for nothing less than a rigorous keeping of the covenant vows sworn at Shechem, faithful implementation of the teaching of the LORD through his servant. Where stone memorials earlier in Joshua reminded Israel of their LORD's mighty acts (4:21–23), the stone at Shechem and the altar the Jordan witnessed Israel's vows of covenant loyalty not to surrender to the seductive promises of other gods, not to abandon the tradition of Moses, not to become relevant in the world's eyes (22:27–30; 24:19–24). By their vows God's people commits itself to resist assiduously the temptation of Canaan's spiritual powers, to perfect holiness out of fear and reverence for God, and to be prepared to defend the hope of the fullness of God's promised rest. The exilic and diasporic audience today will do so with grace, so that "when you are slandered, those who revile your good behavior in Christ may be put to shame. For it is better to suffer for doing good, if that should be God's will, than for doing evil" (1 Pet 3:16–17 ESV). Faithfully keeping the vow not to worship other gods is the price discipleship pays the LORD of the vineyard who, when he returns, will ask his servants for an accounting of his gift of rest from the enemy all around.

6

Judges

Israel Does What Is Right in Its Own Eyes

Summary: After Joshua's death Judah took possession of the hill country, but Benjamin fails to take Jerusalem. Living among the Canaanites, the tribes fail to break down their altars but press them into forced labor; the angel of the LORD declares the Canaanites will a stumbling block for Israel. The generation after Joshua serves the Canaanite gods provoking the LORD to anger. He sends enemies to punish them and judges to save them, but they return to their evil ways. God lets the Canaanite nations remain to test Israel's faithfulness to the covenant (Judg 1:1—3:6).

When Israel does evil in God's eyes, he sends enemies and judges to save them: Othniel from Aram Naharaim; the left-handed Ehud from the Moabites; Deborah from the commander of Jabin's army, Sisera; and Gideon from the Midianites. Gideon's son Abimelech murders his brothers to govern Israel for three years; he dies when a woman drops a millstone on his head. Jephthah rescues Israel from the Ammonites, but foolishly sacrifices his daughter. The angel of the LORD tells Manoah's wife she'll give birth to a son she must raise as Nazirite. Samson's love for women is the reason he fights the Philistines. Tricked into disclosing the secret of his strength, the Philistines imprison him. At a feast to their god Dagon, Samson kills many Philistines in revenge for their taking his eyes. Upon all these the Spirit of God came to save Israel from her enemies. Israel enjoyed respite from war while the judges lived; after their deaths the people returned to their evil ways (Judg 3:7—16:31).

There was no king in Israel in those days. An Ephraimite hired Micah, a young Levite, to be his personal priest. Another Levite, who stayed overnight in Gibeah of Benjamin with his unfaithful concubine, was threatened with rape by the local men. They rejected the virgin daughter of the master of the house, but accepted the Levite's concubine, whom they left dead at the door. Because Benjamin refused to surrender the rapists, the Levite cut his concubine's corpse into twelves pieces to the induce the other tribes to destroy Benjamin. All Israel then swore not to let any of their daughters marry men from Benjamin; they kidnapped women from Jabesh Gilead and Shiloh and gave them to Benjamin. In those days Israel had no king; everyone did what was right in their own eyes (Judg 17:1—21:25).

Central Narrative Interest: Israel needs a king to rescue her from doing what is right in its own eyes.

Opening Sentence and Connection with Antecedent Narrative

LIKE JOSHUA, JUDGES OPENS noting the death of its leader: "After the death of Joshua, the people of Israel inquired of the LORD, 'Who shall go up first for us against the Canaanites, to fight against them'?" Unlike with Moses, Joshua's death leaves a vacuum, there is no successor. Rather than deciding for themselves, as they had with the Gibeonites (Josh 9:14), Israel consults its covenant LORD, thereby demonstrating faithfulness to the vows made before Joshua's death. God's reply indicates a tribe, Judah: "I have given the land into his hand" (1:2), not a person. Later, Judah will lead Israel in a punitive expedition against Gibeah of Benjamin "for all the outrage they have committed in Israel" (20:10, 19).

Although far from a seamless transition, chronological and thematic connections associated with Joshua's instructions and his death link Joshua and Judges. First, after Joshua's death and in accordance with his instructions (Josh 23:4–11), Judah (along with Simeon) successfully drives out the Canaanites in its territory (Judg 1:17, 19). Benjamin fails, as do Manasseh and other tribes; they lived among the Canaanites (1:29, 32, 33) without destroying their altars (2:2). Second, contrary to the vows made at Shechem, the people began to worship other gods after Joshua and his generation died (Judg 2:10; Josh 24:16–18). Where Joshua depicts Israel obediently following the servant of the LORD, Judges depicts the next generation's failure to drive out the nations and its subsequent abandoning of the LORD to worship the gods of the local culture. Because the generation after Joshua gave their children in marriage to the sons and daughters of the Canaanites, contrary to Deut 7, God will no longer drive out the nations (2:3; cf. 3:5), in effect postponing the fullness of the rest he had given his people (*nwḥ*, Josh 21:44–45), and award-ing it to Israel's enemies (*nwḥ*, 2:23; 3:1). Where Joshua depicts faithfulness to the Teaching of the LORD, Judges describes a people at odds with the Teach-ing received from the Servant of the LORD.

Challenges to Reading Judges

Judges presents three challenges that illustrate the conflict between God and Israel: vows and oaths representative at once of the human and divine wills; the conflict between what is right in God's eyes and in the eyes of his people; and, the total corruption of God's people within one generation after the death of the servant of God. As in Joshua, the challenge is the reader's relationship to the God of Scripture, OT and NT.

Covenant Vows

Where Joshua emphasizes God's just response to the nations who serve other gods, Judges turns that justice against God's own people for violating their covenant oath. The reason for God's response to Israel's disloyalty is clear to the exilic audience of Judges: God is faithful to the covenant curses proclaimed in Deut 28:15–68. This description of God holding in abeyance the fullness of the promised gift of rest from the enemy all around is sober-ing: God will no longer drive out the enemy, declares the divine messenger. Indeed, he will allow them to stay (2:3, 21) to test his people, to "see whether they will keep the way of the LORD and walk in it as their ancestors did" (2:22; 3:1). Israel's waywardness and God's response is concretely summa-rized in Judg 2:10–19, and the consequences in 2:20–3:6.

The challenge for committed readers is two-fold. First, in the bibli-cal world vows always involve the divine. One says, for example, "As the LORD lives"; vows are not merely individual or personal utterances. That's why Deut 23:21–23, for example, instructs the Israelites to pay any vows they make: the guarantee of the vow between you and your neighbor does not depend on your goodness or will, but on the LORD; you have sworn loyalty with all you heart, soul, and mouth (Prov 12:22; 13:2–3), and the LORD stands behind the words of his vassals. The sages also remind God's people that "it is a snare to say rashly 'It is holy,' and to reflect only after making vows" (Prov 20:25 ESV). Oath-bound commitments seem quaint to twenty-first-century readers of Judges: no one, *ni Dieu ni maître*, has the right to hold me accountable for what I say or what I mean it to say: "My speech is mine, and only mine and I will tell you what I mean." Vows made willingly before God must be paid. Foolish vows have terrible consequences. Jephthah's sacrificed his daughter because of his foolish vow, and all Israel's oath not to let their daughters marry men from Benjamin led to wholesale slaughter and kidnapping (Judg 11:29–35; 21:16–34, esp. v. 18). The instrument of the vow, the tongue, is dangerous, with it we praise God and curse people made in God's image (Jas 3:3–12); it is a spark that can set a forest on fire. Think only of the contemporary debates about intersectionality, the social media wars, and old-fashioned gossip.

Second, God's response to Israel's disloyalty—treating Israel like their Canaanite enemies, and their enemies like Israel—[1]raises questions about God: Did God break his vow to be Israel's LORD? And, if so, can Israel depend on the God who covenanted with them? What kind of God would allow this to happen? Although Israel addresses God with such questions (Pss 10, 13), they are not motivated by the suspicion that drives modern questions about God. Rather, they are grounded in the confidence that by covenant oath (although violated) they are bound to God, and, more importantly, God to them. Therefore, when God's disciplinary visitations become unbearable, they cry out to their covenant LORD who sends deliverers, time and again (3:9, 15; 4:3b; 6:7–14; 10:10–17). God's people and their saviors may be addicted to what is right in its own eyes, but God's self-maledictory covenant oath with Abraham (Gen 15:17–19) to be their God overwhelms any question of divine rejection or caprice. The words of that covenant and those at Sinai (including, and especially, the blessings and curses of Deut 28) describe the covenant LORD as faithful, dependable, not capricious. God is Israel's LORD in blessing its land and families and in the disciplinary curses whose purpose is to move them to repentance. Thus, when in their distress God's people do turn to him and call upon his name (1Kgs 8:46–49) he will hear them, for he will never break his covenant (Judg 2:1).

The challenge for the reader who acknowledges the God of Scripture as the Father of Jesus Christ, is twofold. With respect to oneself, disciples vow to own what it means to be an oath-bound vassal of God the Father of Jesus Christ. In covenant theology the vassal is completely the property of the Over-LORD. NT covenant theology, an aspect of the theology of divine presence, depicts the Over-LORD as indwelling the body of Christ and the individual Christian by the Holy Spirit. Because the land-LORD thus indwells his people, our bodies are not our own to do with as we please (1 Cor 3:16; 6:15, 19–20), including especially, according to Judges, what we do with our eyes. With respect to the LORD, faithful disciples vow to refuse the transfer of suspicion of human authority and relationships to our covenant

---

1. Note the ironic use of the verb *nwḥ* ("to remain, to rest") in Judg 2:22; 3:1.

LORD. That is, to discipline the eyes to see what is right in God's eyes, and tame the tongue, for "truthful lips endure forever" (Prov 12:19a).

Eyes of God and Israel

Judges uses the metaphor of sight to define its narrative problem from both the divine and the human side. By repeating the phrase "Again Israel did evil in the eyes of the LORD" (2:11; 3:7, 12; 4:1; 6:1; 10:6; 13:1), Judges reminds its audience of their failure to harness its passions. The Jephthah narrative, in addition to portraying Jephthah as a self-interested guerrilla, also employs the verb "to see" to underscore this judge-savior's rashness. Seeking victory over the Ammonites, Jephthah swears an oath to sacrifice as a burnt offering "whatever comes (*hywṣ᾽*) out through the doors of my house to meet me" (11:31). When the victorious Jephthah returns home only to see his daughter greet him first, he is dreadfully dismayed, but fulfills the careless vow he made before the LORD (11:35; cf. Deut 23:23). The metaphor of sight also portrays the defeat of Israel's enemies: Eglon's servants saw him dead (3:25), and Jael shows Barak the defeated Sisera pinned to the tent floor (4:22); and, the appearances of the Angel of the LORD to Gideon and Manoah's wife (6:12, 21–22; 13:3).

As befits the climax of a series of flawed saviors of Israel, the Samson narrative employs the metaphor of sight unusually. Beginning with the typical introduction of Israel's wickedness it unexpectedly shifts to heaven's announcement of Samson's nativity and his dedication from the womb as a Nazirite; the other narratives describe the enemies who punish that wickedness and/or the nature of Israel's wickedness. The Samson narrative, however, does not portray Israel in this way; here the metaphor of sight depicts Israel's wickedness in the person of the judge himself. With heaven's announcement of Samson's nativity and dedication the reader expects good things from the judge whom the Spirit of the LORD began to stir in Mahaneh-dan (13:25). The Samson episode, however, begins and ends with his eyes: the forbidden Canaanite woman Samson saw was "right in [his] own eyes," despite his parents' warnings (14:1–3); his final victory over Israel's enemy is an act of revenge for the loss "my two eyes" (16:21, 28). Samson's "she is "right in my eyes" also anticipates the pervasive corruption in Israel when "everyone did what was right in their own eyes" (17:6; 21:25). In the Nazirite Samson's eating honey from a carcass, Israel, herself dedicated to God from Sarah's womb, is confronted with her own passion for Canaan's carcass-defiled honey (Lev 11:35, 39–40).

Nevertheless, Samson's passions become occasions for the LORD's destruction of Israel's enemies, the Philistines (14:4, 19; 15:14–17; 16:30).

The contrast between what is evil in God's and good in Israel's eyes in
the biblical world of Judges portrays a hierarchy in which heaven evaluates
earthly decisions of his people according to the mutually sworn covenant
that regulates the relationship. The depicted consequences of divine evaluation of earthly human decisions makes sense to the exilic audience of Judges
but challenges contemporary readers who are encouraged to believe that human decisions belong to none other than the self.[2]

Although "doing what is right in your own eyes" may be liberating
today, consider the metaphor of sight and its limitations: "The eye that
sees all things else, sees not itself," "There is none so blind as those who
will not see," "The blind should not judge colors," and "The blind eat many
a fly." These sayings enunciate general but undeniable truths: no one sees
themselves or the world as others do. Indeed, these sayings argue that it's
unwise to depend only on one set of eyes, that we need another set of eyes
to illuminate our lives and to avoid trouble. The biblical wisdom tradition
in Proverbs, for example, seldom consulted in connection with biblical
historical narrative,[3] provides a set of eyes that illuminates the metaphor of
sight in Judges. The repeated phrases "Israel did what was wicked in God's
eyes" and "everyone did right in their own eyes" evoke, for example, the
following wisdom sayings: "All the ways of a man are pure in his own eyes,
but it is the LORD who tests the spirits" (Prov 16:2), "Answer a fool according to his folly, lest he be wise in his own eyes" (Prov 26:5), and "The poor
and the rich man meet in this: the LORD gives light to the eyes of both"
(Prov 29:13). This contrast between God's and human eyes should not be
attributed to the modern exegete's understanding of the tension between
"faith and thought, between reason and revelation." Rather, for "Israel
there was only one world of experience and this was perceived by means
of a perceptive apparatus in which rational perceptions and religious perceptions were not differentiated."[4] The challenge Judges' metaphor of sight
presents to the contemporary reader, encouraged to satisfy what is right
in a post-modern self-pleasing culture, is "not the quantitative limitation

---

2. Mann, *The Book of the Former Prophets*, 32, writes, "There is an assumption of
historical causation operative here that many contemporary people do not hold—at
least, not so explicitly. To us war is the result of political policies, foolhardiness, natural
aggrandizement, long standing ethnic feuds, etc."

3. For a discussion wisdom in the shadows of salvation historical theology and
historical methodology in the OT, see Perdue, *Wisdom & Creation*, 20–48. Crenshaw,
"Method in Determining Wisdom Influence," 129–42.

4. Von Rad, *Wisdom in Israel*, 61.

of human capabilities which forbids self-confidence and self-glorification; it is, rather something which can be explained only in theological terms: self-glorification cannot be combined with trust in Yahweh."[5]

True wisdom, lasting insight, cannot begin and end with human experience, for "the beginning of wisdom is the fear of the LORD" (Prov 1:7; 9:10) where the phrase "the fear of the LORD" refers to the instructions of the LORD. That, the prophet proclaimed at Bokim (Judg 2:1–5), was Israel's folly, time and again. Israel's seeking the "honey" of the Canaanite gods, a practice prohibited by covenant instruction, because it was right in her own eyes brought divine discipline, time and again. Wisdom observes: "Like a dog that returns to its vomit is a fool who repeats his folly" (Prov 26:11).

Corruption of God's People

The three major sections of Judges each end with a devastating portrayal of Israel. First, it describes Israel's laissez-faire attitude to complete the conquest and ends with a summary description of Israel's cyclical disobedience and the LORD's judgment to give her enemies rest (1:1—3:6). Second, following Othniel, the narrative depicts unusual, reticent, manipulative, and hedonistic judges, reaching a nadir in its depiction of Samson embodying Israel's repeated folly (3:7—16:31). And, finally, the awful portrayal of Israel's unrestricted cultic and social corruption (17–21). "The editorial in 2:11–23 leads us to expect a cyclical plot, but overall, the plot is a spiral with a plummeting trajectory."[6]

Taken separately or together, the salvific actions of the judges are sometimes ribald, as in Eglon's death in the bathroom at the left hand of the Benjamite Ehud; ugly in Jael's spiking of a sleeping Sisera; puzzling in Gideon's reticent testing of divine instructions; horrifying in Jephthah's sacrifice of his daughter because of a foolish vow; and, Samson's unsavory womanizing. Notably absent from these accounts is any reference to Israel's repentance, neither before crying to the LORD in her distress nor after her salvation[7] by the judges; there is only a respite for some years.[8] Where, however, the judges' salvific acts are troubling, Judg 17–21's portrayal of

5. Von Rad, *Wisdom in Israel*, 102.

6. Mann, *The Book of the Former Prophets*, 65.

7. The verb is "to save" (*yšʿ*) used of Othniel, Shamgar, and Samson (3:9bis; 3:31; 13:5), and ironically of the other gods (10:14); and the verb "to rescue" (*nṣl*) of God and Israel (8:34; 10:14).

8. The verb usually translated as "rest" in these comments is *šqṭ* (3:11, 30; 5:31; 8:28) not *nwḥ* as in 2:23; 3:1. The Jephthah and Samson accounts end with the comment that they had "judged" Israel for 6 and 20 years respectively.

cultic corruption, the sexual and physical abuse of the Levite's concubine, and the easy slaughter of Benjamin and Israel's kidnapping of virgins to provide wives for the devastated tribe of Benjamin, raise serious questions. Why these stories are remembered at all is a problem. Can they be material for a Christian sermon?

Any answer to these questions must begin with Scripture's unceasing and honest depiction of human nature, whether of the nations: "The LORD saw that the wickedness of man was great in the earth, and that every intentions of the thoughts of his heart was only evil continually" (Gen 6:5 ESV); or God's chosen people, as described in Judg 17–21, and the prophetic denunciations of the kings (2 Kgs 17:13, 23). Ignoring Scriptures' depiction of God's OT people's repeated wickedness would make it impossible to understand Isaiah's proclamation of double comfort for all of Jerusalem's sins (40:1–2); salvation and comfort for Jerusalem has little meaning outside of her corruption. The NT people of God is no less corrupt as Paul's warnings against sexual licentiousness among the Corinthians, or John's exhortation to the seven churches (Rev 2–3) demonstrate. "All of Scripture," Paul tells Timothy, ". . . is useful for teaching, for reproof, for correction and for training in righteousness" (2 Tim 3:16). Scripture will not allow those who read it as God's word to escape the awful truth that "all have sinned and come short of the glory of God." The problem is that Judges is devastatingly honest about the nature of the sin of God's people and its leadership. It does not, however, leave its audience without hope.

The editorial framing of Israel's cultic and moral corruption with "in those days there was no king in Israel" (17:6; 21:25) suggests national leadership, human kingship, as the solution to Israel's constant rejection of their covenant Over-LORD. By refusing the offer of such kingship, "I will not rule over you and my son will not rule over you; the LORD will rule over you" (8:23), Gideon stated the ideal; Abimelech's murder of his brothers to assume the kingship, states the problem of kingship. Nevertheless, the described successes of Judah and failures of Benjamin in Judg 1 and the contrast between the cities of Gibeah, Saul's birth-place, and Bethlehem, argue in favor of David's and not Saul's kingship. Samuel would describe Saul's rule negatively: "there was hard fighting against the Philistines all the days of Saul" (1 Sam 14:52); of David we read that he "administered justice and equity to all his people" (2 Sam 8:15). Even so, David's own reign was flawed (2 Sam 10–20), and his dynasty is ultimately characterized by Manasseh's desecration of God's presence in the Jerusalem temple, a wickedness "in the eyes of the LORD" (2 Kgs 21:1, 6, 15) that provoked God to remove Judah from his presence (2 Kgs 23:27; 24:3, 20). Though flawed, Judges recommends human kingship to rescue Israel from her moral corruption and the oppression it brought on them; David did, because "the LORD gave victory to David wherever he went" (2 Sam 8:15).

Judges' unappetizing portrayals of God's people as repeatedly prostituting[9] themselves with other gods, and the flawed judges who rescued them from their oppressors, anticipate the disloyalty of the kings of Judah and Israel. Neither God's people nor its leadership can escape its dedication to cling to what is "right in their own eyes." Should Israel then continue to sin so that God's compassion may abound (Judg 2:18c; cf. Rom 6:1)? By no means!

What Is Judges about Today?

Barry Webb writes that "[T]he challenge for those of us who read [Judges] as Scripture is not whether we can identify with the violence, but whether we can identify with the theology that frames and interprets it."[10] The abiding theological claim of Judges arises from the portrayal of Israel's moral and religious corruption in Judg 17–21: more than the repeated rescue from her oppressors by flawed saviors, Israel needs to be rescued from herself. Incapable of responsible stewardship of her covenant vows without the national leadership of a Moses or Joshua to oversee her torah faithfulness, Israel is "a wild donkey used to the wilderness, in her heat sniffing the wind! Who can restrain her lust?" (Jer 2:24 ESV). Flawed kingship, argues Judg 17–21, is better than everyone doing what is right in their own eyes, for: "Better a little with righteousness than great revenues with injustice" (Prov 16:8; cf. 2 Sam 8:15). In the meantime, Judges confronts its exilic and diasporic audience with the uncomfortable claim of the profound wickedness of her covenant disloyalty and the immorality it spawns.

Compared to the writing prophets Judges' claims are unique, for it accuses the post-Joshua generation, a generation that it "did not know the LORD or [know] the work that he had done for Israel" (2:10). Dozeman, commenting on a similar use of the verb "to know" in "a new Pharaoh who did not know Joseph" (Exod 1:8), suggests it points to a loss of memory, a gap between the generations. William Propp suggests this text means that "the new king ignored Joseph's former salvation of Egypt and did not acknowledge the benefits conferred upon the Hebrew vizier and his kin." Lillian Klein, pointing to the substitution of the verb "to see" (2:7) by "to know," suggests that the second generation did not have first-hand experience of

---

9. This verb (*znh*, 2:17; 8:27, 33; 19:2) defines Israel's disloyalty. Jephthah's prostitute mother and Samson's taking a prostitute (*zwnh*, 11:1; 16:1) ironically exemplify these judges' mirroring of Israel's disloyalty.

10. Webb, "Judges as Christian Scripture," 61.

what Joshua's generation "saw."[11] There is, of course, a gap and memory loss between the generations: Walter Brueggemann writes that "the central temptation of the land for Israel is that Israel will cease to remember and settle for how it is and imagine not only that it was always so but that it will always be so."[12] Imagining "it will always be so" obliges a constant adjusting to the local culture's values established and defined by its ruling deities, the gods and goddesses of fertility; it produced a compromised loyalty that sought blessings from the Baals and Ashtaroth not from the LORD of Israel's salvation. Although an a-theistic twenty-first century will not grant the existence of "other gods" never mind their pernicious pressure on the faith, the old world's search for fertility, blessing, and pleasure[13] is alive and well, the boundaries the old gods established for body, soul, and mind erased for maximum enjoyment of the material self, until death.[14]

All this began with the post-Joshua generation. The compromises of religious syncretism are not, however, just the problem of the generation after Joshua. God's exiled and diasporic people, Gentile and Jew, are under similar pressure to adjust their covenant loyalties to the "realities" of their environments. Ezra's requirement to put away their foreign wives reminded the returned exiles of the divine instructions against intermarriage, so easily forgotten far away from Jerusalem. Paul reminds the Corinthians not to let local values of sexuality compromise their bodies, temples of the Holy Spirit (1 Cor 3:16; 6:18–20), and the Ephesians not to embrace the futility of Gentile thinking, for they "did not come to know Christ that way" (Eph 4:20; cf. Rev 2:1–7). Beyond the NT, church history is replete with reflections on and warnings against the cultural pressures on God's people: Augustine's *City of God*; the numerous revivals and reformations that addressed compromised faith and practice, in monasteries and among church officials; the decline of the post-Enlightenment Western Church and Bonhoeffer's *Cost*

---

11. Dozeman, *Exodus*, 70; Propp, *Exodus 1–18*, 130; Klein, *The Triumph of Irony*, 32.

12. Brueggemann, *The Land*, 54.

13. See the discussion of ethical hedonism in Brandt, "Hedonism," 432–35.

14. "Enlightenment thinkers believed that if Earth comes to an end, it will be brought to an end not by God's Messiah but purely by natural causes such as the gradual extinction of the sun . . . . The world is shaped not by divine Providence but by natural forces and by human actions . . . . The famous analogy was that it was set in motion by a great clockmaker. This is the foundation for modern physicalism—the view that the only things that can exist are physical objects and forces, and that the only true knowledge we have is drawn from observation of these physical objects and forces . . . [although] the mechanistic model of the world was later demolished in twentieth-century physics, that model has persisted in the popular imagination into the twenty–first century." Russell, *Paradise Mislaid*, 43–44.

of Discipleship; the unwelcome impact of churches from the 10/40 regions of Africa and Asia on progressive western Christianity.[15]

The abiding claim that God's people needs salvation from itself is accompanied by the covenant LORD's response to their cries of distress, time and again, cries the exilic audience is encouraged to direct to God's dwelling place (1 Kgs 8:46–53), though it lies in ruins. Against the severe limitations of the temporarily Spirit-filled saviors like Jephthah and Samson, God promises the exiles to "put my Spirit within you, and you shall live" (Ezek 37:14), a promise fulfilled by the Pentecostal indwelling of the body of Christ by the Holy Spirit. This Spirit intercedes (Rom 8:26–27) for the living temple of God which, in its disciplined desire to separate itself from unbelief, seeks "to cleanse [itself] from every defilement of body and spirit, bringing holiness to completion in the fear of God" (2 Cor 6:14—7:1). But then, it is also this Spirit filled community that receives the warnings from Paul about abusing their bodies, the temple of the Holy Spirit.

What Is Judges 10:4—12:7 About?

Context of Judges 10:4—12:7

Although it begins with the typical narrative introduction of Israel's wickedness in God's eyes, the Jephthah episode adds two unexpected elements: a list of the Canaanite fertility gods Baal and Asherah, and the nations—Syria, Sidon, Moab, Ammon, and Philistia—whose deities Israel also served; and a comment not found in the other introductions: "And they forsook the

---

15. http://home.snu.edu/~hculbert/1040.htm. "Representatives of the United Methodist Church voted Tuesday to uphold traditional church bans against homosexual clergy and same-sex marriage—a move that could lead to a schism in the second-largest Protestant denomination in the United States.

"Delegates at the church's international summit in St. Louis voted 438 to 384 to adopt the Traditional Plan, after earlier having rejected the bishops-approved One Church Plan, which would have allowed individual congregations to decide whether to allow gay pastors and same-sex marriages in their churches.

"The vote was pushed predominantly by members of delegations from *African and Southeast Asian* countries, where homosexuality is criminalized, and by conservative church representatives from the Southern U.S. It signals a deep and perhaps unbridgeable divide between American Methodist churches, which have widely accepted and supported LGBT members and leaders, and the more conservative international congregations, which have adhered to and enforced traditional church teachings that their liberal brethren in the U.S. have ignored. If the bans were eased, 'the church in Africa would cease to exist,' said the Rev. Jerry Kulah of Liberia. 'We can't do anything but to support the Traditional Plan. It is the biblical plan.'" Emphasis added. *https://www.washingtontimes.com/news/2019/feb/26/united-methodist-church-vote*

LORD and did not serve him" (10:6c). Only then does the narrator turn to the LORD's response to Israel's apostasy. The reference to the Baals and Ashteroth recalls their appearance in the summary of 2:11–20 and in the Othniel narrative. The unusual addition of the five nations adds a geographic element indicating that Israel is hemmed in by her disloyalty, at home and abroad. Second, the depiction of Israel surrendering to the culture and the gods that define its socio-political values, is followed by God's abandoning them to these gods for rescue from their distress (10:14). Although Israel put away the other gods to serve the LORD, God becomes impatient over his people's misery (10:16) and speaks no more. Third, in ironic evocation of requests for leadership from the LORD that frame Judges—"Who shall go up first for us against the Canaanites," with the LORD responding "Judah shall go up" (1:1–2 and 20:18)—Gilead's leadership asks: "Who is the man who will begin to fight against the Ammonites" (10:18), but God does not answer. Samson and Gideon become saviors through divine visitations; the LORD "raises up" Ehud and Othniel; and, the prophetess Deborah appointed Barak in the name of the LORD. But the narrator keeps the LORD far from active involvement in Jephthah's appointment. Nevertheless, he indicates divine support for Jephthah's victory over Ammon (11:32), places divine approval in the mouths of Jephthah and his daughter ("now that the LORD has avenged you on your enemies, the Ammonites," 11:36), and Jephthah ("the LORD gave them [the Ammonites] into my hand," 12:3). The unexpected divine silence prepares the reader for the LORD's explicit withdrawal from Samson: "*but he did not know* that the LORD had left him" (16:20; cf. 14:4: "*but his father and mother did not know* that it was from the LORD," 14:4[16]), and, finally, the absence of the recurrent "Israel did what was wicked in God's eyes" in Judg 17–21, for in those days Israel did what was right in their own eyes (17:6; 21:25).

When the Spirit of God came on Othniel "he judged Israel" (3:10); clothed by the Spirit Gideon "sounded the trumpet" (6:34); the Spirit enabled Samson to kill a lion, strike down thirty men, break his Philistine bonds and slay a thousand at Lehi (14:6, 19; 15:14). However, the text that depicts the Spirit Jephthah moving toward battle with the Ammonites also introduces his vow to sacrifice whatever meets him on returning home victoriously (11:29–32). It leaves the reader asking: What is the relationship between God's Spirit and Jephthah's vow? The text gives no answer, as it does with the aside that points to Samson's lustful eyes as the occasion for God's dealing with Israel's enemies (14:4). Jephthah's rash vow and the fate of his virgin daughter also anticipate the foolish hospitality of the

---

16. "Yahweh is underway in the world to free his people from Philistine tyranny though not a soul in the story knows it and his chosen instrument looks very like an oversexed buffoon," Wharton, "The Secret of Yahweh," 58.

man from Gibeah who offered his virgin daughter to be abused (19:24), the murder of women and children that required the kidnapping of four hundred virgins plus the daughters of Shiloh for the widowers of Benjamin (21:12, 20–24), and Saul's oath to execute anyone who eats before battle, a vow that would have sealed his son Jonathan's fate, except for the people's ransom of Jonathan (1 Sam 15:24–46, esp. 45c).

Who Does What in Judges 10:4—12:7?

IS GOD OR JEPHTHAH THE MAIN CHARACTER?

After the initial exchange between God, Israel and its leaders, Jephthah takes center stage, never to relinquish it. When the narrator introduces Jephthah, the deity has begun to move into the background by refusing Israel's cynical profession of faith as the basis for another rescue: let the "other gods" you worship rescue you. A second confession of sin and abandoning the other gods only elicits God becoming impatient with Israel's misery, no direct appointment of a savior-judge (10:10–18). Indirect, behind-the-scenes involvement becomes the deity's mode of involvement in the Jephthah episode, possibly indicated by a passive verb in the clause following the depiction of God's impatience: "Then the Ammonites were called to war, and they encamped in Gilead" (10:17). Similarly, the last episode of the narrative: Ephraim "was called to arms" (12:1). The passive verb ($ṣ^cq$) could function as an impersonal call to arms by an implied leader, but since the one calling to arms is clearer elsewhere (Judg 6:34, 35; 7:24; 18:23 [z^cq]),[17] it does raise a question: if Ammon did not gather itself for war, who did? Is this a subtle reference to the LORD? Did the LORD "incite" them to war?[18] Given the developing unobtrusiveness of the deity in Judg 10:4–18, he passive verbs "were called to arms" in 10:17 and 12:1 may be construed as elements in characterization of the deity who occasions conflicts suited to Jephthah's unusual strengths.[19] Divine silence also abandons the people and its leaders

17. Thus Webb, *The Book of Judges*, 19n13. However, in Judg 6:34, 35; 7:24; 18:23 [z^cq] the one calling to arms is clear (Gideon's trumpet, messengers, Gideon, Micah), less so in 7:23 and 18:22 [z^cq]. Not so in 10:17 and 12:1.

18. There is no clear connection as in 2 Sam 24:1, "and he [i.e., the LORD] incited David against them [i.e., Israel]," (2 Sam 24:1). Nevertheless, the comment that "The LORD gave [the Ammonites] into his hand" (12:32), links the victory and the preceding vow, contra Webb, *The Book of Judges*, 62–63.

19 Not unlike the description of the Israel's defeat by the Philistines with a passive verb, subsequently understood as the LORD's work (*wygnp yśr'l*, 1 Sam 4:2; *lmh ngpnw yhwh*, 4:3).

to the question, "Who is the man *who will begin to fight* (*lḥm*) against the Ammonites"? (10:18; 14:5[20]).

The narrator answers this question by introducing Jephthah as a mighty warrior (*gbwr ḥyl*, 11:1), not "man of valor" (*ʾyš ḥyl*) a term applied to Gideon and other able–bodied men (6:12 and 3:29; 18:2; 20:40, 46; 21:10; and see Ruth 2:1; 3:11). Like Saul and David (1 Sam 9:1; 16:18) and later Jeroboam (1 Kgs 11:28), Jephthah was a successful warrior. The immediately following disjunctive clause, however, introduces a worrisome element of Jephthah's *curriculum vitae*: "but he was the son of a *prostitute*" (*znh*, ESV[21]), fathered by Gilead, whose other sons disinherit Jephthah because he is the "son of another woman." Crudely short, Jephthah's nativity evokes the first part of Israel's "*whoring* after other gods," (*znh*, 2:17 ESV; 8:27, 33; 16:1), and his half-brothers' "son of *another woman*" (*bn ʾšh ʾḥrt*, 11:2[22]) the second part of "whoring after *other gods*." This savior-judge knows whereof Israel suffers. They drive him away (*grš*, 11:2, 7; cf. 2:3; 6:9; Gen 3:24) into exile. Fleeing from his brothers like Jotham from Abimelech,[23] Jephthah lives in the land of Tob where "men of low character" (*ryqym*, 11:3 JPS) gather around him, as did such men (*ryqym*, 9:4 JPS) around Abimelech in his quest for kingship.[24] The noun "good" (*ṭwb*) in land of Tob (=Good, 11:3, 5) recalls the elders' request that God "do to us what is good (*ṭwb*) in your eyes" (10:15; a phrase that typically uses "wickedness" (*rʾh*) or right (*yšr*) in Judges. Along with Gideons' wondering "if I have found favor (*ḥn*) in your eyes" (6:17), the elders' request is the second of two times that God's eyes are described positively in Judges. Is Jephthah's dwelling in the land of Tob/Good a subtle hint at God's approval of Jephthah? Perhaps, but if so, it would only underscore the unobtrusive role of the deity.

After presenting Jephthah's qualifications the narrative depicts him as a shrewd bargainer with Gilead's elders and his demands (*dbrym*) of the LORD (11:11); a knowledgeable diplomat to the king of Ammon who hears

---

20. Not "save" as when the divine messenger tells Samson's mother that her son "shall *begin to save* (*yšʿ*) Israel from the hand of the Philistines" (13:5).

21. So also, Butler, *Judges*, 272.

22. In the appeal of two prostitutes before Solomon, the king does not award the living child to the "other woman" (1 Kgs 3:22). The daughter of an Israelite who becomes a prostitute defiles the land (Lev 19:29), such and other forbidden sexual relations pollute the land on pain of suffering exile ("vomit out," Lev 18:28; 20:22). Torah forbids sacrificing "any of your seed" to Molech (Lev 20:1–5). Moses instructs Israel to redeem its first-born, female and male (Ex 13:1–2, 11–16).

23. With the same verb, Jacob from Esau (27:23; 31:21–22, 27; 35:1, 7) and Hagar from Sarah (Gen 16:8).

24. On the run from Saul, "mean and churlish fellows" (here: *kl-ʾyš-rʿ wblyʿ ʿl*, 1 Sam 30:22 JPS) also gathered around David.

JUDGES: ISRAEL DOES WHAT IS RIGHT IN ITS OWN EYES   101

the name of the LORD from Jephthah's mouth (11:21, 24, 27); and a deadly opponent of Ephraim (12:1–6). With the LORD moving behind the scenes Jephthah appears to be the main character but that would overlook the role of his daughter.

OR JEPHTHAH'S DAUGHTER?

Phyllis Trible argues that Jephthah's daughter is the protagonist of Judg 11:29–40, but that "throughout the centuries patriarchal hermeneutics has forgotten the daughter of Jephthah, but remembered her father, indeed exalted him."[25] Nearly every pre–Reformation scholar John Thompson examines in *Reading the Bible with the Dead*, however, considers Jephthah's daughter to be the protagonist.[26] Esther Fuchs seeks to restore this unnamed woman whose words are "an extension of and reflection of her father's words," who was "sacrificed as part of a general strategy to defend the father at the daughter's expense."[27] Cheryl Exum writes that readers resisting the "dominant (male) voice . . . can give the victim a voice that protests her marginalization and victimization—one that claims for her a measure of that autonomy denied her by the narrative that sacrificed her to her father's word."[28] Reclaiming autonomy for Jephthah's daughter, however laudable, is a post-Enlightenment *desideratum* absent from the time when there was no king in Israel. In the ancient world, not even royalty contemplated autonomy from the gods; worshiping other gods in Israel was not an act of freedom but covenant rebellion; a vow freely given inevitably involved the covenant Sovereign. Moreover, although the text acknowledges the father-daughter relationship, it is Jephthah the savior-judge of Gilead who vows the sacrifices. Male abuse of women as such is unconscionable; by males with religious or social authority—the Levite, the master of the house, the tribes of Israel—worse; sacrificing a first-born in

25. Trible, *Texts of Terror*, 93, 107.

26. Thompson, "Sacrificing Jephthah's Daughter," 45. For a similar study of post-Reformation exegetes, see Knapp, "Jephthah's Daughter in English Post-Reformation Exegesis," 279–97

27. Fuchs, "Marginalization, Ambiguity, Silencing," 125–30. For attempts to fill in the gaps to work out ambiguities and silences in devotional literature, see Houtman, "Rewriting a Dramatic Old Testament Story," 167–90.

28. Exum, "On Judges 11," 143–44. Davis, "The Condemnation of Jephthah," 16, considers feminist and evangelical readings of the text. After considering the text against the background of Genesis 22, she concludes that "[T]he narrator has no need to justify Jephthah because Jephthah is presented as utterly despicable. Neither ought we, as readers, attempt to exonerate him. There is no excuse. In this sense, the text is just as feminist as the feminists, condemning the sacrifice of Jephthah's daughter as an abominable exemplar of unfaithfulness."

Israel aching for a fruitful future with her friends is worst of all, especially by a father overshadowed by the Spirit of the LORD. Not abuse of women by men as such, but named corrupt and flawed Spirit-filled leadership, that informs the spiral of degradation in Judges that almost reaches its nadir with Jephthah's sacrifice of his daughter.

The horror of the daughter's sacrifice[29] is that 1) she is Jephthah's only child,[30] 2) who "had never known a man," and 3) echoes Jephthah's rash vow. The daughter's near repetition of her father's words is undeniable. But are they "an extension of and reflection of her father's words"? Was she "sacrificed as part of a general strategy to defend the father at the daughter's expense"?[31] It is better to understand that "Jephthah and his daughter display some nobility in this story, though of a pagan variety."[32] Gileadite society was thoroughly dedicated to other gods; Jephthah could have redeemed his vow, as did Jonathan's companions (Lev 27:1–13; 1 Sam 14:45), but didn't. Moreover, in sacrificing his "only one" who "had never known a man," she becomes the embodiment of Israel herself: barren, without a future, not sacrificed according to the LORD's instructions as did obedient Abraham. Unlike Sarah, Rebekah, Rachel and Samson's unnamed mother, this barren daughter of Israel, the un–Isaac, will not yet rejoice (Isa 54:1). Rather she'll become a byword (Deut 28:37; 1 Kgs 9:7); a foreshadowing of the abuse anonymous men perform on the anonymous women in Judges:[33] the Levites' concubine, the master's virgin daughter, and the six-hundred kidnapped women of Judg 19 and 21 as wives for the unnamed men from Benjamin in a punitive war against them for permitting the abuse of the concubine. And the horror of it all is that these unnamed abusers and abused are God's own people; a not-to-be-forgotten description of what

29. Translating the *waw* in 11:32 as "or" to read Jephthah's vow "whatever comes out of the doors . . . shall be the LORD's *or* I will offer it up for a burnt offering" is rejected because "a burnt offering is not an alternative to a dedication" according to Lev 1. See Gane, *God's Faulty Heroes*, 96n7.

30. Exegetes point to Gen 22, the sacrifice of Abraham's "only son," as background Jephthah's sacrifice of his daughter. Trible, *Texts of Terror*, 105; Webb, *The Book of Judges*, 335–36; Davis, "The Condemnation of Jephthah," 1–16, understands Jephthah to be an inversion of Abraham.

31. Fuchs, "Marginalization, Ambiguity, Silencing," 125–30.

32. Smit and Fowl, *Judges & Ruth*, 133.

33. Unnamed women: Gideon's female servant (9:8), the woman who threw the millstone (9:53); a prostitute (11:1), Gilead's wife and another woman (11:2), Jephthah's daughter (11:34), Manoah's wife (13:2), a daughter of the Philistines (14:1), a prostitute (16:1), a woman from the Valley of Sorek (16:4), Micah's mother (17:2), a concubine (19:1), a virgin daughter (19:1).Unnamed men: the man the spies saw (1:24), a prophet (6:8), Gideon's servant (6:27 [Purah?], 7:10), a man from Succoth (8:14, 21), a Levite (17:7), Levite's father-in-law (19:4), an old man (19:16);

saved-from-Egypt Israel did to its own when it turned to other gods. And its savior Jephthah reflected this corruption.

Jephthah is the main character throughout; of all that he did, keeping a rash vow to sacrifice his daughter stands out as the climax of all the words that came out of his mouth: "I have opened my mouth to the LORD, and I cannot take back my vow"; and so did his daughter: "You have opened your mouth to the LORD; do to me according to what has gone out of your mouth" (11:35–36 ESV). Far from exalting or exonerating him, Judges memorializes Jephthah's onerous deed for all the generations of God's people, and to see mirrored in this savior-judge their own manipulation of God to escape the consequences of their apostasy. "In those days," intones the narrator, "there was no king in Israel. Everyone did what was right in his own eyes" (21:25).

Jephthah Today: Leadership during Corrupt Times

Can corruption produce incorruptible leadership? Can making careless vows to serve God harvest a leadership whose vows are spoken with integrity? Can those who sacrifice their daughters and sons to other gods through intermarriage with worshipers of those gods (3:5–6) expect its leadership to do less? How sincere are God's people's cries to save them from their consequences, time and again? Judges confronts every generation of God's people and its leaders with the uncomfortable truth of their corruptibility: "the time is coming when people will not put up with sound doctrine, but having itching ears, they will accumulate for themselves teachers to suit their own desires, and will turn away from listening to the truth and wander away to myth" (2 Tim 4:3–4).

The Jephthah narrative invites honest self-examination of what God's people seeks, or not; and how their leadership will satisfy those desires, or not. If it's true that "Like a dog to its vomit, so a fool returns to his folly" (Prov 26:11) wisdom also teaches that "The way of a fool is right in his own eyes, but a wise man listens to advice"; and, "The wise lay up knowledge, but the mouth of a fool brings ruin near" (Prov 12:15; 10:14 ESV). More particularly, the Ecclesiast warns: "Be not rash with your mouth, nor let your heart be hasty to utter a word before God" and "It is better that you not vow than that you should vow and not pay . . . why should God be angry and destroy the work of your hands" (Eccl 5:2, 6 ESV). More so if the fool has leadership responsibilities, for "The eyes of the LORD are in every place, keeping watch on the evil and the good" (Prov 15:3 ESV). Finally, after the pouring out of the Spirit (Acts 2:14–21) on the body of Christ, the Jephthah's overshadowing by the Spirit invites the spirit-filled people of God and their leaders to evaluate themselves: are they quenching or grieving the Spirit of God who guides Christ's disciples in truth (1 Thess 5:19–22; John 16:13)?

Waiting for the Rest That Still Remains: A Time of Self-inflicted Testing

The generation after Joshua and his contemporaries fouls its covenant loyalty, seeking the good life promised by the teaching of Canaan's deities. Becoming good Canaanites was wicked in God's eyes; the LORD would no longer dispossess the nations but employ them to test Israel's covenant vows (2:22). God's leaving Israel's enemies in their place—the same verb used to indicate Israel's rest in Josh 21:44—ironically reverses the situation at the end of Joshua: divine abeyance grants the Canaanites rest from *their* enemy, Israel. Withdrawal of divine favor initiated a time of testing (*nsh*, 2:22; 3:1) that was intended to show "whether they will take care to walk in the way of the LORD." Sadly, it revealed the second generation's true commitment: after the death of the divinely appointed savior–judge who rescued them from divinely imposed distress, God's people returned to more profound corruption (2:19). Exchanging its pot of lentil stew for the sweetness of stolen water and bread eaten in secret and refusing to acknowledge that Folly's "guests are in the depths of Sheol" (Prov 9:18), Israel suffered the consequences: God sold his foolish people to its enemies, for as "a whip for the horse, a bridle for the donkey, [so] a rod for the back of fools" (Prov 26:3).

God's permitting the nations to punish Israel in the time of the Judges was harsh, but assuaged by the savior-judges through whom the LORD provided respite; not so with the exile: "Judah . . . dwells now among the nations, but finds no *resting* place," (Lam 1:3 ESV; cf. Deut 28:65), and later, "our pursuers are at our necks; we are weary, we are given no *rest*" (Lam 5:5 ESV). Divine withdrawal of rest during the time of the judges came to an end, through David's defeat of Israel's enemies, and, finally, the ark's arrival in the Holy of Holies of Solomon's temple (2 Sam 7:1; 1 Kgs 8:56). The dove Noah sent from the ark could find no place for its feet to *rest*, but could return to the ark (Gen 8:9); but the divinely constructed redemptive space for the speakers of Lamentations lies in ruins (Lam 2:6–9).

Judges confronts its exilic and diasporic audience with several truths about the generation that inherits what God accomplished through his chosen servant Joshua, that "not one word of all the good promises that the LORD had made to the house of Israel had failed; all came to pass" (Josh 21:45). First, Judges encourages every generation of God's people to see itself as the generation that arose after Joshua died, that is, the generation that

betrays its covenant vows to the Teaching of God's servant suffers the consequences of rest held in abeyance. Second, and related, Judges suggests that
loyalty to covenant vows is only one generation deep, a reality reflected by,
for example, Solomon's foolish son Rehoboam under whom the kingdom
was divided, and Manasseh's wicked reign after his father Hezekiah's righteous rule (1 Kgs 12:1–15; 2 Kgs 21:2; 18:3; cf. Ezek 18).

Because every generation of God's people is tempted to reformulate the
teaching, or to reject "the good way . . . and find rest for your souls" (Jer 6:26;
Ps 78:9–64; Matt 11:28), the psalmist encourages one generation to catechize
the next (Ps 78:1–8) in the Teaching of the LORD. Third, testing the loyalty of
his people is natural to covenant discipleship, rooted in Abraham's sacrifice of
Isaac (*nsh*, Gen 22:1), and necessary, for God's people is stubbornly ungrate-
ful to God and his servants, as Israel showed by the waters of Marah (Exod
15:25). The LORD's testing exposes the easy surrender to spiritual values of
the culture, easy because of God's people's demonstrated penchant for cultic
and moral corruption. Fourth, the Jephthah episode reminds Israel that self-
ish and reckless vows contribute to Israel's distress. Attributing Jephthah's
daughter's failure to assent and not to object to her sacrifice to androcentric
victimization is an easy and anachronistic rereading. The textual fact is that
she surrendered to her savior-judge's folly.[34] Careless speech and vows unravel the warp and woof of the covenant community because they subvert the
Teaching once for all delivered to the saints (Jude 3). Finally, the irony of the
Canaanites receiving rest and Israel suffering attacks from other enemy nations, teaches that God may abandon his people to the terrible consequences
of their apostasy and corruption. The voices of Lamentations articulate this
truth; Paul reminds the church at Rome that it should take counsel from the
partial hardening of Israel (Rom 11:25). Judges also teaches that when God's
people cry to him for mercy, he sends his savior-judges, for God loves his
stubborn people, ultimately for the sake of his Beloved Son, the Savior-Judge

---

34. Jonathan does not submit to Saul's vow, but says "My father has troubled the
land." Later, perhaps speaking in self-defense, Jonathan says: "See how my eyes have
become bright because I tasted a little of this honey? How much better if the people
had eaten freely today of the spoil of their enemies that they found. For now the defeat among the Philistines has not been great" (1 Sam 14:29–30 ESV). Eating the right
amount of honey is wise (Prov 25:16–17, 27). Saul grudgingly gave in to advice, but the
episode shows his kingship is no better at rescuing Israel from her enemies than were
the savior-judges, "for there was hard fighting against the Philistines all of Saul's days"
(1 Sam 14:52). Goering, "Honey and Wormwood," 30, writes that the phrase "lightens
the eyes" "connotes the reception of divine instruction (Ps 19:9) or of wisdom (Qoh
8:1)." Contrast this with Samson's eating honey defiled by the lion's carcass, the riddle
he proposes and the destruction that follows.

whose sacrifice brings the eternal rest which all Israel, Jew and Gentile awaits (Rom 11:26; Lam 5:20–22).

Meditating on the enduring claim of Psalm 95:7–8, 11, "Today, if you hear his voice, do not harden your hearts, as at Meribah, . . . they shall not enter my rest," Hebrews encourages God's people to "strive to enter that rest, so that no one may fall by the same sort of disobedience. For the word of God is living and active, sharper than any two-edged sword" (Heb 4:11–12).

7

Ruth

Covenant Piety in the Fields of Bethlehem

Summary: Because of a famine in the time of the judges Naomi of Bethlehem moves to Moab where her sons marry Moabite women. Her husband Elimelech and sons die, leaving Naomi empty of family. Naomi returns to Bethlehem, with her daughter-in-law Ruth. They arrive at the beginning of the barley harvest (Ruth 1).

Going out to pick grain in the harvest fields Ruth finds herself in the field of Boaz, who tells his servants to be kind to her. When Ruth tells Naomi that she had gathered grain in Boaz' fields, Naomi praises God. Ruth stays in Boaz's fields until the end of the harvest (Ruth 2).

Naomi tells Ruth to visit Boaz that night on the threshing-floor. When Boaz discovers Ruth at his side, she asks him for help as a close relative. Boaz promises to deal with a closer relative. Boaz gives Ruth six measures of barley so she does not have to return to Naomi empty-handed (Ruth 3).

At the city gate Boaz acquires Ruth and Elimelech's property. The elders at the gate wish that Ruth be a mother in Israel like Rachel, Leah and Tamar. The LORD blesses Ruth and she gives birth. The neighboring women express the wish that this child may fill Naomi's emptiness, because she now has a son, Obed. He becomes father of Jesse, who becomes the father of David (Ruth 4).

Central Narrative Interest: Ruth and Boaz's covenant piety fill Naomi's emptiness with food and family.

Opening Sentence and Connection
with Antecedent Narrative

OPENING WITH "IN THE days when the judges were judging there was a famine in the land," the narrator evokes the consequences of Israel's covenant disloyalty (Deut 28:38–42). That this opening immediately follows Judges' conclusion that "In those days Israel had no king, everyone did what was right in his own eyes" (Judg 21:25) links Ruth to the theme of kingship, evoked by the city of Bethlehem, which Elimelech ("God is my king") abandons, and the reference to David as Ruth's and Obed's distant descendant (4:18–22). Where the geography of Judges moves from one region of the land to another, Ruth's main actions occur on the journey from Moab and in Bethlehem of Judah.

Moab and Bethlehem allude to events in the antecedent narrative. Moab was Lot's son by incest (Gen 19:30–38); his female descendants had sexual relations with Israelites who then worshiped the Baal of Peor (Num 25:1–5). Moabites were not allowed in the assembly of the LORD because they were inhospitable to Israel and because they hired Balaam to curse Israel (Deut 23:3–6). The Benjamite savior-judge Ehud rescued Israel from Moab (Judg 3:12, 30). Jacob's wife Rachel died and was buried in Bethlehem (Gen 35:19; 48:7).

Challenges to Reading Ruth

Ruth presents several challenges for contemporary readers. First, it raises the question of what it means to abandon your people as Ruth did when she insisted on clinging to Naomi. Second, Ruth's submission to Boaz and the covenant institutions of levirate marriage and property redemption suggests Ruth is merely an object in the ancient Israelite economy. Third, the emphasis on Ruth and Boaz's faithfulness to divine instruction does not demonstrate a justification by works, but those that proceed from faithful discipleship.

Leaving Your Past/Culture

Throughout history peoples have experienced cultural diversity and ethnic identity through social groups—family, tribe and clan (patriarchal and matriarchal)—not, however, without contact with others who in one or another way joined those groups. With varying degrees of success modern nation states have assimilated such groups and those who crossed their borders legally. Massive people movements in the first quarter of the twenty-first century have raised questions about the political identity and rights of such peoples, shaped and/or imposed by early modern, mostly Western, colonial powers.[1] During the last quarter of the twentieth century a post-colonial biblical hermeneutics has emerged to challenge such assumptions by emphasizing and elevating cultural-ethnic particulars over identities defined by the colonial powers. About the same time feminism emerged to challenge received assumptions about the social role of men and women; in its biblical hermeneutical form this included reclaiming the role of women depicted in the biblical text.[2] Reading Ruth today cannot avoid these cultural and hermeneutical developments.

Ruth and Naomi "reinterpret the language of a man's world to preserve the integrity of a woman's story . . . [t]he absence of misogyny, violence and vengeance . . . speaks a healing word in the days of the judges . . . it does show both the Almighty and the male establishment a more excellent way."[3] In her discussion of Ruth's vow Katharine Doob Sakenfeld writes that "commitment to another people across ethnic and cultural lines does not mean abandoning one's own identity (people today often speak of their 'dual identity')"; and, "Asian-American theologians have highlighted the danger of using Ruth's decision as a warrant for an assimilationist, melting-pot view of the proper role of immigrants to the United States."[4] Of course, Ruth's abandoning her Moabite past is not a biblical warrant for assimilation, but neither does her apparently trouble-free crossing from Moab to Bethlehem warrant contemporary immigration policies. Neither Ruth, Boaz, nor Naomi are stand-in-solutions for contemporary socio-political problems. Rather, they dramatize Scripture's solution to an ancient problem it defines in Gen 2–3: the good life in God's presence is not the result of autonomous human decisions, but of compliance with God's will. This brings us to the biblical understanding of human identity.

Ruth's abandoning her past is inescapably socio-cultural, but not merely so, for it is not what she leaves behind but to whom she avowedly clings, Naomi: where Naomi goes and lodges, Ruth will; she vows to own Naomi's people, God, and land as her burial place; not even death will separate her from Naomi (1:16–17). What defines Naomi—her land, people, God, and

---

1. This is not a peculiarly Western problem. Cultural and social impositions were and continue to happen: the tribal clashes between Islam and Christianity in Nigeria, the Chinese government's treatment of the Uighur peoples, the inter-Islam conflicts.

2. See Brenner, *A Feminist Companion to Ruth*, and the literature cited in chap 1 above.

3. Trible, *Texts of Terror*, 85. Trible includes the women of Bethlehem and Hannah.

4. Sakenfeld, *Ruth*, 31, 32.

grave—Ruth vows, now defines her; but she is still called a Moabite (1:22; 2:6, 21; 4:5, 10). Furthermore, Naomi's land, people, God, and grave are not components of a chthonic identity, as they would be in Moab, but the inheritance all descendants of Abraham and Sarah receive (Gen 15:18–20; 23:19–20). By clinging to Naomi Ruth joins Abraham's journey from Ur: Abraham heard and obeyed, "Leave your country (ʾrṣk), your kindred (mwldt) and your father's house" (byt ʾb; Gen 12:1). Ruth heard Boaz enunciate her identity when he told her, "how you left your father and mother (ʾbyk wʾmk) and your native land (ʾrṣ mwldtk) and came to a people you did not know before" (2:11). When Abraham abandoned Ur he also left behind "the other gods" (Josh 24:2, 14–15), but he took along his language, clothing, tents, cattle and sheep, and presumably all the equipment necessary to manage the journey. Unlike his ancestors on the plain of Shinar Abraham did not build a city, but an altar to the LORD who appeared to him at Shechem (Gen 12:7–8). Centuries later his descendants worshiped "the other gods" at Canaanite altars they should have destroyed; they also allowed their children marry into the Canaanite families, an act of religious assimilation consequent on their serving "other gods" (Judg 3:5). Not Ruth's ethnicity, but the God to whom she clings is constitutive of her identity; she remains a Moabite even as Rahab remained a Canaanite.

Ruth's clinging to Naomi and her theological declaration to Naomi depicts her conversion: she rejects the old gods in favor of another source of blessing and preservation of order (ṣdqh) against chaos. In her socio-religious context, Ruth the Moabite's clinging to Naomi represents a rejection of the theology of the Baal of Peor whose female adherents seduced Israel in the desert (Num 25:1–9), including the sacrifice of children, evoked by the realization of Joshua's curse over the rebuilding of Jericho (Josh 6:26; 1 Kgs 16:34). With her vow to Naomi, Ruth the Moabite joined the people whose hope lies in what God began to do with Abraham: "In you [i.e., Abraham and his descendants] all the families of the earth shall be blessed." In her persona Ruth brought Moab into the presence of God.

The NT reminds its audience that Rahab and Ruth are ancestors of Jesus the Christ who, abandoning his equality with God to take on the form of a servant, became God with us. All his disciples imitate him: Peter did not stop being a fisherman but learned his vocation anew; Saul abandoned his prestigious religious identity and sacrificed his Scripture learning to the LORD he met on the way to Damascus. Having left his past, Paul taught the Roman church: "Present your bodies as a living sacrifice, holy and acceptable to God, which is your spiritual worship. Do not be conformed to this world, but be transformed by the renewal of your mind, that by testing you may discern what is the will of God, what is good and acceptable and perfect" (Rom 12:1–2).

Ruth's Body and Covenant Polity

Sometime after she learns that Ruth gathered barley in the fields of Boaz, Naomi says, "My daughter, should I not seek rest for you?" (3:1), but then asks Ruth "to wash and anoint yourself" (3:3), to go to Boaz while he's asleep on the threshing-floor and await his instructions. As it turns out Ruth's petition "to spread [his] wings over his servant" (3:9) moves Boaz to redeem Elimelech's land; he will also acquire Ruth and father a child by her to perpetuate her dead husband's name. None of this violates OT covenant morality. Moses teaches Israel that if a man's brother dies childless, his widow may not marry a stranger but "her husband's brother shall go in to her and take her as his wife and perform the duty of a husband's brother to her. And the first son whom she bears shall succeed to the name of his dead brother, that his name may not be blotted out of Israel" (Deut 25:5–6 ESV). Although the phrase "to uncover another man's nakedness" refers to adultery (Deut 22:30; 27:20), the prophet Ezekiel depicts the LORD as spreading his cloak (wing) over Israel's nakedness, pledging himself to his people (Ezek 16:1–14). "Ruth is in effect inviting Boaz to play the role of the LORD to her Israel, to offer her marriage, security, and a covenantal relationship."[5] In this context Boaz calls her a worthy woman (3:11).

As with the unnuanced readings that fear Ruth's behavior supports assimilation, so Ruth's submission to levirate marriage without objections may raise suspicions about this story's potential contribution to abuse of women and their bodies.[6] The hermeneutic of suspicion—associated with the thought of Marx, Nietzsche, and Freud—is rooted in the ancient question, "Did God really say?" (Gen 3:1b). That is, if divine instruction says "Thus and so," it cannot really mean "Thus and so." Or, if it meant "Thus and so" then, surely, it cannot in any way mean "Thus and so" today. Reading an ancient document for meaning today is complicated, but not without sophisticated resources.[7] Understanding Scripture as normative for faith

---

5. Smit and Fowl, *Judges & Ruth*, 237.

6. Many questions about Ruth's depiction of levirate marriage and the buying back of land have no satisfactory answer; the book of Ruth remains silent. See Smit and Fowl, *Judges & Ruth*, 234–57, for a discussion of these matters, including the history of interpretation.

7. See, for example, Baker, *Two Testaments, One Bible*; Gane, *Old Testament Law for Christians*.

and conduct does not bind contemporary Christians to the particulars of Deuteronomy's dicta on levirate marriage; it does to Scripture's underlying teaching about the descendants (zr^c) of Abraham, that is, the future of the covenants between God, Abraham (Gen 15 and 17), and Abraham's descendants (Gal 3:29).

Where contemporary Western society understands human reproduction as the province of the autonomous self, *ni Dieu ni maître* tell me what to do with my body, Scripture teaches that the human body and its reproductive processes, like any other creaturely thing, were created to serve God's purposes (Gen 1:28). Eve's fecundity populates the earth east of Eden, but her descendants, like Eve and Adam themselves, attribute their fertility to "other gods" whose favors they court with altar-cities such as Babel. In Pauline terms, they "exchanged the glory of the immortal God for images resembling mortal man and birds and animals and reptiles" (Rom 1:23 ESV). God's water judgment on the nations for filling the earth with rebellion (Gen 6:11, 13) did not damage their fecundity: from Noah's sons "the nations spread abroad on the earth after the flood" (Gen 10:32). Abraham's ancestors have many sons and daughters (the verb "to father" occurs twenty-five times in Gen 11:10–26), even Abraham's brothers have families (Gen 11:26–29), but Sarah, removed from the Babel culture with Abraham, was barren, as were Rebekah and Rachel. Their descendants subsequently fill the earth (Exod 1:7), but God makes possible their motherhood (Gen 17:19; 25:21; 30:22).[8] Pharaoh's and Abimelech's endangerments of Sarah and Rebekah, and the Dinah-Shechem and Judah-Tamar affairs underscore the unique origin of and concern that the growth of covenant descendants not be attributed to "other gods" (Judg 3:5). Levitical instructions about the womb (Lev 12)[9] support this concern, especially in relationship to the sexual practices of the nations (Lev 18:24–30; 20:22–27). The prohibition against offering children (zr^c, "seed," Lev 20:1–5) to Molech also reminds Israel that such sacrifices do not secure fertility, for God alone is the source of the growth of his people. That Hiel of Bethel, when rebuilding Jericho during the reign of Ahab, "laid its foundation at the cost of Abiram his firstborn, and set up its gates at the cost of his youngest son Segub" (1 Kgs 16:34), illustrates the depth of Israel's covenant disloyalty. After Abraham obediently offered his firstborn, the LORD told him, "because you have done this and have not withheld your son, you only son, I will surely bless you, and I will surely multiply your offspring

8. On the role of the divine in human reproduction, see Leder, "Who builds the house of Israel?"

9. See Whitekettle, "Levitical Thought and the Female Reproductive Cycle," 376–391; Whitekettle, "Leviticus 15.18 Reconsidered: Chiasm, Spatial Structure and the Body," 31–45.

as the stars of the heaven" (Gen 22:16–17 ESV). A later firstborn son would secure this commitment with his own blood.

Ruth's submission to the law of the levirate without objection portrays her participation in the unique growth of God's covenant people. Thus, the elders say to Boaz: "May the LORD make the woman, who is coming into your house, like Rachel and Leah, who together built up the house of Israel" (4:11 ESV). And although Leah was not barren, "God listened to [her], and she conceived and bore Jacob a fifth son" (Gen 30:17). Similarly, Ruth: "So Boaz took Ruth, and she became his wife. And he went into her, *and the Lord gave her conception*,[10] and she bore a son" (4:13 ESV). Rather than giving her body to the purposes defined by Moab's Chemosh,[11] she surrendered it to Naomi's God, became a mother in Israel by giving Naomi a son. Obed, like Isaac and later Jesus Christ, is not merely a product of the human reproductive process, but of God's redemptive way among the nations: "And if you belong to Christ, then you are Abraham's offspring (lit. "seed"), heirs according to the promise" (Gal 3:29). The bodies of Abraham's seed—female or male, Jew or Greek, slave or free—are not their own: "Do you not know that your body is a temple of the Holy Spirit . . . so glorify God in your body" (1 Cor 6:19–20 ESV). At great cost to his own financial future Boaz also surrendered himself to the divine purposes, and "fathered" a son for Naomi.

Loving God's Instructions

Luther did not pass on Ruth as he did Esther and James,[12] nevertheless, Ruth may be troubling in its depiction of "women working out their own salvation with fear and trembling, for it is God who works in them."[13] Echoing Paul, Phyllis Trible does not argue that these women saved themselves from original sin, justifying themselves by works of the law. Rather, Naomi, Boaz and the women of Bethlehem belong to the covenant people whose normal vocation it is to comply with the divine instructions of the Sinai covenant. Ruth joined that people by abandoning her past as did Abraham, but without explicit divine direction. Leaving one's past to join the journey to the future promised by the God of Abraham, Isaac, Jacob, and Jesus Christ

---

10. Because this phrase is not a normal element in birth reports, its insertion here heightens the role of the LORD.

11. The king of Moab sacrificed his firstborn to secure success in battle against Israel (2 Kgs 3:26–27).

12. Ruth's focus on righteous works of the covenant polity depicts that faith without works is dead, but does not say this in so many words.

13. Trible, *God and the Rhetoric of Sexuality*, 196.

defines salvation: a turning around, conversion. Working out that conversion or salvation, is walking toward that future on the way designed by torah, divine instruction: "For I have chosen [Abraham], that he may command his children and his household after him to keep the *way of the Lord by doing righteousness and justice*" (Gen 18:19). Abraham's descendant Jesus Christ told Thomas, "I am the way, and the truth, and the life," and, "If anyone loves me, he will keep my word" (John 14:7, 23; 15:10–17).

Theologically speaking Ruth, Esther, and James depict sanctification, not justification: "Be holy as I am holy" (Lev 19:2), and, "let us cleanse ourselves from every defilement of body and spirit, bringing holiness to completion in the fear of God" (2 Cor 7:1 ESV). The book of Ruth shows that loving God means nothing less than loving his covenant instructions by embodying them; such love interrupts and challenges the violent world created by covenant disloyalty in the days of the judges. Judges often uses the verb "to save" to describe Israel's salvation from her oppressors:[14] God justified Israel once for all at the sea by enabling it to walk through the waters that drowned Pharaoh; from her covenant disloyalty she was saved daily (Ps 7:1; 34:6; 59:3). Ruth the Moabite's covenant love (*ḥsd*, 3:10) astonishes the Israelite audience: a foreign woman, a Moabite at that, complies with divine instruction to give life to barren Naomi. Thus, the book of Ruth urges the exiles to be saved again, that is, repent and return to the covenant loyalty of loving God's instructions.

Ruth is a story of a woman in a patriarchal culture; Naomi tells Ruth to visit Boaz on the threshing floor; Ruth's visit calls forth Boaz's covenant responsibility; the women of Bethlehem do give Naomi's son a name, traditionally the role of the father. But Trible's description of Ruth as "the stories of women in a man's world," in which Ruth and the women of Bethlehem are "paradigms of radicality,"[15] recontextualizes the over-arching canonical narrative through the feminist or womanist lens of contemporary egalitarian culture. This overlooks the women's stand-in function for larger concerns in the covenant community: Naomi evokes barren, exiled Israel; Ruth, like Rahab, speaks to the Gentiles who gain rest as descendants of Abraham; the women of Bethlehem exalt the barren one whose future is uniquely dependent on divine instruction for the salvation of God's people, "for the children of the desolate one will be more than of her who is married" (Isa 54:1). In a time of confused clinging to feelings, the clear voice of the great shepherd of the sheep brings salvation to all who loving God's word, hear and do it; it is more desired than gold and sweeter than honey (Ps 19:9–10).

14. *yš*, Judg 2:16, 18; 3:9, 15, 31; 6:14, 15, 31, 36, 37; 7:2, 7; 8:22; 10:12, 14; 12:2, 3.

15. Trible, *God and the Rhetoric of Sexuality*, 184, 196.

What Is Ruth about Today?

The opening clauses, "in the days when the judges were judging, there was a famine in the land" (1:1ab), define the narrative setting: the days of the judges, morally corrupt, and the consequences of covenant betrayal, famine (Deut 28:38–42). These historical references contextualize the subsequent action whether the book of Ruth follows Song of Songs (JPS), Proverbs (BHS) or Judges (LXX).

Nevertheless, canonical location matters. Following Proverbs 31:10–31's meditation on a worthy woman (ʾšt ḥylh), Boaz's description of Ruth as a worthy woman (ʾšt ḥylh, 3:11) suggests an intertextual reading that reflects Proverbs' teaching on Lady Wisdom and Lady Folly. Both Ruth and Boaz illustrate wisdom's fear of the LORD—a reference to covenant polity— as the beginning of wisdom (Prov 1:7; 9:10) and how walking in the way of Wisdom and declining Folly (Prov 9:1–6; 13–18) fills Naomi's emptiness. Following Judges, another intertextual theme emerges: the phrase "worthy woman" and its close parallel description of Boaz as a "worthy man" (gbwr ḥyl, 2:1) now recall Gideon and Jephthah (gbwr ḥyl, Judg 6:12; 11:1). This intertextual connection reinforces the opening reference to the time of the judges, and encourages the reader to view Ruth and Boaz as savior-judges, but with crucial differences. First, the saviors of Judges only defeat Israel's oppressors militarily; Ruth and Boaz illustrate how compliance with divine instruction yields sweet life in the bitter days of the judges. Second, the last two judges, Jephthah and Samson, are unsavory rescuers whose torah piety is at best ambiguous; worthy Ruth and Boaz demonstrate torah piety. Third, the savior-judges rescued larger Israelite communities with little concern for the local, excepting Gideon and the altar of Baal; the savior-judge pair Ruth and Boaz rescue a widow from Bethlehem of Judah. Finally, where Judges subtly hints at David as Israel's hope, Ruth explicitly links its savior-judges with David.

Comparison with Judges uncovers other differences between the two books. First, the text indicts neither Elimelech, Naomi or their sons for covenant disloyalty. As in the days of Elijah when seven thousand faithful Israelites suffered the consequences of Ahab's corruption, so this family from Bethlehem suffered the consequences of Israel's disloyalty: famine was the occasion for Elimelech's family to sojourn ([ger, 1:1] like Abraham and Jacob to Egypt in a foreign land). The text notes the deaths of Elimelech and his sons without attributing the cause. Naomi, however, is twice described as a remnant (šʾr, 1:3, 5)[16] of this family from Bethlehem. Second, foreign op-

---

16. The noun "remnant" (šʾryt) refers to the faithful remnant of God's people in 2 Kgs 19:4, 31; Ezra 9:14; Isa 46:3; Jer 23:3; 31:7; Mic 2:12; 5:7–8; 7:18; Zeph 2:7, 9; 3:13;

pression in Judges is clearly the result of the divine judgment that Israel was wicked in God's eyes, not so Ruth. Naomi does attribute her emptiness to the LORD (1:13, 20–21), but she does not restate her bitterness. Rather, her bitter complaint and the women's praise of God in chapter four frame the narrative with elements typical of a lament: complaint and praise (e.g., Ps 13:1–2, 6). Third, Ruth's determination to find someone "in whose eyes I shall find favor" (2:3) contrasts with Judges' repeated "Israel again did what was wicked in God's eyes" and "everyone did what was right in his own eyes," especially in respect of the person who resolves Naomi's barren future, the righteous savior-judge, Boaz. Ruth's seeking favor also anticipates Hannah's appeal to Eli: "let your servant find favor in your eyes" (1 Sam 1:18).

Naomi went to Moab with her family; she returned to Bethlehem empty (1:21), a widow without sons to support her. However, she enters Bethlehem at the beginning of the barley harvest with a Moabite daughter-in-law clinging to her; two childless widows facing a barren future. As it turns out the widow from Moab rescues the widow from Bethlehem, who in turn provides rest for her daughter-in-law (*mnwḥ*, 3:1). Nevertheless, Ruth is not a story of two women, but of one woman, the LORD's bride in the person of Naomi, the remnant who occasions Israel's (the women) praise of God (4:14–15; Isa 54:5–8) for saving her from barrenness.[17] The enduring claim of Ruth is that God provides an unexpected savior-judge whose covenant piety secures a satisfying and joyful future for his barren people. Ruth 4:17–22 explicitly points to Naomi's great-grandson, David; Matthew 1:5–16 to her even greater grandchild, Jesus Christ, through whom the Father looks favorably on his errant people.

Zech 8:6, 11, 12.

17. This fits the late exilic date proposed for Ruth. About the dating and purpose of Ruth, Sakenfeld (*Ruth*, 5) writes that Ruth "could have been read as a challenge to community purity perspectives of the late pre–exilic Deuteronomistic History, with its emphasis against relationships with the local Canaanites. Or it might have addressed in story form the tensions arising already in the early post-exilic era between Jewish returnees from Babylon and those who had remained in the land after the fall of Jerusalem. Noting the repeated need to challenge narrow exclusivism in the life of the ancient community should remind readers that the story of Ruth addresses a perennial issue in the *human community*." Emphasis added. While true, the last statement removes the concerns of Ruth from the particulars of the covenant community, whether understood in OT or NT terms.

What Is Ruth 2:1–23 about Today?

Context of Ruth 2:1–23

Ruth 1 defines the narrative problem in terms of a question, "What does the future hold for Naomi, bereft of a husband and sons?" Juxtaposed to Judges and in the light of the introductory clauses "in the days when the judges were judging, there was a famine in the land," other questions arise: Will Naomi's accusation that God has treated her bitterly (1:13, 20) receive a response from the God who rescued Israel from Egypt's bitter oppression (*mrr*, Exod 1:14; 12:8; 15:23–24), and who repeated saved wayward Israel in Judges? If so, what form will that response take? And, why does the narrator describe Ruth the Moabite as "the one who returned" (*hšbh*, 1:22) with Naomi to Bethlehem?

Ruth 1:6–22 portrays Naomi's return to Bethlehem, a return occasioned by the LORD's blessing Bethlehem (lit. "the house of bread") with bread. Occurring twelve times (1:6, 7, 8, 10, 11, 12, 15bis, 16, 21, 22bis), the verb "to return" forms a narrative thread that runs from Naomi's intent to return (*lšwb*, 1:6) to its completion in 1:22a, and finishes with Ruth's "returning" (1:22c) to Bethlehem. Interwoven in the movement towards Bethlehem are mentions of Naomi's daughters-in-law returning with her (1:7), Naomi urging them to return to Moab (1:8, 11, 15bis), and Naomi's complaint that the LORD "caused me to return" empty (1:21). Elsewhere in the OT the verb "to return" (*šwb*) portrays "turning from sin" or "repent" (Jer 5:3; 8:5). Solomon's dedicatory prayer employs both senses: if Israel *turns* from sin and acknowledges the LORD, "then hear in heaven and forgive the sin of your people Israel and *bring them again* (Heb. "cause them to return") to the land that you gave to their fathers" (1 Kgs 8:33–34). Especially in the light of 1 Kgs 8, exilic and diasporic audiences would hear God's "causing" Naomi to return to Bethlehem from a foreign land as a returning from exile, from a place where "other gods" set the norms for faith and conduct, Moab for Naomi or Cyrus' Persia for Judah and Benjamin (Ezra 1:5). The double use of the verb "to remain" (1:3, 5) reinforces Naomi's return as the remnant of Israel. When Ruth 1:22c states that "Naomi returned and Ruth the Moabite her daughter-in-law with her, *the one who returned from the fields of Moab*," the narrator includes Ruth in Naomi's return from exile to the land God gave to their fathers. Bitter Naomi is unaware that the rescuer from her emptiness came home with her,[18] is standing beside her at the beginning of Bethlehem's barley harvest.

---

18. Mann, *The Book of the Former Prophets*, 98.

A narrative aside—"Now Naomi had a relative of her husband's . . . whose name was Boaz" (2:1)—interrupts the narrative flow from 1:22: "and they came to Bethlehem at the beginning of the barley harvest," to 2:2: "And Ruth the Moabite said to Naomi, . . . ," to introduce to the audience a character whose distant relationship to Elimelech hints at the possibility of hope. Naomi's bitter lament turns to joy when she learns that Ruth gleaned in the fields of this Boaz (2:19–20).

Armed with this knowledge Naomi shrewdly moves Ruth to awaken Boaz's interest in performing his role as the kinsman-redeemer, that is, to rescue Elimelech's property from debt. The word "rescue" or "redeem" occurs seven times ($g^{\jmath}l$, 3:9, 12bis, 13[4x]) in chapter three, once in Ruth's request, and six times in Boaz's response. Boaz seals his vow to pursue Ruth's request with *six* measures of barley (3:13, 15), a reflection of his intent to redeem and an anticipation of the fullness of Naomi's rescue portrayed by the women's "He (Boaz or Obed) shall be to you a restorer of life and a nourisher of your old age, for your daughter-in-law who loves you, who is more to you than *seven* sons, has given birth to him" (4:15 ESV). Shrewd negotiation at the gate reveals the fulness of this redeemer's "worth" (2:1): Boaz will redeem ($g^{\jmath}l$, 4:1, 3, 4[4x], 5, 6[4x], 8, 14) the land, and acquire (qnh, 4:4, 5bis, 8, 9, 10) Ruth ("I have bought" 4:9, 10 ESV), with whom he will have a child. As Mahlon's and Naomi's son, Obed will inherit the land Boaz acquired at great personal cost. Even as Ruth and Boaz resolved Naomi's problem of a barren future, Naomi's descendant David ends the oppression of Israel's enemies and rules with a righteousness also displayed by David's Moabite ancestor in the fields of the righteous Boaz.

Who Does What in Ruth 2?

Several features identify Ruth as the main character in this chapter: she initiates the action, gleaning "after him in whose sight I shall find favor" (2:2); her gleaning in the field of Boaz draws Naomi's relative into the drama; and, upon bringing the barley home, Naomi learns from Ruth that her lack of bread was solved by "one of our redeemers" (2:20). Like the verb "to return" in chapter 1, the verb "to glean" (*lqt*, 2:2, 3, 7, 8, 15bis, 16, 17bis, 18, 19, 23) forms the narrative thread that connects the characters unassumingly embodying divine instruction concerning the poor: "you shall not reap your field right up to its edge, neither shall you gather the gleanings after your harvest . . . You shall leave them for the poor and for the sojourner. I am the LORD your God" (Lev 19:9–10; Exod 23:10–11). Ruth gleans the heads of grain the harvesters missed or dropped. Landowner Boaz facilitates Ruth's gleaning by urging her to stay in his fields, warning the harvesters not to touch her, and inviting her to join the harvesters at mealtime. Boaz tops off his hospitality by exceeding divine instruction, telling his young men "to pull out some from the bundles for her and leave it for her to glean, and do not rebuke her" (2:16). This is Boaz's down payment on the LORD's recompense for all Ruth has done for Naomi, including leaving "her father and mother and your native land" (2:11–12). Gradually, the wings of the Almighty begin to spread over her (2:12; 3:10).

Naomi's response to Ruth's good news brings the gleaning episode to a conclusion: Ruth gives her about three-fifths of a bushel of grain in addition to the leftovers from the meal (2:17–18), which included roasted grain, wine, and notably, bread. Aside from its appearance in the name Bethlehem, the word "bread" (*lḥm*) occurs twice in the Ruth narrative: when Naomi heard the LORD had given his people bread she returns to Bethlehem; and when Ruth joins eats the bread Boaz and his harvesters received from the LORD (1:6; 2:14). The first mention indicates the famine's end by divine intervention, and the second foregrounds a Moabite's tasting the goodness of the LORD before Naomi, as Rahab enjoyed rest before Israel. Naomi's bitterness begins its transformation when she praises the LORD's covenant faithfulness (*ḥsd*, 2:20) for Ruth's happening "to come to that part of the field belonging to Boaz, of the clan of Elimelech" (2:3), explaining that this "man is *our* close relative, one of *our* redeemers" (2:20). The plural "our" further defines Ruth's clinging (*dbq*, 1:14) to Naomi, especially because she tells Ruth to *stay close* to the young women, and then to *stay close* to the young men until harvest's end. The narrator ends the episode with Ruth *staying close* to the young women until the end of the harvests (*dbq*, 2:8, 21, 23).

Woven into the narrative word-thread "to glean," the phrase "to find favor in the eyes of" adds a distinctive color. Ruth uses it when asking permission to glean "after him in whose eyes I shall find favor" (2:2), when neither Ruth nor Naomi were narratively aware of their close relative. It also occurs in her question "*Why* have I found favor in your [i.e., Boaz] eyes?" and in her affirmation, "I have surely found favor in your eyes, my LORD" (2:10, 13). The phrase "to find favor in the eyes of" typically occurs in biblical depictions of superior-subordinate social relationships (LORD-Noah and Potiphar-Joseph, Gen 6:8; 39:4; Ahasuerus-Esther, Esth 5:8) where the social superior has resources to grace the recipient or petitioner with a gift whose benefits unfold in the subsequent narrative. Noah and Joseph were unknowing recipients of divine favor that saved the nations from world-wide disasters; Esther depended on Ahasuerus' favor to plan an escape from Haman, "the enemy of the Jews." Ruth herself intends to be the recipient of someone's favor. Unlike the audience—who knows about Boaz from the narrative aside and Ruth's "happening" to glean the field of Boaz (2:1, 3)—Ruth has no idea who that might be, not even when she meets him. To Ruth's question why she, a foreigner, had found favor in his eyes, Boaz answers with language reminiscent of Abraham's leaving his clan and native land (Gen 12:1). In Boaz's eyes, Ruth's clinging to Naomi was not merely an act of personal courage and patient gleaning, but of covenant piety. In clinging to Naomi and gleaning on Bethlehem's harvest fields, Ruth defined herself as a Gentile daughter of Abraham: she joined the journey Abraham began by leaving her clan, family and land, and she follows the way of righteousness (*drk* and *ṣdqh*, Gen 18:19) defined by divine instruction for feeding the poor. Favor had found Ruth before she found it.

Ruth's affirmation "I have surely found favor" (2:13) emphasizes a confident assurance in the gift of favor, "though I am not even one of your servants"; *de facto* Ruth conducts herself as a covenant vassal who loves the instruction of the LORD and lives by its letter and spirit. Through Boaz's favor emerges the almost unobtrusive action of the Almighty in Ruth: "The eyes of the LORD are everywhere; he examines the wicked and the good" (Prov 15:3). When Naomi saw (2:18) the gleanings Ruth brought home and heard about Boaz, she knew that her Moabite daughter-in-law *Ruth had found favor with Naomi's redeemer*. That answers the question, "Who, does what?," but not without raising another: what is God's role in Ruth 2? Why is God not the mover of events in Ruth 2? Doesn't focusing on human character promote a works righteousness?

God's Role in Ruth 2

This section addresses the *literary* role of God in biblical narrative where, like human characters, God speaks, responds to human actions, appears to the patriarchs and Moses, and speaks through prophets. Genesis, Exodus, Jeremiah and Ezekiel depict God as interacting explicitly with these human characters. Although Boaz and Naomi refer to God, there is no explicit divine-human interaction in Ruth 2; rather, it foregrounds Ruth, Boaz, and Naomi, and, of these three Ruth initiates and completes the narrative action. Therefore, she is the main character. Nevertheless, the text does not exclude God. How is this so? The book of Esther illuminates the matter.

The MT of Esther goes one step further than Ruth 2: the characters do not interact with God, nor does the narrator inform the audience of God's role in Esther and Mordecai's defeating Haman, the enemy of the Jews. The narrator resolutely veils God, leaving Mordecai and Esther to their own devices. The poetics of irony: Mordecai in the position of power Haman schemed for; and peripety: Haman hanging on the gallows he prepared for Mordecai, are often taken to imply the presence of God. More persuasive, however, are the numerous textual allusions to events narrated by the PH. Thus, for example, Mordecai is a descendant of King Saul, who refused to execute Agag the Amalekite (1 Sam 15:10–35; Esth 2:5–7), a people with whom the LORD had sworn eternal enmity (Exod 17:8–16); Haman the Agagite is a descendant of the Amalekite king (Esth 3:1). Haman's plot to kill the Jews, then, is rooted in Mordecai's refusal to honor the sworn enemy of the LORD (3:2b). Israel's separation from other peoples—central to Leviticus, mentioned in Ezra–Nehemiah, and thus to Israel's covenant distinctiveness—is the reason Haman tells the king that "it is not to the king's profit to tolerate them" (3:8 ESV[19]). The proposed date for the Jews' destruction (3:13) evokes the date of the Passover and the phrase "no one could stand against" the Jews because they feared them (9:2; Josh 1:5; 23:9;) recalls the fear of the Canaanites (Josh 2:9; 5:1). Finally, the Jews' relief from their enemies (*nwḥ*, 9:16, 22,) recalls the rest God gave Israel (*nwḥ*, Josh 1:15; 21:44), a rest Haman publicly opposed (3:8). These poetics and textual allusions inform Esther's audience; unaware of these allusions, Esther's characters operate in the veiled presence of God, normal for the audience of Esther and Ruth 2 to this day.[20]

Textual allusions to the deity in Ruth 2 include Boaz and Naomi's mentioning God in greetings and wishes, and Boaz's declaration that Ruth has taken refuge under the wings of the God of Israel. Ruth's exilic and diasporic audience know that gleaning fallen grain and Boaz's extraordinary kindness on the harvest fields allude to divine instructions that the poor may gather the fallen ears of grain and that the land owner's laborers may not pick them up, neither may they harvest to the edges of the fields (Lev 19:9; Deut 24:19–22). Foregrounding Ruth the Moabite's covenant piety provokes the exilic and diasporic audiences, for they know who did what was right in its own eyes in the days of the judges. By doing God's will Ruth and Boaz brought sweetness to bitter Naomi, for keeping the statutes of the LORD brings life (Lev 18:5; Ps 1), they are sweeter than honey that "enlightens the eyes" (Ps 19:8, 10) for those who seek God's favor. Ruth's "happening" on Boaz's fields, occurring just after the disjunctive introduction to Boaz in 2:1, also argues that it was not mere happenstance, but divine providence, that brought Ruth to Boaz's fields. Although a fundamental Christian belief, divine providence

---

19. The verb is *nwḥ*, translated as "to tolerate." In concert with this verb's use in Esth 9:16, 22, the clause might be better translated as "it is not in the king's interest to give them relief."

20. On rest in Joshua and Esther, and on the veiled presence of God, see Leder, "Hearing Esther after Joshua," 267–79.

is a theological statement about God's unobtrusive involvement in human affairs, not an exegetical explanation of the narrative depiction of a text's characters, including God.

The narrator's explanation that God restored the fields of Bethlehem and gave Ruth life (1:6; 4:13), and that God blessed Joseph (Gen 39:5, 21, 23), are textual indicators of God's explicit involvement, and only thus clear examples of providence. Although these examples demonstrate that human experience is fraught with the divine, these narrative comments only inform the audience; the characters themselves remain unaware of this activity. Christian belief in divine providence does not obviate the expectation that covenant believers love and execute God's instruction. Ruth's initiative to "glean . . . after him in whose sight I shall find favor" alludes to the divine and is central to what Ruth 2 means today.

RUTH 2 TODAY: WISELY SEEKING HIM IN WHOSE EYES I MAY FIND FAVOR

The narrative worlds of Ruth and Esther are similar to our own. Special divine disclosures are not the norm; biblical revelation and theological reflection guides faith and conduct. As in Esther, God is not absent from our world, but his presence is veiled. Still, humanity is responsible to God the Creator (Rom 1:18–20) and his people committed to the Creator-Redeemer by means of sworn covenants. Paul argues that Gentiles who have not received the covenants can make good decisions (Rom 2:14–15); Judges teaches that having God's instructions is no guarantee of righteous decision-making. Given that Naomi, Ruth, Boaz and Esther made decisions without explicit, that is, textually indicated, divine influence, and that Esther also sought divine favor, how do we understand "seeking him in whose eyes I may find favor?"

Veiled means of divine favor continue to this very day, but to identify a contemporary Cyrus, Darius, Boaz, or Ahasuerus as the instrument of this favor is fraught with difficulty. Was God's use of Nebuchadnezzar to destroy Jerusalem and bring Judah into exile *only* a sign of judgment and not of God's favor? Amos confidently warns God's people of such connections: a famine is God's instrument to bring Israel to repentance (Amos 4:6). But which contemporary events are evidence of God's favor or judgment? Since Simon the magician (Acts 8:18–24), attempts to manage the power of the Holy Spirit or discern his reshaping the church in new socio-historical situations, continue unabated. But the uncontrollable Spirit moves like the wind to bring about new birth and teach disciples the truth of Christ and his Word (John 3:8; 14:26). Christian believers may be certain of God's favor in and for the world in the birth, death, resurrection and ascension of God's only Son, as revealed in Scripture. It is better to intentionally seek God's favor in the Christ Scripture reveals, to eat this Bread of Life (John 6:35), than to bake your own spiritual bread and dig new wells (Jer 2:13) in failed attempts to identify contemporary favors of God through the Spirit.

Ruth did not know from whom to seek favor. Esther, being favored in the king's court (2:9, 15, 17), knew from whom to seek favor, but it was dangerous (Esth 4:11, 16). Both women shrewdly pursued favor to escape destitution and/or maintain hope for a restful future for God's people in the land and the diaspora, and both sought favor without explicit awareness of divine influence. Seeking and finding favor does not require discernment of divine irruptions into daily life, but a canonical self-understanding, an identity rooted in the mighty acts of God revealed in Scripture. The narrative allusions reveal Esther and Mordecai's awareness of that identity, Ruth assumes it in complying with divine instruction. Whatever socio-cultural situation asks for a decision, divine instruction teaches God's covenant people to accept the invitation of Lady Wisdom to drink her wine, not Lady Folly's appeal to drink stolen waters (Prov 9:1–6; 13–18).

From the persecution in Persia by Haman, "the enemy of the Jews," to that of Rome's emperors, the pressures on members of the Three-Self churches and believers in tightly controlled Muslim and Hindu areas, the community of Christian believers today cannot avoid seeking favor from authorities. The wisdom that comes from generations of social experience warns those seeking such favors from earthly authorities to be careful: "A servant who deals wisely has the king's favor, but his wrath falls on one who acts shamefully" (Prov 14:35), and "Do not put yourself forward in the king's presence or stand in the place of the great, for it is better to be told, 'Come up here,' than to be put lower in the presence of a noble" (Prov 25:6–7 ESV). Seeking favors can get complicated: "By justice a king builds up the land, but he who exacts gifts tears it down" (Prov 29:4 ESV). Failure to return the favor has its own rewards, think of the horse-head episode in *The God Father. Part One.* If the price is high, one does what divine instruction permits, potential consequences understood: "If I perish, I perish" (Esth 4:16). Esther's dangerous decision to go to the king, points to the truth that "many seek the face of a ruler, but it is from the LORD that a man gets justice" (Prov 29:26).

No matter how righteous or self-serving, earthly authorities can only bestow penultimate favors. Boaz, a worthy man who loved God's instructions, bestowed unconditional favor on Naomi and God's people. Note, however, that while Ruth seeks refuge under the wings of her redeemer Boaz (3:12), Boaz himself identifies that refuge with the wings of the LORD God of Israel (2:12). Thus, Ruth's seeking to find and Boaz's granting her favor is nothing less than a Moabite's petition to find favor with Israel's covenant LORD. That a Moabite, prohibited from the presence of the LORD, receives divine favor and rest in the home of Naomi's redeemer, reflects *God's unmerited favor* to his own people.

The Rest That Still Remains for the Daughters of Lot

While Canaanites enjoy rest (*nwḥ*, Judg 2:23; 3:1) from Israelite conquest, Moab attacks God's people with the support of Ammon and Amalek (Judg 3:12–14). This enemy triad has a sordid history in relation to the covenant people: Moab and Ammon are Lot's descendants by incest and are prohibited from entering the presence of the LORD (Gen 19:36–38; Deut 23:3), and the LORD swore eternal enmity against Amalek (Exod 17:14–16). Against this background the benevolent depiction of Ruth the daughter of Lot joining a righteous Israelite to save Naomi, i.e., Israel, from distress is unexpected, more so given Naomi's initiative to find rest (*mnwḥ*, 3:1) for Ruth. But Ruth is not the first Gentile to enjoy such rest: Rahab the Canaanite and her family enjoyed in the rubble of Jericho.

Words for "rest" occur only twice in Ruth. Naomi urges Ruth and Orpah to return home, wishing that "the LORD grant that you may find rest (*mnwḥh*), each in the *house* of her husband" (1:9). Daughter of Lot Orpah returns to Moab, but Ruth clings to Naomi and "returns" to Bethlehem. Ruth's bountiful gleanings from the harvest fields of Elimelech's kinsman-redeemer impels Naomi to seek rest (*mnwḥ*, 3:1) for Ruth in the *house* of an Israelite husband. Indeed, the elders at the gate describe this daughter of Lot as building the *house* of Israel, along with Rachel and Leah from Paddan-Aram and the Canaanite Tamar. In the days of the judges, when the LORD holds Israel's rest from the enemy in abeyance, a daughter of Lot receives rest in the house of Naomi's redeemer. What does it mean for Ruth the Moabite to be at rest in the home of Naomi's Israelite redeemer (i.e., the historical enemy)? What about Orpah who went home to find rest in the home of another Moabite husband? And, what about the other daughters of Moab and Ammon?

Like the other nations of the earth, Lot's daughters will escape the curse on all nations only through God's blessing of Abraham (Gen 12:3), he is their divinely appointed kinsman-redeemer. The way towards rest for the nations is the one depicted by Ruth, the daughter of Lot who became a daughter of Abraham by abandoning the gods that defined her and clinging to the God of Naomi/Israel. Her former divine antagonist became her LORD, her former lord an antagonist. Like Noah's dove who could not find rest for soles of its feet anywhere in post-diluvian world and could only return to the divinely designed vehicle of salvation (Gen 8:9), so Ruth finds ("returns," 1:22) rest in the divinely created vehicle of salvation, the house of Israel, built by the LORD's protection of the blessed descendants ("seed," Gen 12:7; 22:15–18) of Abraham. Israel owes its unique identity to the house of the LORD, the divinely created space for God's dwelling in Israel's midst, first through Sinai's tabernacle (Exod 25:8), and later after the ark entered the Jerusalem temple. At that time Solomon thanked the LORD for giving Israel rest (1 Kgs 8:56). About this house, Scripture declares, peoples will say "Come, let us go up to the mountain of the LORD, . . . he will judge among the nations and will settle disputes" (Isa 2:3–4; 19:18–25).

Along with Ruth the Moabite, the other daughters of Lot and of Ammon will find rest from the false values of their gods in the place the LORD has chosen as a dwelling place for his name. By following Ruth on the way of Abraham (*drk*, Gen 18:19) those who were "not my people" may become "my people." Salvation from distress is from the Jews (John 4:22), but being Jewish is not a necessary condition (Gal 3:29). And so "all Israel" will enter the rest that remains (Rom 11:26–27).

8

Samuel

Of Prophets and Kings

Summary: During the days of the judges, when Eli was priest in Shiloh, Elkanah's childless wife Hannah finds favor in God's eyes, gives birth to Samuel and dedicates him to the LORD. Unlike Eli's wicked sons, Samuel grows in favor with the LORD and becomes the instrument of God's word to Israel. During war with the Philistines the ark of the covenant was taken into the temple of Dagon. Finding their god fallen and broken in pieces before the ark, the ark is moved to other cities, none of which escape God's punishment. The Philistines send the ark back to Israel, where it remains for twenty years in the house of Abinadab. As savior-judge Samuel acknowledges God's help in subduing the Philistines (1 Sam 1:1—7:17).

Although the LORD is Israel's king, the wickedness of Eli's sons as savior–judges impels Israel to ask for a king like the nations. Although displeasing, the LORD condescends to the request, Samuel anoints Saul the donkey-herder king, and Saul defeats the Ammonites. At Gilgal Samuel declares he has faithfully executed his ministry, the people agree, and Samuel charges them and their king to serve the LORD faithfully. While battling the Philistines Saul's rash vow endangers the life of his son Jonathan. Saul fought the enemies of Israel valiantly, but did not defeat the Philistines (1 Sam 8:1—14:52).

Samuel announces that Saul will lose the kingdom be-cause he took Amalekite plunder and failed to put Agag their king to death. Samuel anoints David, who becomes Saul's mu-sician and warrior; he defeats Goliath. Saul's jealousy forces David to flee for his life. Saul pursues him, repents, pursues again and kills those who help David; David spares the life of God's anointed several times. In the meantime, Jonathan has become David's friend, Michal and Abigail his wives, and he has many followers. After Samuel's death, Saul seeks his counsel through the witch of Endor; Samuel tells Saul that he and Jonathan will die. After this David defeats the Amalekites; Saul and his sons die fighting the Philistines (1 Sam 15:1—31:13).

Seeking to maintain the kingship after his death, the house of Saul opposes David. After defeating Saul's son Ishbosheth, David is anointed king of Judah and later over Israel. God refuses David's offer to build him a house, but pledges to give David rest from his enemies and to maintain his throne forever. Following a list of David's military victories, the narrator notes that David administered his kingdom with justice and righteousness (2 Sam 1:1—8:18).

Thereafter David pays respect to Jonathan's memory by having Mephibosheth eat at the king's table. The Ammonites repay David's kindness to their late king Nahash by shaving the beards of David's emissaries. David sends Joab to war against Ammon, but he remains in his palace. David's adultery with Bathsheba reaps a terrible harvest: the treacherous murder of Uriah and the death of their child. The prophet Nathan's parable brings David to repentance and God grants David and Bathsheba another child, Solomon. Absalom kills his brother Amnon for violating his sister Tamar; Absalom rebels against David by seeking the kingship and dies at the hands of Joab and his men. Having fled before Absalom, David returns to Jerusalem only to confront Sheba's rebellion (2 Sam 9:1—20:26).

The narrative ends depicting earlier episodes from David's reign: his avenging the Gibeonites, war against the Philistines, his songs of deliverance, a list of his mighty men, and David's census of Israel and surrendering himself to God for this sin, and his building of an altar on the threshing floor of Araunah the Jebusite (2 Sam 21:1—24:25).

Central Narrative Interest: God ends the chaotic days of the judges by defeating his adversaries through his servants Samuel and David.

Opening Sentences and Connections
with Antecedent Narrative

THE OPENING SENTENCES OF Samuel identifies "a certain man of the Zuphites from Ramathaim of the hill country of Ephraim . . . an Ephratitite" as Elkanah. Phrases similar to "there was a certain man" at the beginning of the Samson story, "there was a certain man from Zorah," (Judg 13:2), and of the Saul story, "there was a man from Benjamin" (1 Sam 9:1),[1] provide close links between Samuel and Judges in the MT.[2] That Elkanah is identified as an Ephratite, i.e., from or associated with Bethlehem,[3] echoes Ruth's references to Bethlehem and David in the Christian Scriptures. Ramathaim (Twin Heights), the other designation of Elkanah's home, appears in the dual form only here (Ramah in 1 Sam 1:19; 2:11; 7:17; 8:4; 15:34; 16:18; 19:18, 19, 22bis, 23bis; 20:1; 22:6; 25:1; 28:3; not in 2 Samuel).

Stanley Walters argues that the use of the dual form alludes to two episodes, 1 Sam 19:18–24 and Jeremiah 40:1–6, "which together show the Spirit and the Word as essential features of biblical prophesying. Elkanah thus appears as part of a trans–generational study and spiritual revitalization, to which the canonical book of Samuel continues to call us."[4] Elkanah's name, "God creates," indicates that "through him and his family God is creating the public prophetic movement in ancient Israel, and through it the life that only the Spirit and the Word can bring."[5] Walters' provocative reading of Ramathaim would be strengthened by defining twin episodes within 1 Samuel. I would replace Jer 40:1–6 with 1 Sam 28, which Walters dismisses as a geographic reference. Samuel's last prophetic word (*dbr*, 28:11, 17, 20, 21; esp. 28:18) against Saul, from the grave, is a better candidate for the Word controlling rashness, of the Spirit or of Saul, than that of Nebuchadnezzar.

Walters' reading is illuminating for another reason: it identifies Elkanah first as a prophetic figure, and only then as the husband of Hannah. Elkanah speaks tenderly to Hannah (1:8), but his most important words to Hannah are prophetic: "may the LORD establish his word" (*qwm* + *dbr*, 1 Sam 1:23; *qwm* + *dbr* bis, Deut 18:18), a word that later came to Samuel, through whom God spoke again to all Israel (*dbr*, 1 Sam 3:19—4:1).

The opening episodes of 1 Samuel recalls themes from Ruth. The abusive Peninnah contrasts starkly with Ruth's selfless devotion to Naomi. Barren Hannah's bitter lament and God's gift of Samuel, who would begin to unravel the chaos of the time of the judges, continues the theme of bitter Naomi's receiving a son through the righteous kinsman-redeemer who acquired (*qnh*, 4:4, 5bis, 8, 9, 10) Ruth while redeeming the property of Elimelech. Where

---

1. Tsumura, *The First Book of Samuel*, 106.

2. Jobling, *1 Samuel*, 41–76, discusses 1 Sam 1–12 as an extension of the Judges.

3. Tsumura, *The First Book of Samuel*, 107.

4. Walters, "Twain Heights," 60. For Walters' definition of five narrative *episodes* from which he selects two, see Walters, "Twain Heights," 62–63.

5. Walters, "Twain Heights," 75–76.

Boaz acquires Ruth and thus facilitates turning Naomi's lament to praise, El-kanah ("God acquires," or "creates") is instrumental in the birth of the prophet through whom God began to put an end to the chaotic time of the judges. In the MT, without Ruth's literary interruption, Penninah, Eli and his sons continue the moral and cultic disorder of the days when Israel did what was right in its own eyes. Hannah's request to find favor in Eli's eyes (1 Sam 1:18) recalls the sight metaphor in Judges, but suggests Eli himself was not wholly corrupt; his sons committed great sin in the eyes of the LORD (2:17). Hannah's paying her vow to dedicate Samuel continues the theme of paying one's vow as depicted in Joshua (22–24) and Judges, Jephthah's rash vow to dedicate his daughter to the LORD as a sacrifice.

The most distant allusion may be the curt "but Hannah had no chil-dren" (*wlḥnh ʾyn yldym* 1:2) after describing Penninah's fecundity, for the phrase is similar to the brief description of Sarah, "she had no child" (*ʾyn lh wld*, Gen 11:30), after a description of her sisters-in-law's fertility. Like Sarah, whose Isaac Abraham offered to the LORD, Hannah gives birth to Samuel, a Nazirite from birth (1 Sam 1:11, 27–28). Unlike Samson, Samuel judges Israel all his life as a faithful Nazirite (1 Sam 7:15–17; Judg 13:5).

Challenges to Reading Samuel Today

The Challenge Defined

Scripture depicts the creation and its creatures as part of an orderly whole, whose natural processes and materials are given to the man to work and keep according to the divine will (Gen 2:15–17). This is the origin of earthly polity, the human organizing and resultant organization of the earthly states of affairs in the presence of and according to the will of God. Further de-velopment of polity in Eden is unknown. East of Eden, however, Adam and Eve's descendants generated a polity unavoidably rooted in God's will and his creation, but profoundly altered by human autonomy (3:6; 6:1–7) and the divine curse (*ʾrr*, Gen 3:14, 17; 5:29; 4:11; 9:25). The Creator decisively rejected Babel's polity, but initiated a redemptive polity rooted in God's oath-bound commitments to bless Abraham and his descendants (*brk*, Gen 12:1–3; 15:17–21). Still east of Eden but under the wings of the Almighty, the Creator-Redeemer revealed his covenant polity at Sinai, a polity that administered Israel's faith and conduct by Moses himself in the desert and his teaching (*spr trt mšh*, Josh 1:6–8) in the land of promise.

Joshua–Judges demonstrates that God's people are incapable of complying with covenant polity without leadership, but that even that leadership is seriously flawed. Samuel in particular focuses on a leadership reflective of God's heavenly rule of the universe: an earthly king who rules according to heaven's direction, the covenant polity rooted in Sinai (Deut 17:14–20). But before Samuel develops its argument for kingship it focuses on the covenant official whose task it is to remind the king of his covenant obligations: the prophet. Samuel's depiction of prophets and kings ruling and speaking in the name of heaven challenges not only his contemporaries, but also the modern cultured despiser of heaven and the Christian attracted to such views. Questions arise. How do contemporary polities and notions of leadership affect one's understanding of prophetic and royal leadership of God's people? What does such leadership do today, and according to which or whose norms? Who or what evaluates prophetic and royal leadership and how? And, what are the consequences of failed prophetic and royal leadership?

The Conflict of Heavenly and Earthly Polities: Thinking Outside the Box

Genesis 4:1–11:26 acknowledges the earthly polities of ancient city–states such as Akkad, Calneh, Erech and Nineveh (10:9–10), but the Babel episode illustrates how this polity challenges heaven. Beginning with Abraham's uprooting from Babel's polity, but without neglecting the continuing impact of such polities (Jericho, Assur, Babylon, Susa, Rome), Scripture focuses on the community rooted in the redemptive polity God declared to Abraham: the OT and NT people of God and its polities.[6] The ancient world's conflict of polities centered on their deities' will as divined in nature; Israel's polity was based on divine speech in conflict with the polities of "the other gods" (Exod 23:20–33; Judg 2:11–15). Contemporary conflict of polities centers on earthly constitutions that seek to organize religiously plural societies inclusive of Christian, atheist, Hindu, Muslim, animist, and Confucian peoples. Within this pluralist society, the polity of the Israel of God (Gal 6:16), i.e., the church of Jesus Christ, is anchored in the truth of Christ revealed in Scripture for post-Pentecostal life among the nations led by the Spirit, and as such "not . . . conformed to [the mind of] this world" (Rom 12:2). In principle, the polity of the church of Christ—Episcopalian, Presbyterian-Reformed, or Congregational—is anchored in revelation from heaven as depicted in Scripture and historically elaborated in various theological traditions, all focused on the kingship of Christ; the polities of societies and

6. Scripture depicts a variety of pre- and post-Sinai and pre- and post-Pentecostal human polities, as do the post-canonical polities developed in Judaism and Christianity. All, however, in some sense insist on heaven's will as their anchor.

government—democratic, republican, monarchical, socialist—in human development of creation. The former polity administers a redemptively-created community, the latter polities administer communities developed in the course of human affairs, usually but not necessarily without reference to the divine since the Enlightenment. The redemptive origin and resultant peculiar polity of the church of Christ needs a leadership that differs significantly from that of other social organizations, beginning with Abraham's separation from the polity of Ur.

God's covenant polity is unambiguous; execution of that polity after the death of Joshua and his generation was disastrous, except for that of Ruth and Boaz. Unlike Moses and Joshua, the savior–judges displayed no interest in covenant polity, or, as the audience hears from Samuel's opening chapters, were corrupt. Nearly blind Eli fails to acknowledge the distress of God's people in the person of Hannah, nor does he correct his sons' abusive leadership (1 Sam 2:12–17). Samuel's sons are so corrupt ("they took bribes and perverted justice (*mšpṭ*)" [1 Sam 8:3]) that the people ask Samuel to "give us a king like the nations to judge (*špṭ*) us" (1 Sam 8:5). That is, rather than seek a ruler from among God's people, they ask for what the covenant polity of Deut 17:15 prohibits, a foreigner to lead them. If Israel's public demand for adapting the received covenant polity to the values of other gods is an example of thinking "outside the box," it no less illustrates a covenant people in fundamental conflict with the revealed will of God. When God told a displeased Samuel to grant the people their wish and explain "the ways of the king who will reign over you" (1 Sam 8:10–18), the exilic and diasporic audience is reminded of the crucial role of the prophet in the administration of an earthly covenant polity rooted in heaven's will, and of how the syncretistic ways of the kings begot the exile, a judgment prescribed by the covenant polity detailed in Lev 18:28 and 20:22–23.

Covenant polity teaches that when the king "sits on the throne of his kingdom, he shall write for himself in a book a copy of this law . . . and he shall read in it all the days of his life, that he may learn to fear the LORD his God by keeping all the words of this law . . . and that he may not turn aside from the commandment" (Deut 17:18–20). David's reign is righteous and just (*ṣdqh wmšpṭ*, 2 Sam 8:15), fulfilling in part what the people asked from Samuel, someone to judge (*špṭ*) them. Hezekiah and Josiah also ruled like David. Others, like Solomon in his old age (1 Kgs 11:1–40), and Ahab and Manasseh who ruled by the polity of other gods, paved the cruel road to a schism (1 Kgs 11:11–12) and exile. Unlike David, Hezekiah and Josiah, they rejected the word of the LORD himself or that of his prophets (1 Kgs 11:9–10; 2 Kgs 17:13, 23; 21:10–15). The relationship between prophets and kings poses another question.

Prophets and Kings: Charisma versus Institution?

Samuel's solution to the corruption of the days of the judges—a kingship dedicated to defeat Israel's enemies all around according to covenant polity—becomes a problem for contemporary readers in the West for social and/or historical exegetical reasons. First, the metaphor of kingship depicts an autocracy at odds with the various contemporary democratic polities that grant the people a greater role in selecting candidates for and removing from leadership. Second, a polity in some sense originating in heaven conflicts with the Western polities whose elevation of naked reason and feeling slowly undermined earlier faith shaped polities. Varieties of Christian and secular polities were adapted to a developing pluralism and toleration, among them the cultural polity of a self-esteem that refuses all boundaries to the self's identity-orientations, except perhaps ethnicity and culture. This provides opportunities for the contemporary reader to ignore the history of interpretation and its various methodologies to hear Scripture only within the reader's own echo chamber. Third, recent sociological and biblical exegesis argue that original ecclesiastical authority is charismatic, not institutional. In this vein scholarly reconstructions of the rise of the monarchy insist that the origin of kingship lies with the Spirit-endowed judges such as Saul, not the David whose scribes imposed a dynastic ideology on the charismatic origins of authentic Israelite leadership.[7] Consequently, Scripture becomes an institutional artifact that needs salvation from reading it as the church's canon, a rescue performed by charismatic "outside the box" interpretations and deconstructions. But, is the view that original ecclesiastical authority is charismatic correct such that it warrants an anti-institutional revisioning of the church? Does canonical Scripture warrant such a reading?

Rodney Hutton[8] understands charisma "not primarily as a personal trait exhibited by a 'charismatic' individual independent of social context but rather as an essentially social phenomenon that is a function of the broader group dynamics and fixed social relationships."[9] Hutton continues, "if one can legitimately speak of the judges as 'charismatic,' it is only in the sense that they represent the centering principles of cosmic justice and

7. Hutton, *Charisma and Authority*, 1–16, briefly describes the historical background and then discusses various proposals about the authority of Moses, the judges, kings, prophets, and priests. The last chapter looks at wisdom, "the charisma of order."

8. Priestly agents, for example, are understood against the background of a dialectic of nature (myth, abstraction, priestly ritual, eternity, institution) and history (narrative, becoming, prophetic critique, charisma). Hutton, *Charisma and Authority*, 164–70.

9. Hutton, *Charisma and Authority*, 8.

order in the mind of the author and his intended audience."[10] Kings and prophets similarly represent and enact these "centering principles."[11] Priests taught Torah and administered its centering principles at the temple, officiating at sacrifices, pronouncing people and objects "clean" or "unclean," and were concerned about "the sanctity of the cult and the maintenance of a strict separation of distinct realms, symbolic of the manner in which Israel sought to frame its conceptual universe and maintain cherished patterns of order."[12] Rather than being opposed to the institution, charisma is exercised within the community's organizational self-understanding based on its foundational documents. That is, Israel's centering principles, its covenant polity or Torah, administered by priests, kings, prophets and sages, is rooted in the community's documented self-understanding. The administration of this documented self–understanding functions authoritatively only within the belief that it is an authoritative word the LORD revealed to Moses from Sinai (Exod 19:1—Num 10:10) which the different agents of the covenant polity in the land were expected to execute (Josh 1:8–9; 2 Kgs 17:13). The books of Judges and Kings show that these agents more often than not did so corruptly (cf. Jer 2:26).

Contemporary readers of Scripture no less than Israel challenge the covenant polity by admixing it with forbidden polities, with one major difference: contemporary readers, culturally trained to believe that not heaven but humanity itself administers all of life, tend to subordinate heaven's interests to that of an earthly community of believers that has progressed from the primitive beliefs of Israel to a more sophisticated understanding of administering socio-religious affairs. This often includes a rejection of the God of the OT, a Marcionite heresy, and a redefinition of Jesus Christ as a sophisticated religious man from Bethlehem who dispenses wisdom, but is not divine, an Arian heresy. This reduces Christ's authority to the merely human and permits a development of authority in the body of Christ to the merely horizontal. Christ is LORD only in the sense of his sophisticated teaching. Furthermore, the Spirit of God—who endowed judges, prophets, and kings with authority—sent by Christ to guide his disciples in the truth, is transformed into a sort of cultural force that enables contemporary disciples to recognize progress.[13]

---

10. Hutton, *Charisma and Authority*, 69–70.

11. Hutton, *Charisma and Authority*, 79, 130–31.

12. Hutton, *Charisma and Authority*, 154–55.

13. This is nowhere more clearly stated than in recent leadership literature challenging the post-Christendom world to adapt to changes or die. For example, Bolsinger (*Canoeing the Mountain*, 23), writes that "The Spirit of God goes before us. The mission of Christ will not fail . . . [T]his moment requires those of us in positions of authority . . .

The church is an historical institution but, unlike other human institutions, is not merely the product of human historical political developments. Rather, it is the body of Christ and the temple of the Holy Spirit, a community gathered by the Holy Spirit and thus by nature charismatic, no matter its institutional form. It is also the community that understands the books of Samuel to be authoritative for faith and conduct, above all about the nature and behavior of the agents of the LORD's covenant polity.

What Is Samuel About?

The repeated "in those days there was no king in Israel, everyone did what was right in his own eyes" (Judg 17:6; 21:25) raises the expectation that Samuel in the MT canonical order depicts the rise of kingship. Nevertheless, besides a reference to God's anointed in 1 Sam 2:10d, the narrative moves to kingship only in 1 Sam 8, and then not in the Davidic terms Judges' preference for Judah over Benjamin leads the audience to expect. Samuel does open with an episode linked to Bethlehem, but 1 Sam 1:1—7:17 do not present kingship as the solution to Israel's wickedness in the days of the judges. Rather, these chapters explicitly depict the covenant Overlord himself opening a new era in the chaotic days of the judges: the miraculous nativity of Samuel, Hannah's God-centered prayer, the divine judgement on Eli's house, the LORD's call of Samuel in the temple, the ark's defeat of the Philistine pentapolis, and the LORD's defeat of the Philistines at Mizpah mediated by Samuel. Having heard the cry of his barren people in the person of Hannah heaven answers with the nativity of a prophet like Moses, in fulfilment of the words spoken on the plains of Moab, "And I will put my words in his mouth" (*dbrym*, Deut 18:16; 1 Sam 1:23a). In the days when the word of the LORD was rarely heard (*dbr*, 1 Sam 3:1) the word of the LORD came to Samuel who brought it to Israel (1 Sam 3:19—4:1a; 7:3). Not kingship, but the birth and ministry of a prophet sets the narrative stage of Samuel.

The Samuel narrative names three prophets: Samuel, Nathan and Gad; and two kings: Saul and David. Samuel interacts with Saul and David,

---

to embrace an *adventure-or-die* mindset, and find the courage and develop the capacity for a new day. We are heading into uncharted territory and are given the charge to lead a mission where the future is nothing like the past" (emphasis included). Bolsinger's administrative wisdom, based on the challenges Lewis and Clark faced during their explorations, ends as follows: "Perhaps this spirit of exploration—this adventure-or-die attitude—is the great gift uncharted leaders can give to the church in a post-Christendom world." Bolsinger, *Canoeing the Mountains*, 207. Note the move from "Spirit of God" to "spirit of exploration." Furthermore, Bolsinger does not engage Joshua–Kings nor church history, both of which are replete with examples of misguided adaptation. You have to understand the box before you think outside of it.

Nathan and Gad only with David. An unnamed man of God announces
judgment on Eli and his sons, a judgment Samuel subsequently reveals to
Eli. Samuel's ministry as judge and prophet among God's people is suc-
cinctly illustrated by his call to repentance, leading Israel in confession of
its sin, and calling upon God to defeat the Philistines at Mizpah. All me-
morialized at Ebenezer. As long as Samuel lived the hand of the LORD was
against the Philistines and Samuel went on a circuit to Bethel, Gilgal and
Mizpah to judge Israel (1 Sam 7:3–17).

Only with 1 Sam 8 does the narrator depict Samuel in relationship to
the kingship of Saul: he anoints Saul (1 Sam 9:27), but the king's subsequent
follies and disobedience yield a prophetic announcement of the end of Saul's
house (1 Sam 15:26; 28:20). By divine instruction Samuel then anoints David (1 Sam 16:12–13) but has no further dealings with him. After the LORD
gives him rest from his enemies (nwḥ, 2 Sam 7:1) David plans to build a
house for the LORD with the support of Nathan ("for the LORD is with you,"
2 Sam 7:3), but a subsequent word from the LORD through Nathan rejects
David's proposal. Instead, the LORD promises to build David's house and
that his descendant will build the LORD's house (2 Sam 7:4–17). David's response to the word of the LORD through Nathan—"O LORD God, you are
God and your words are true, and you have promised this good thing to
your servant" (2 Sam 7:28)—stands in stark contrast with Saul's responses
to Samuel. When Nathan next appears to confront David with his adultery,
he repents and humbles himself before God (2 Sam 12:1–15), unlike Saul.
Finally, in the aftermath of his census of Israel (2 Sam 24:1–9), David responds to the disciplining word of the LORD through Gad by giving himself
and his people into the hands of the LORD. After seventy thousand die David
confesses his sin and implores the LORD to direct his punishment against
him and his father's house (24:17). At the word of the LORD through Gad
(2 Sam 24:18–19), David went up to Araunah the Jebusite's threshing floor
where God responded to his offerings and stayed the plague. Without the
prophets Israel's kings, even David, will surely be like those of the nations, as
the places of sacrifice and prayer in Samuel suggest.

Sacrifice and prayer frame Samuel: the tent at Shiloh presided over by
Eli, and Araunah's threshing floor (1 Sam 1:3, 9; 2 Sam 24:18)—Solomon
would build the temple there (2 Chr 3:1)—where David offered sacrifices
of reconciliation. The cultic corruption of Hophni and Phinehas and Eli's
failure to rebuke them begets the LORD's judgment on Eli's house (1 Sam
3:13–14). David's respect of Saul's house, his patient waiting for Judah and
Israel to accept his kingship, God's promise of to build David a house,
and his military prowess beget the judgment that David's rule was just
and righteous (2 Sam 8:15). But this just and righteous David is scarcely

recognizable in 2 Sam 9–20. Except for brief descriptions of his stead-fast loyalty to Jonathan and his military prowess in 2 Sam 9–10, David's stewardship of the kingship takes one bad turn after another. Adultery with Bathsheba begets Uriah's murder and the death of their child. Sub-sequently, and like Eli, David fails to discipline Amnon for his ruinous love of Absalom's sister Tamar, Absalom for murdering Amnon and later his open rebellion. But David's Eli–like behavior is not Samuel's last word about him, that is reserved for a comparison with Saul rooted in the ca-nonical narrative's last episode, 2 Sam 24:1–25.

David acknowledging his folly (*skl*, 2 Sam 24:10) in the matter of the census recalls two earlier episodes where the verb "to be foolish" occurs, one with Saul (*skl*, 1 Sam 13:10, 13) and the other with Ahithophel (*skl*, 2 Sam 15:31b). Saul offers burnt and peace sacrifices before engaging the Philis-tines, without waiting for Samuel. When Samuel arrives, Saul acknowledges he did not seek the LORD's favor but went ahead with the sacrifices. Samuel then tells Saul, "You have done *foolishly*. You have not kept the command-ment of the LORD your God, with which he commanded you" (*skl*, 1 Sam 13:10, 13). Had Saul been obedient, Samuel continues, "the LORD would have established your kingdom over Israel forever. But now your kingdom shall not continue" (13:13b–14). Saul's folly, offering sacrifices without the prophet's presence, lost him the kingship. David's folly, the census of Israel, also occasions a word of the LORD from the prophet Gad (24:11), but the king chooses punishment at the hands of the LORD. When death takes a heavy toll of the people, David acknowledges his sin and asks God to punish him, not the people. In this context Gad instructs David to build an altar on Araunah's threshing floor, where he brings burnt and peace offerings which the LORD accepts. The comparison between Saul and David discloses a crucial difference in royal responses to foolish decisions: David submits to the prophet and brings sacrifices from a broken and contrite heart (Ps 51:17); Saul brings offerings impetuously.

The third use of the verb "to be foolish" in Samuel depicts an Eli-like David who refuses to discipline Absalom for usurping the king's authority (*špṭ*, 2 Sam 15:1–6; 13–17). Absalom offers sacrifices at Hebron and asks David's counsellor Ahithophel for advice on overthrowing David. Upon hearing that Ahithophel's had joined the conspiracy, David asks the LORD to turn it in to foolishness (*skl*, 2 Sam 15:31b). The LORD hears David's petition and frustrates Ahithophel's superior counsel (2 Sam 17:13), for "no wisdom, no understanding, no counsel can avail against the LORD. The horse is made ready for battle, but victory belongs to the LORD" (Prov 21:30–31). Fear of the LORD cultivates true wisdom (Prov 1:7; 9:10), a fear David demon-strated by submitting to the word of the LORD and seeking the LORD's will in prayer. Flawed like Eli and Saul, David keeps his house by submitting to the word of the LORD brought by Nathan and Gad. David wisely submits to prophets; Saul does not. Faithful agents of covenant polity submit to its discipline, foolish agents refuse it.

During the days of the judges the LORD initiates an era of hope for his people by establishing David's kingship, an agency of covenant polity that submits itself to that polity as administered by the prophets Samuel, Nathan, and Gad. This is what Samuel is about. This takes us to a reading of 1 Sam 3.

Reading 1 Samuel 3 Today

Context of 1 Samuel 3

The call of Samuel follows a description of abuse and barrenness in Elkanah's house and priestly incompetence at Shiloh, a microcosm of Israel in the days of the judges. Samuel's birth and dedication mark the LORD's response to Hannah's barrenness (1:19) and her prayer of trust in the LORD: "The barren one has borne seven, but she who has many children is forlorn," for "the LORD makes poor and makes rich; he brings low and he exalts" (1 Sam 2:5, 7 ESV). This prayer, along with the psalms of 2 Sam 22 and 23:1–7, forms another frame that unmistakably identifies the LORD as Israel's sovereign, who "will give strength to his king and exalt the power of his anointed" (1 Sam 2:10), as illustrated by his delivering David from his enemies (2 Sam 22:1–7) and exalting him as the LORD's anointed (2 Sam 23:1).

After the opening element of the frame, the narrative compares Eli's sons and Hannah's Samuel, the former wicked in the eyes of the LORD (cf. Judg 3:7, 12; 4:1; 6:1; 10:6; 13:1), the latter growing in the presence of the LORD and blessed by Eli (1 Sam 2:17, 21b). Eli's sons also refuse their father's rebuke, "for it was the will of the LORD to put them to death" (1 Sam 2:25; cf. 2:6). A man of God declares that the LORD has rejected Eli's priestly house, because you "honor your sons above me by fattening yourselves on the choicest parts of every offering of my people Israel" (1 Sam 2:29). The observation that "the young man Samuel was ministering to the LORD under Eli" (3:1a) prepares the reader for the climactic episode in a series depicting the LORD's initiatives. The episode begins with "And the word of the LORD was rare in those days" (3:1b) and ends "the LORD revealed himself to Samuel at Shiloh by the word of the LORD" (3:21). Shiloh, where inconsiderate Eli and corrupt Hophni and Phinehas irresponsibly administered covenant polity, had received a new agent of covenant polity.

The narrator limits his description of Samuel's prophetic ministry to one sentence, "And the word of the Lord came to all Israel," and follows it with an extensive narrative of Israel's loss to Philistia and the capture of the ark (1 Sam 4:1–7:2). Israel's removal of the ark from Shiloh illustrates their rejection of the word of the Lord that came to them through Samuel. Only after the ark's return does the narrator summarize Samuel's judging of Israel, highlighted by the defeat of Philistia at Mizpah and commemorated by Ebenezer (1 Sam 7:3–17).

Who Does What in 1 Samuel 3?

First Samuel 3:1b–3 states the theme, the word of the Lord was rare in those days and visions were scarce, and then elucidates the problem with the metaphor of sight in the person of Eli: "his eyes had begun to dim so that he could not see" (*r'h*). The almost extinguished lamp of God in the tabernacle underscores Eli's nearly dark eyes. The opening paragraph concludes with a Samuel sleeping in "the temple of the Lord by the ark of God," that is, the Holy of Holies.[14] By contrast, Eli is sleeping "in his place," not specifically identified. First Samuel 3:19–21 concludes the narrative by noting that the Lord was with Samuel as he matured, that he did not let one of his words "drop to the ground,"[15] that all Israel recognized Samuel as a faithful prophet of the Lord, and that "the Lord appeared (*r'h*) again in Shiloh because the Lord revealed himself (*glh*) to Samuel in Shiloh by the word of the Lord" (1 Sam 3:21). Although Eli is no longer the authorized agent of covenant polity at Shiloh, his last words, spoken in response to Samuel's delivering the Lord's word about the house of Eli (1 Sam 3:11–14, 18ab), are revelatory in their use of the metaphor of sight: "He is the Lord, he will do what is good in his eyes" (1 Sam 3:18c–e; 3:2). Eli acknowledges that God's judgment on him and his sons is deserved, that they had blighted their stewardship of covenant polity of right, and, that God justly revealed his word to Samuel. Eli's inability to see (*r'h*, 1 Sam 3:2) in the episode's statement of the problem, becomes God's solution by causing himself to be seen in Shiloh (*r'h*, 1 Sam 3:21). Between the narrative introduction and conclusion three scenes and three characters develop the action: God calls Samuel and, in his final priestly

---

14. The MT separates the phrase "Samuel was sleeping" from the phrase "where the ark of God was" with a major accent (*'athnaḥ*) thereby keeping Samuel from sleeping in the Most Holy Place. JPS translates, "sleeping in the temple of the Lord by the ark of God." Most other translations place a comma after "the temple of the Lord."

15. That is, given Eli's use of *dbr* in 3:17, Samuel did not hide the word of the Lord from him. He fulfilled his prophetic duty.

action, Eli instructs Samuel how to respond (1 Sam 3:4–9); God tells Samuel of his judgment on Eli's house (1 Sam 3:10–15); and, Eli asks for and Samuel delivers the LORD's word to him (1 Sam 3:16–18).

The narrator explains why Samuel runs to Eli three times: "Now Samuel did not yet know the LORD, and the word of the LORD had not yet been revealed to him" (1 Sam 3:7). That is, Samuel had not yet had any prophetic experience. The priest-judge Eli, however, should have understood what was happening. That he understood what was happening only after the third call illustrates the consequences of the scarcity of the word of the LORD (1 Sam 3:10). Nevertheless, Eli performed his priestly service one last time by telling Samuel how to respond properly to God's call: "Speak LORD, for your servant is listening" (1 Sam 3:8d; note *šmᶜ* in 3:11c). Samuel returns to sleep "in his place," previously identified as the Holy of Holies, to wait upon God; Eli has lost his privileged place in the LORD's presence to Hannah's son, a Nazarite from birth.

The theophany legitimates Samuel as the LORD's messenger: he receives "the word of the LORD" from the LORD himself. As the LORD called Moses from the burning bush, so now "the LORD came, and stood there, and He called as before" (JPS),[16] "there" referring to the place where Samuel was sleeping, the Holy of Holies. And Samuel responds as instructed by Eli. Like prophets before and after him—Moses, Elijah, Micaiah, Isaiah and Jeremiah—his first message is one of judgment,[17] on Eli's house. The typical prophetic phrase "on that day" (*bywm hhᵓw*, 1 Sam 3:12, cf. 3:2)[18] anticipates the deaths of Eli, Hophni and Phinehas "on that day" (*bywm hhwᵓ*, 1 Sam 4:12). After receiving the word of the LORD Samuel sleeps until the morning (1 Sam 3:15), the time when significant events happen in Scripture:[19] the morning after the theophany Samuel opens the doors to the house of God (1 Sam 3:15). The tabernacle is open for prophetic business, for the LORD revealed his word to Samuel in the Most Holy Place. Samuel is afraid to convey his vision, but Eli urges him to declare the LORD's word. Like other reluctant prophets, Samuel tells Eli every *word* (*kl–dbrym*, 1 Sam 3:18) of

16. The theophany at Bethel, "the house of God" (Gen 28:13) uses the same verb to depict the LORD standing either at the top of the staircase (ESV), or beside Jacob (JPS).

17. Thus in Exod 5:1; 1 Kgs 17:1; 22:19–23; Isa 1:2–20; Jer 1:9–10.

18. The phrase is part of a cluster that refers to "the day of the LORD," a time of judgment and/or of blessing. Sæbø, "*ywm*," 31.

19. Abraham saw Sodom and Gomorrah's destruction (Gen 19:27); Jacob names the place where he slept at the gate of heaven, Bethel (Gen 28:18); in the morning David wrote Joab a letter about Uriah (2 Sam 11:14); hope comes with the morning (Ps 130:7); those who rule justly experience God like the morning dawn or a cloudless morning (2 Sam 24:5); early on the first day of the week women saw an open tomb (Matt 28:1; Mark 16:2; Luke 24:1).

the *word* (*hdbr*) the LORD has *spoken* to him (*dbr*), he did not hide a *word* from every *word* which the LORD *spoke* (*dbr*, 3:17). In the summary conclusion the narrator adds that Samuel did not let any of his *words* drop to the ground" (*dbryw*, 1 Sam 3:19).

God's people had never been without divine guidance, they had the instructions revealed at Sinai but abused or ignored them. Eli, Hophni, Phinehas, and Penninah are emblematic of the covenant-polity-laziness in the time of the judges when God abandoned his people to the consequences of their sins (Judg 2:14–15). The phrase "in those days" (*bymym hhm*, 1 Sam 3:1; cf. Judg 17:6; 21:25) evokes that time of God's abandonment and further identifies it as a time when the word of the LORD was scarce (1 Sam 3:1). The narrative then moves on to one of those days (*bywm hhw'*, 1 Sam 3:2) to describe Eli in his place, almost blind, unable to see. On that day the word of the LORD breaks through to Samuel with a word for Eli and his house; they will die on that day (*bywm hhw'*, 1 Sam 3:12; 4:12). The LORD's subsequent appearances at Shiloh established Samuel as the LORD's prophet. During the days of the judges, when everyone did what was right in his own eyes, the LORD revealed himself again at Shiloh, to Samuel, by the word of the LORD.[20] That answers the question, "Who, does what?"

Reading 1 Samuel 3 Today

Whether the audience is exilic, diasporic or post-Pentecostal, 1 Sam 3 claims that at the right time God appeared in his temple again and spoke to his servant Samuel who communicated the word to Eli and then to God's people. In his appearance to the prophet Samuel God answered the deep distress of Israel in the person of Hannah who prayed at Shiloh to be delivered from barrenness. Samuel's birth and subsequent opening of the temple doors signaled a new time in God's dealings with Israel: the rise of a leader who, though flawed, conformed to covenant polity, David, son of Jesse. Subsequently, however, the agents of covenant polity—prophets, priest and kings—surrendering to the gospels of prosperity flowing from the altars of Baal and Asherah, sought repeatedly to adapt covenant polity to their syncretistic polities (Jer 2:8, 26–28; Lam 1:19; 4:13). Hearing 1 Sam 3, exiled Israel can only wonder: How long before God appears again to speak a word to his distressed people? And, because the temple lies in ruins, where will he appear?

20. The phrase "the word of the LORD" typically introduces the communication a prophet receives, for example, Jer 1:4; 46:1; Ezek 15:1; Hos 1:1; Joel 1:1. The phrase "*by* the word of the LORD" (3:21) suggests distance between the LORD and the prophet.

The Christian OT canon ends with Malachi's pointing to the prophet Elijah,[21] who will prepare the way of the LORD and come unexpectedly to the LORD's temple (Mal 3:1); Haggai and Zechariah also point to a future day of the LORD. Moreover, the temple itself, zealously rebuilt under the direction of Haggai, Zerubbabel, Ezra and Nehemiah, remains empty of the glory of the LORD that indwelt Solomon's temple. In the shadows of the holy city, Israel renews its commitment to covenant polity with a self-maledictory oath (Neh 10:29). In particular they swear not to marry foreigners, not to defile the sabbath, and to maintain the house of God (Neh 10:30–39). Having broken their oaths (Neh 13:4–13, 15–22, 23–28), God's people awaits in exile and diaspora for God to appear again in his holy temple. But their waiting is anchored in the canonical memory of his appearances to Samuel at Shiloh, to Moses at Sinai, and to Abraham by the oak at Shechem. At the right time, he will appear again to save his people from distress.

When Gabriel appeared to Zechariah in the temple and announced the birth of a son "who will go before (God) in the spirit and power of Elijah," he could not believe that his and barren Elizabeth's prayers had been heard, as Hannah's had been. And, like Hannah, he also praises the LORD after John's birth. And, as Hannah's prayer speaks of the power of the LORD's anointed (1 Sam 2:10b), "Zechariah . . . filled with the Holy Spirit . . . prophesied . . . you child, will be called the prophet of the Most High; for you will go before the LORD to prepare his ways" (Luke 1:76 ESV). Even as the word of the LORD Samuel prepared the way for David, so John prepared the way for Jesus Christ who was born at the right time (John 1:23; Gal 4:4a) for the salvation of all people, "a light for revelation to the Gentiles, and for glory to your people Israel" (Luke 2:32). As with Samuel, God appeared again in his holy temple: Gabriel to the righteous priest Zechariah, and "the LORD's Christ" to Simeon and Anna. The birth and ministry of Jesus is the divine response to those who had been waiting in the temple for "the consolation of Israel" and "the redemption of Jeru-salem" (Luke 2:25, 38). In that temple Zechariah had been, Eli-like, un-able to pronounce the priestly blessing; in that same temple the disciples continually praised God after Jesus's blessing them as he ascended from Bethany. But a new temple would replace that house of God.

The post-Pentecostal audience hears the enduring claim of 1 Sam 3 that God responds to his people's distress with a temple appearance in the person of Christ who built a new temple, of his body (John 2:21)[22] with

21. For the significant difference between the endings of the Christian and the MT canons, see Josipovici, *The Book of God*, 29–49.

22. Kerr, *The Temple of Jesus' Body*, 65–101, where he discusses John 2:13–22.

living stones (1 Cor 3:16; 6:19–20; John 15:26; 16:7–11; 1 Pet 2:4–5), indwelt by the Holy Spirit (John 15:26; 16:7–11). Anchored in the canonical
memory of Scripture, especially the defiling of the Jerusalem, the post–canonical audience hears the prophetic challenges to keep the body of Christ
holy and undefiled (1 Cor 3:16–17; 6:12–20; 2 Cor 6:14—7:1; 1 Pet 4:1–11)
until Christ comes again (Acts 1:11).

This Holy Spirit-endowed body of Christ ordains agents to execute the
LORD's received covenant polity in his name, rooted in various ecclesiologies and polities, not to adapt the faith once for all delivered to the saints
in a charismatic anti-institutional purge of the church for the sake of the
kingdom. Prophetic leadership in ancient Israel was not one of charismatic
prophets against the institutionalized priests and kings; charisma was not the
special province of prophets (1 Sam 10:9–13; 16:13, 14; Judg 13:25; 14:6, 19;
15:14). The challenge for contemporary agents of covenant polity is to live
in a given socio-cultural present, there to be guided by a divinely revealed
authority given scriptural form in the past and to be faithful to the confessions of the church. Above all not to play off the Spirit against the Word or
the spirit of the age, but to evaluate claims of the Spirit's moving in terms of
the Word, not socio-cultural developments. It has been ever the challenge for
God's people: "my people have committed two evils: they have forsaken me,
the fountain of living waters, and hewed out cisterns for themselves, broken
cisterns that can hold no water" (Jer 2:13). In the post-Pentecostal diaspora,
God's people hear: "Today, if you hear his voice, do not harden your hearts,
as at Meribah, as on the day at Massah in the wilderness . . . [when] I swore
in my wrath, they shall not enter my rest" (Ps 95:8, 11). Post-Pentecost, OT
and NT Scripture is the prophetic word proclaimed in and out of season to
and in the body of Christ, the temple of the Holy Spirit. Ordained agents of
the temple of the Holy Spirit thus guard against quenching the Spirit's work
through the Word or resisting him (Acts 10:38).

Waiting for the Rest That Still Remains
beyond David's Kingship

Samuel's faithful judging of Israel (*špṭ*, 1 Sam 7:13–17) and the just and righteous rule of David (*mšpṭ wṣdqh*, 2 Sam 8:15) resolved the problem of everyone doing what was right in his own eyes when there was no king in Israel.
Moreover, the LORD gave David rest from his enemies (*nwḥ*, 2 Sam 7:1), a
rest divinely held in abeyance during the time of the judges because of Israel's
covenant disloyalty. David's rest from the enemy is a present reality with a
future rooted in the LORD's commitment to David's house: "I will appoint a

place for my people Israel and will plant them, so that they may dwell in their own place, and be disturbed no more. And violent men shall afflict them no more, as formerly, from the time that I appointed judges over my people Israel. I will give you rest (*nwḥ*) from all your enemies, and the LORD declares to you that he will build you a house" (2 Sam 7:10–11 ESV). Israel's rest from its enemies all around is no longer dependent on its compliance with divine instruction as in the days of Joshua, but on the LORD's covenant with David and his descendants (*nwḥ*, 1 Chr 22:9; Isa 11:2).

The end of Samuel depicts a David in whom Israel's hope is well-founded. David pays the vow Saul swore to the Gibeonites but broke, thus making atonement for Saul's bloodguilt (2 Sam 21). He acknowledges that the LORD gave him victories over his enemies (2 Sam 22) and that his house stands with God because the LORD has made an everlasting covenant with him (2 Sam 23:1–7). David's military successes were supported by loyal mighty men, including Uriah the Hittite, the last mentioned (2 Sam 23:8–39). David submits to the prophet Gad, places himself in the merciful hands of God to accept the just consequences of his sin, and offers sacrifices of atonement at the place where Solomon would build the temple. David looks like the right kind of king for the quarrelsome people of God that Psalm 95 warns about entering into God's rest.

Beginning with Solomon and his Egyptian wives, David's descendants became more like the kings of the nations who worshiped other gods. So much so that Manasseh led God's people "to do more evil than the nations had done whom the LORD destroyed before the people of Israel" (2 Kgs 21:9). In response, the LORD sent enemies against the king of Judah (2 Kgs 24:2) as he did in the time of the judges: Nebuchadnezzar destroyed Jerusalem with its temple, and David's descendant Jehoiachin went into captivity. Lamentations depicts the consequences as follows:

> Judah has gone into exile
> because of affliction and hard servitude;
> she dwells now among the nations,
> but finds no resting place (*mnwḥh*);[23]
> her pursuers have all overtaken her
> in the midst of her distress. (Lam 1:3 ESV)

> Our pursuers are at our necks;
> We are weary; we are given no rest. (*nwḥ*, Lam 5:5 ESV)

David could not bring rest to God's people. But Israel's kingship was not about David as such, but God's oath to keep a descendant of his on

23. An evocation of Deut 28:65 which in alludes to Gen 8:9.

the throne. Those awaiting the fulfilment of that promise ask, "How long, LORD? Will you hide yourself forever? How long will your wrath burn like fire? . . . LORD, where is your steadfast love of old, which by your faithfulness you swore to David?" (Ps 89:46, 49 ESV). They are also encouraged to plead with God: "Arise, O LORD, and go to your resting place (*mnwḥh*), you and the ark of your might . . . For the sake of your servant David, do not turn away the face of your anointed one" (Ps 132:8, 10 ESV).

9

Kings

If They Repent and Pray toward your House

Summary: In David's old age Adonijah usurps the throne, but Nathan's intervention leads to Solomon's anointing and the establishment of his kingdom. God gives Solomon wisdom and understanding beyond measure. Solomon builds the LORD's house. After the ark enters the Holy of Holies Solomon asks God to hear prayers of repentance directed to this house. In old age Solomon turns his heart away from God who raises up enemies against him. Rehoboam his son becomes king (1 Kgs 1:1—11:43).

Solomon's kingdom suffers a schism at the hands of Rehoboam's foolish policies. Rehoboam remains king over Judah but Jeroboam rules the northern tribes, builds golden calves in Bethel and Dan and so makes Israel sin against the LORD. The prophet Ahijah curses the house of Jeroboam for making Israel sin against the LORD. Under Rehoboam Judah began to worship other gods; Jeroboam's descendants did evil in God's sight (1 Kgs 12:1—16:28).

Ahab and his wife Jezebel of Sidon zealously promote Baal and Asherah worship. The prophet Elijah announces the LORD's judgment of famine against Ahab, and demonstrates the LORD's power to bring rains at Mt. Carmel, thereby defeating Jezebel's priests of Baal. Ahab, successful in war, pouts because Naboth will not sell his inheritance; Jezebel solves the case by having Naboth accused of blasphemy and then executed. Elijah curses Ahab's house, but because Ahab humbles himself before the LORD the curse is postponed until after his death. Ahab dies in war, as Micaiah prophesied. Elisha, succeeding Elijah, works with widows, the sons of the prophets, and Naaman the Syrian, and anoints Jehu king over Israel. Jehu fulfills the Elijah's curse over the house of Ahab, destroys the prophets of Baal, but Jehu does not turn from the sin of

Jeroboam. The prophet Elisha dies. In Judah some kings rule as did David, Ahaz burns his son as an offering and redesigns the altar of the LORD. Because of her idolatry and not listening to the prophets' calls to repent, God removed Israel from his presence to Assyria. The king of Assyria settles foreigners in Israel (1 Kgs 16:29—2 Kgs 17:41).

When Sennacherib attacks Judah and his commander insults the LORD God, Hezekiah of Judah trusts the LORD. The prophet Isaiah announces God heard his prayer in the temple and the angel of the LORD destroys Sennacherib's army. His son Manasseh defiles the LORD's house with altars of Baal and Asherah; his rule in Judah is as wicked as Ahab's was in Israel. Manasseh's grandson Josiah repents, rebuilds the temple, destroys the high places, and restores the book of the law to its preeminence. But Manasseh's wickedness had so provoked the LORD that he removes Judah from his presence as he had Israel. Nebuchadnezzar destroys Jerusalem, the house of the LORD, and takes king Jehoiachin captive. After 37 years in exile, Nebuchadnezzar exalts Jehoiachin above other captive kings (2 Kgs 17:1—25:30).

Central Narrative Interest: Hope for God's exiled people and the agents of covenant polity resides in prayers of repentance toward the ruins of the house of God in Jerusalem.

Opening Sentence and Connection
with Antecedent Narrative

KINGS BEGINS WITH "Now David was old and advanced in years" (1 Kgs 1:1). David is no longer the mighty warrior and sweet singer of Israel, the Eli-like father of 2 Sam 13:1—19:8 is in the past, as is the humble servant of the LORD depicted in 2 Sam 21-24. In contrast to his vigor with Bathsheba, Abishag's lying in his bosom (cf. 2 Sam 12:3) reveals his impotence.[1] First Kings 1:1-4 signals a danger associated with an aging and impotent David: What will happen to the rest from the enemy God bestowed on him (2 Sam 7:1, 11)? Even more important, what does the future hold for God's covenanted promise to establish David's throne forever (2 Sam 7:16)?

---

1. "The life and blessing inherent to the king from birth are bestowed in their enthronement . . . Beauty presupposes blessing, and *vice versa*. The king is beautiful *ex officio*," Keel, *The Symbolism of the Biblical World*, 280. Saul (1 Sam 9:2) and David (1 Sam 16:12) are so described before their enthronement.

The aftermath of the Bathsheba affair—Amnon's incest, Absalom's murder of Amnon and his attempt to usurp David's throne—fulfills the word of the LORD through Nathan: "I will raise up evil against out of your own house . . . you did it secretly, but I will do this thing before all Israel" (2 Sam 12:11-2 ESV). The prophetic judgment carries on into David's old age when Adonijah takes advantage of his father's impotence "to exalt himself (ns') by saying I am king" (1 Kgs 1:5). With Nathan's intervention, Solomon becomes king (1 Kgs 1:11-40; cf. 1 Chr 28:2-10) after Bathsheba reminds David of his promise that Solomon would succeed him (1 Kgs 1:13). When Adonijah asks Solomon for permission to take David's young woman Abishag as wife, Solomon executes him for *lèse majesté* (1 Kgs 2:22-25). With the assassination of Manasseh's son Amon, Nathan's prophecy is fulfilled,[2] but the house of David looks anything but secure.

Adonijah's exalting himself (ns', 1 Kgs 1:5) to the kingship[3] anticipates a monarchy repeatedly compromising the covenant polity—from Solomon's building altars for his foreign wives to Manasseh's building altars to Baal in the LORD's temple. Kings ends with Jehoiachin exiled, but hope flickers when Nebuchadnezzar exalts (ns', 2 Kgs 25:27) captive Jehoiachin by placing him on a throne higher than those of the other kings at Nebuchadnezzar's table. God's alien work through this unexpected servant (Isa 28:21; Jer 25:9) reminds the exilic audience of God's promise to David (2 Sam 7:12-15), but in exile Jehoiachin is as impotent as David was in his old age. Like their exiled king, the exilic audience can only wait for God to keep his promise to keep a descendant of David on Israel's throne.

What Is Kings About?

Judges depicts God's people persistently turning to other gods; it ends pointing to kingship as the solution to covenant disloyalty. Samuel reinforces Judges' hope in kingship by describing the rise of David's house. The books of Kings theologically evaluate the kings' execution of covenant polity with a focus on their worship of other gods. "The chief, indeed, almost exclusive, concern in those evaluations (of the kings) is sacerdotal—the worship of Yahweh alone, at the proper place, in the proper manner, conducted by the proper personnel."[4] These evaluations rate David's royal descendants (and

---

2. And other prophets: 1 Kgs 15:28-31; 16:11; 2 Kgs 11:1; 12:19-21; 14:17-20; 15:10; 16:25, 30; 21:23-24.

3. Walsh argues that Adonijah's "I and no one else will be king," "is a self-satisfied comment on his status as heir, not a statement of rebellious intent." Walsh, *1 Kings*, 7.

4. Mann, *The Book of the Former Prophets*, 244.

those who broke with the house of David) in terms of David's just and righteous rule (2 Sam 8:15) or Jeroboam's idolatrous rule characterized by the golden calf altars at Bethel and Dan.

Bound to rule according to covenant polity according to Deut 17:18–20, especially that of undefiled loyalty to their covenant Overlord enthroned above the cherubim in Jerusalem, Kings argues that monarchical leadership of God's people, the solution Judges hoped for (Judg 20:25), compromised its loyalty by worshiping at the altars of other gods, with the result that, like their ancestral parents Adam and Eve, God removed his people from his presence.

Like Judges before it, Kings links marriage with foreigners with the worship of other gods,[5] beginning with Solomon, through Ahab (Judg 3:6; 1 Kgs 11:1–8; 16:29–34), to Manasseh's defiling of the temple. Thus Kings signals the inherent weakness of human leadership of God's people, including the Davidic dynasty, and thus raises the question of a secure future of God's covenanted promise to David. The introduction to Solomon's dedicatory prayer at the altar in Jerusalem reminds the audience that the Davidic dynasty itself will not secure the LORD's promise to David. Rather, Solomon's double[6] request is that *God* confirm[7] his covenant with David that "you shall not lack a man to sit before me on the throne of Israel" (1 Kgs 8:25–26). Solomon asks that heaven itself fulfill the covenant with David because the Davidic dynasty itself is powerless, especially the newly exalted Jehoiachin in Babylonian exile. Solomon's prayer at the altar in Jerusalem also challenges the efficacy of prayers at the altars of Bethel, Dan and those of other gods.

Kings explores this flawed royal leadership in three narrative sweeps: Solomon's building of God's house (1 Kgs 3:1—11:43), Ahab's kingship as a devotee of Baal (1 Kgs 16:29—22:40), and the reigns of Hezekiah, Manasseh, and Josiah (2 Kgs 18:1—23:30). With God's house in ruins and David's distant descendant Jehoiachin in Nebuchadnezzar's court, Kings develops its answer to the question: What does the future hold for God's covenant promise to keep one of David's descendants on Israel's throne forever?

---

5. "The core problem with intermarriage is not ethnic purity but theological orthodoxy." Mann, *The Book of the Former Prophets*, 267.

6. The phrase "now, therefore" ($w^{e}th$, 8:25 and 26) signals the drawing of a conclusion. See also Josh 1:2; 24:14; 1 Sam 12:16; Neh 9:32, and (*kai nun*) John 17:5; Acts 3:17

7. The verb $h^{a}mn$ is translated variously: "let it be fulfilled," JPS; "let your word be confirmed," NRSV, ESV; "let your word . . . come true," NIV; "let thy word be verified," KJV. Alfred Jepsen, "^{a}mn," 302, the Niphal of $h^{a}mn$ means "to be reliable, trustworthy."

What Is Kings about Today?

Kings argues that Israel's royal leadership compromised its stewardship of the LORD's house as a place of prayer, beginning with Solomon himself. The chaos within David's house when he was old, ends centuries later with the destruction of the royal palace and Jehoiachin's humiliating captivity. Nebuchadnezzar raises Jehoiachin's throne (*ks³*, 2 Kgs 25:28) above the other kings at his table, but he's as impotent as David with Abishag. Worse yet, the house of the LORD lies in ruins (2 Kgs 25:9) and the exiles are hemmed in by altars which, unlike Josiah (2 Kgs 23:10), they have cannot defile, and the pressure to pray at those altars almost irresistible. Only a disciplined covenant piety—Shadrach, Meshach, and Abednego in the furnace (Dan 3:8–30)—will expose the weakness of those gods. Like Daniel, the exilic and diasporic audience can only pray *towards* Jerusalem.

Post-exilic biblical literature places its hopes in a rebuilt temple at Jerusalem and a leadership descendant from David (Hag 1:1–15; Zech 8:1–8, 11:10; Mal 3:1–4), but, according to Nehemiah that temple is soon defiled and marriage with foreign women becomes a common practice again (Neh 13:23–27). The NT argues this hope is realized in Jesus Christ, the son of David. Christ is the incarnate solution to exile from God's presence, he is Immanuel, God with us to the end of the age. The apostle John not only declares that the Word "dwelt among us," but that this Word replaces the temple with his body (John 2:21). Neither Jerusalem nor Samaria will be the place to worship the LORD God (John 4:21), but a spiritual house of living stones from which rise "spiritual sacrifices acceptable to God through Jesus Christ" (1 Pet 2:5). There is no other name through whom to plead with God than Jesus Christ (Acts 4:11–12; Heb 8:1–2).

Even as kingship emerged from the people, not a foreigner (Deut 17:15), so leadership of the body of Christ arises from its members (1 Cor 12:12–31, esp. 27–31). Kings, however, reminds its audience that this leadership led God's people astray more often than not. Similarly, the NT reminds God's people to remain firm, not to surrender to leaders who scratch seductive cultural itches or offer strange teachings (2 Tim 4:3–4; 1 Tim 3:1–12).

The Kings' Incomparable Leadership

The narrator depicts five kings, each incomparable in his own way: Solomon's wisdom (1 Kgs 3:12–13; 10:23–24), Hezekiah's trust in God (2 Kgs 18:5), and Josiah's turning to the LORD (2 Kgs 23:25). Ahab's marriage to Jezebel of Sidon and adding Baal's altar to those at Dan and Bethel was incomparably wicked (1 Kgs 16:31), Manasseh outperformed the nations God had expelled from Canaan in leading God's people astray in wickedness (2 Kgs 21:9).

Solomon: Incomparably Wise, but Not Quite Right in God's Sight

The LORD granted Solomon incomparable wisdom[8] and instructed him to walk in the way of the LORD by "keeping my statutes and my commandments, as your father David walked" (1 Kgs 3:14). This Solomon builds God's house and dedicates it (1 Kgs 6:1—9:9). In old age, however, his "heart was not wholly true to the LORD his God, as was the heart of David his father . . . Solomon did what was evil in the eyes of the LORD" by building altars to Chemosh of Moab, Molech of Ammon for his foreign wives and he himself by worshiping Asherah of the Sidonians (1 Kgs 11:4–7; cf. 16:31). Jezebel would introduce Asherah to the northern kingdom (1 Kgs 16:31). The narrator foreshadows this darker side of Solomon at the beginning of his reign,[9] noting his marriage to Pharaoh's daughter to seal an alliance with Egypt (i.e., Israel's "house of bondage") and the people's worship at high places, both forbidden by covenant polity (1 Kgs 3:1–3; 7:8b; 9:24; Deut 7:1–5; 12:3–4). Even the builder of God's house surrendered to the seduction of cultural correctness. For all his incomparable wisdom, Solomon ended his days an old fool, right in his own eyes (Prov 12:15) but evil in the eyes of the LORD.

Jeroboam: The Altars at Bethel and Dan

Evocative of Judges, the LORD raised up three adversaries (*sṭn*,[10] 1 Kgs 11:14, 24, 25): Hadad of Edom and Rezon disturbed Solomon's rest throughout his reign (1 Kgs 11:25), Jeroboam, rebelled against Solomon to become ruler over the ten northern tribes because, the prophet Ahijah told him, Solomon worshiped other gods (1 Kgs 11:31–33). The consequent isolation of the north from God's Jerusalem presence led Jeroboam to reimagine the received tradition of worshiping the LORD by building altars at Dan and

---

8. For a study on the incomparability of Solomon, Hezekiah, and Josiah, see Knoppers, "'There was none like him,'" 411–31.

9. For a fuller discussion of the narrator's description of Solomon's darker side, see Walsh, *1 Kings*, 65–8, and throughout the commentary on 1 Kgs 3:1—11:13, Walsh, *1 Kings*, 69–138.

10. An ironic commentary in the light of 1 Kgs 5:4 (MT 5:18): "But now the Lord has given me rest (*nwḥ*) on every side. There is neither adversary (*sṭn*) or misfortune."

Bethel.[11] This was not a *per se* rejection of the LORD, but a religio-political adaptation—"Behold your gods, O Israel, who brought you out of Egypt" (1 Kgs 12:28; cf. Exod 32:4)—to prevent the people from going to Jerusalem (1 Kgs 12:26–30). Jeroboam's golden calves undermined a crucial aspect of covenant polity: only the LORD designs the place for covenant worship, "exactly as I show you concerning the pattern of the tabernacle" (Exod 25:9, 40), and chooses the place for his name to dwell (Deut 12:11). But God would not afflict David's descendants forever (1 Kgs 11:39).

Ahab: Jezebel and Baal

Ahab intensifies Jeroboam's paganization of covenant polity by outperforming "all who were before him. And as if it had been a light thing for him to walk in the sins of Jeroboam the son of Nebat, he took as his wife Jezebel, daughter of Ethbaal, king of the Sidonians, and went and served Baal, and worshiped him" (1 Kgs 16:30-31 ESV). By building an altar to Baal and making an Asherah, Ahab "did more to provoke the LORD, the God of Israel, to anger than all the kings who were before him" (1 Kgs 16:33 ESV). Hiel's sacrifice of his sons characterizes Ahab's reign, and anticipates Ahaz's and Manasseh's burning their sons as offerings (1 Kgs 16:34; 2 Kgs 16:3; 21:6). Incomparably wicked prayers at such altars merit physical death, or expulsion from God's Jerusalem presence (Lev 20:1–5, 22).

Built on Jeroboam's apostasy, Ahab's incomparable wickedness defines the fundamental challenge the kings faced since Solomon: which altar supports efficacious prayer, the LORD's or those of other gods. The contest on Mt. Carmel[12] answers: No amount of liturgical blood could persuade Baal to consume the burnt offering. Jezebel's priests fail: "There was no voice. No one answered; no one paid attention" (1 Kgs 18:29 ESV). God answers Elijah's prayer at the reconstructed altar to the LORD with fire that consumes the sacrificial victim and the altar; then "the heavens grew black with clouds and wind, and there was a great rain" (1 Kgs 18:45 ESV). Celebrated in Canaan as the "rider

11. "The plurality of shrines inevitably reflected the local multiplicity of Canaanite Baal worship, implying a Yahweh of Dan and another Yahweh at Bethel. As the Christian church itself has learned, liturgical forms are never without theological implication." Nelson, *First and Second Kings*, 81.

12. It highlights two aspects of this religio-political conflict, securing fertility and maintaining social order by prayer/sacrifice at the deities' altars. In the old world it was the king's responsibility to ascertain harmony with the deity's will, aided by priests and prophets, and so to secure these benefits for the community in the king's role in furthering the powers of life and defense against the enemy. See Keel, *The Symbolism of the Biblical World*, 280–06.

of the clouds," the creator of clouds, wind, and rain, the episode pokes fun at Baal's impotence. A prophetic intervention moves Ahab to humble himself before the LORD (1 Kgs 21:17–29, esp. 27–29), but not before the narrator reminds the audience of Jezebel's role in Ahab's reign.

The worship of other gods as a consequence of intermarriage begins with the second generation of David's house: Solomon built altars for the gods of his foreign wives (11:1–6).[13] Not one foreign wife is named, nor her power and influence described until Ahab takes for his wife Jezebel the daughter of Ethbaal. His submission to and worship of Baal is the syntactical ("and so went and worshiped Baal") and religious consequence of that marriage. Jezebel's oath to kill Elijah after the defeat and slaughter of her priests illustrates her devotion to Baal; the Naboth episode her refusal to acknowledge the LORD's ownership of the land.

After Naboth refuses Ahab's offer of a "better vineyard"[14] in exchange for the inheritance allotted to his fathers by the LORD (Josh 13:1–7), Ahab's pouting spurs Jezebel to give him "the vineyard of Naboth the Jezreelite" (1 Kgs 21:7). As if the land were Baal's to allot.[15] To achieve a "legal" transfer of the inheritance she suborns perjury in Ahab's name (1 Kgs 21:8), whereupon Ahab dispossesses Naboth's divinely granted inheritance. Elijah announces heaven's judgment on this dispossession: Ahab's dynasty has no future and Jezebel will die defiled by dogs (1 Kgs 21:21–24). Ahab humbles himself before the LORD after hearing Elijah's condemnation, but the narrator leaves no doubt about Jezebel's role: this devotee of Baal incited Ahab (1 Kgs 21:25) to accept her subversion of the LORD's land ownership. It also illustrates how marriage to devotees of other gods compromises covenant orthodoxy at the highest level of leadership. Baal's altar would not last. Jehu—having already destroyed Ahab's dynasty according to the word of Elijah (2 Kgs 10:17)—demolished the temple and pillar of Baal, "and made it a latrine to this day" (2 Kgs 10:27). A daily humiliation for the Canaanite deity of rain.

---

13. Like the generation after Joshua that provoked the Lord to anger (Judg 2:10–11; 3:5). Nehemiah decries intermarriage with women from Moab and Ammon using Solomon as an example: "foreign women made even him to sin" (Neh 13:26).

14. Isa 5:7 describes Israel as God's vineyard.

15. To read Jezebel as a modern woman exercising her autonomy disregards the ancient world's belief that land was under divine administration, no matter the deity.

Hezekiah and Josiah: Trust and Repentance

There was none like Hezekiah among the kings of Judah who trusted in the LORD (2 Kgs 18:5),[16] a trust illustrated in the conflict with Assyria and his deadly illness. Faced with the Rabshakeh's declaration that Assyria had defeated all who trusted in their own gods, Hezekiah lays out the Assyrian's challenge before God in the temple and prays for deliverance[17] (2 Kgs 19:4, 14–19; cf. 1 Kgs 8:44–45). Isaiah delivers God's word of salvation from Sennacherib. Sometime during the Assyrian siege, facing death, Hezekiah prays for mercy from the LORD, but this time not in the temple. Rather, he "turns his face to the wall and prayed to the LORD" (20:2), perhaps evoking the directional character of Solomon's prayer (If any one prays "toward this place."[18]). Word of healing comes through Isaiah, but Hezekiah must still go to the temple on the third day when the LORD will rescue Jerusalem and extend Hezekiah's life for David's sake (2 Kgs 20:5–6). Hezekiah's trusting prayer to the LORD at the temple extends the rule of David's house and adds years to Jerusalem's security. But the LORD would not detain Babylon from destroying Jerusalem and David's house (2 Kgs 20:16–18).

The introduction to Josiah's reign reminds the audience of Joshua, whom the LORD instructed "not to turn aside to the right or the left" (2 Kgs 22:2; Josh 1:7–8) from the torah of Moses. The summarizing ending describes Josiah's incomparability in similar terms: "before him there was no king like him, who *turned* to the LORD with all his heart and with all his soul and all his might, according to the Law of Moses, nor did any like him arise after him" (*šwb*, 2 Kgs 23:25 ESV). At the end of the narrative of Josiah's reign his incomparability is depicted with words that recall Deut 6:5:

> You shall *love* the LORD your God with all your heart and with all your soul and with all your might. (Deut 6:5)

> . . . who *turned* to the LORD with all his heart and with all his soul and all his might. (2 Kgs 23:25)

Comparison shows that the verb "to turn" replaces Deuteronomy's verb "to love." Josiah's incomparability consists not in loving God but in repentance, in turning back to the covenant polity his father and grandfather, Amon and Manasseh, had abandoned, a policy he himself presumably

---

16. The verb "to trust" (*bṭḥ*) occurs 9 times (18:5, 19, 20, 21bis, 22, 24, 30; 19:10) in this episode. Not used elsewhere in Kings.

17. The verb "to deliver" (*nṣl*) occurs 12 times (18:29, 30bis, 32, 33bis, 34, 35bis; 19:11, 12; 20:6) in this episode. Once more in 2 Kgs 17:39.

18. Prayer "to the Lord" (*htpll ʾl yhwh*, 2 Kgs 20:2) is a directional parallel of "toward this place" (*htpll ʾl mqwm hzh*, 1 Kgs 8:29, etc.).

followed. It was the eighteenth year of his reign, after the recovered Book of the Law was read to him, that a penitent Josiah sought advice from the LORD. In response, the prophetess Huldah revealed that Judah's worship of other gods would beget an irrevocable judgment, but that Josiah would not experience the disaster because he humbled himself before God. This penitent Josiah read the book of the law in the temple, before all the people, the priests and the prophets, to renew the covenant with the LORD (2 Kgs 23:1–3). Thereafter he commanded a wholesale destruction of altars Manasseh had built, defiled sacred places to prevent the people from worshiping there (the reverse of Jeroboam), including the altars Solomon[19] had built (2 Kgs 23:13–14). Josiah's destruction of altars and establishing the words of the law (2 Kgs 23:24) suggests he "re-conquered" the Judah Manasseh, Amon, and Solomon, had turned into old world Canaan.

Manasseh: Better Than the Nations at Leading God's People Astray

The narrator does not compare Manasseh to other kings of God's people, but to the nations "whom the LORD destroyed before the people of Israel" (2 Kgs 21:9), thereby reminding the audience of Israel's first request for a king: "Appoint for us a king to judge us *like the nations*" (1 Sam 8:5). The point of comparison, however, is that Manasseh led God's people "astray to do *more evil than the nations* had done" and that he had done "things *more evil* than all that the Amorites did, who were before him" (21:11). He employed the culturally approved religious technologies of the day—mediums, wizards, and fortune tellers—to guide his policies; like Ahaz, he burned his own son as an offering, an echo of the days when Ahab ruled (1 Kgs 16:34). He also rebuilt the high places Hezekiah had destroyed and built altars to Baal and Asherah, like Ahab before him. Manasseh intensified this old-style paganization of the LORD by building altars for the "host of heaven in the two courts of the house of the LORD" and placing an image of Asherah in the house of the LORD (2 Kgs 21:5–7). These altars were not supplemental to the traditional religion, typical of syncretism, but a wholesale redesign of the place where the LORD put his name. During Manasseh's reign those who prayed at or toward the Jerusalem temple petitioned the host of heaven and Asherah, not the LORD in his heavenly dwelling. What started with a few altars for Solomon's wives, ended up with the goddess Asherah in the house of the LORD.

During these days of Manasseh's rule, the LORD declared through his prophets that he would judge Jerusalem with "the measuring line of Samaria,

---

19. Essentially framing the narrative in terms of the altars of other gods.

and the plumb line of the house of Ahab" (2 Kgs 21:13 ESV). Like Samaria, Jerusalem would go into exile, at the hands of God's servant Nebuchadnezzar (2 Kgs 24:2; 25:1), and God's defiled house would be destroyed.

The Challenge of Reading Kings Today

From beginning to end Scripture insists that life flows from the LORD God: the rivers from God's throne water the whole earth (Gen 2:8–14; Ezek 47:1–12; Rev 22:1); God alone nourishes life (1 Cor 10:1–5; John 4:7–15). The bitter waters turned sweet at Marah link divine instruction with life-giving water (Exod 15:22–25[20]) and anticipates Sinai's covenant instructions, which, "if you do them, you shall live by them" (Lev 18:5). Psalm 1 renders explicit the relationship between life, water, and covenant polity: whoever mediates upon the LORD's instructions is like "a tree planted by streams of water that yields its fruit . . . and does not wither" (Ps 1:2–3).

Under Joshua, an Israel shaped by desert dependence upon manna from heaven, began to destroy Canaan's sophisticated religio-political culture. But to the generations and their leadership after Joshua, the local religio-political way of doing things proved irresistible for almost four hundred years. The altar contest at Mt. Carmel revealed Baal's empty cisterns; Ahab and Manasseh sought his blessings anyway. God's people, writes Jeremiah, persistently forsakes the true source of life, it seeks "broken cisterns that can hold no water" (Jer 2:13). The epistles to the NT churches and centuries of the church's history depict similar tendencies.

Kings challenges contemporary readers with the inconvenient claim that there is only one source for the good life, that that source is the LORD's heavenly dwelling place, and that the altar at Jerusalem is the only revealed point of contact, not Samaria nor imitations of ancient Babel. Where Baal was a pantheistic personification of "natural" metereological forces, contemporary panentheism[21] and hedonic life-styles similarly deify earthly spiritualities such as aboriginal land, the purely physical body, and the material self. As such they cannot escape partnership in an enterprise that elevates the creature to creator (Rom 1:22–25), witness the self-revelation of numerous sexual orientations. Such creations, it is believed, enable the good life. The old world held sexuality in high esteem also, but perceived its binary male-female expression as the divine means for fertility/blessing: the entire

---

20. The verb "to point" (*yrh*, Exod 15:25) evokes torah (Ps 19:7–10). See Propp's notes on the text in *Exodus 1–18*, 574, 577.

21. For examples, see the treatment of liberation and eco-theologies in Cooper, *The Other God*, 282–300.

world was understood "as a composite of polar sexual forces."[22] Threats to this established communal harmony between heaven and earth were met with deadly force, for life itself was at stake.[23] Contemporary sexual orientation discourse eschews received traditional and communal boundaries as a threat to self-expression; they must be destroyed.

Covenant polity counters the highly sexualized culture of the old world: rain, celestial bodies, fertile fields, and male and female human beings, are not the sexual partners of some deity. Rather, they are creaturely things whose role in producing crops, children, an orderly society, and a satisfying life is defined by complying with the Creator God's will, expressed in covenant polity. From the beginning, the human body, its intellect, emotions, sexuality, and its will were not themselves sources for the good life. Rather, the good life proceeded from working and keeping the garden of Eden as instructed and with the received male and female bodies. Having defiled their bodies by eating prohibited food, God gave Adam and Eve and their descendants, up "to impurity, to the dishonoring of their bodies . . . to dishonorable passions . . . that are contrary to nature; . . . to a debased mind to do what ought not to be done" (Rom 1:24, 26, 28).

Kings challenges contemporary agents of covenant polity, members of the body of Christ and its leadership, to resist the seductive claim that many altars serve the common good, to acknowledge that religious pluralism and faith-based engineering of the creation present only short-term politico-social solutions to the intractable human problem (Gen 6:6), to confess that "all our righteous deeds are like a polluted garment" (Isa 64:6). In short, Kings urges its exilic and diasporic audience, now in the desert of the nations and surrounded by seductive places of prayer, to turn to the LORD, to renew its dependence upon the only source of all good: The LORD God himself. That takes us to Solomon's prayer of dedication.

Solomon's Prayer of Dedication (1 Kgs 8:22–53)

Solomon's prayer is one of several historical rehearsals and speeches located at crucial narrative locations throughout Joshua–Kings (Josh 1, 23; 1 Sam 12 and 1 Kgs 8 and 2 Kgs 17), which function as anticipatory and retrospective reflections.[24] The dedicatory prayer is part of the building and dedication of

22. Keel, *The Symbolism of the Biblical World*, 30.

23. Keel, *The Symbolism of the Biblical World*, 48–56, for a discussion of Yam and Tannin, the expressions of disorder.

24. Noth, *The Deuteronomistic History*, 6. For a brief discussion of scholarly development of Noth's theory, see Satterthwaite and McConville, *A Guide to the Historical*

the temple episode (6:1—7:51; 8:1—9:1) which lies at the structural center of 1 Kgs 1–11. At this center, 1 Kgs 8 "lays out the ideological program by which the rest of the Book of Kings must be understood."[25]

The prayer's anticipatory and retrospective reflections are linked to its location at the end of one and the beginning of a new era, the entry of the ark into the Most Holy Place of the temple Solomon built.

> the Deuteronomist portrays the dedication of the temple as the culmination of Israelite history since the exodus and as the dawn of a new era for king, cult, and people. The author actively promotes the unity of his state by arguing for the temple's centrality to the fate of his people.[26]

The introduction to the prayer focuses on God's promise to David (1 Kgs 8:22–26), lending the prayer its retrospective character; the LORD's response to Solomon's petition at Gibeon similarly recall David (2 Kgs 9:1–9), but emphasizes the importance of ruling like David and consequences of not doing so. This defines the anticipatory character of Solomon's prayer.

What Is Solomon's Prayer of Dedication About?

Where the desert tabernacle was a sacrificial center (Lev 1:1—7:38), Solomon's dedication depicts the temple as a house of prayer, centered on the altar (1 Kgs 8:22). Prayer does not replace sacrifice, for the two are intimately related: Hannah prayed during the family's yearly trip to Shiloh to offer sacrifices; David's sacrifice at Araunah's threshing floor pled for salvation from the plague. Solomon also offered massive sacrifices before and after the dedicatory prayer (1 Kgs 8:5, 62–66), but these sacrifices and prayer do not coincide at the temple's dedication. Rather, the emphasis falls on the temple as the place God chose for his name to dwell (1 Kgs 8:16, 18–20, 29, 33, 44; 9:3); it is the directional ground zero for petitions. Like Sinai and the tabernacle before it, the Jerusalem temple is the earthly place where heaven and earth meet.[27] Indeed, it is the only place *at* (1 Kgs 8:31, 33) and *toward*

Books, 199–219.

25. Walsh, *1 Kings*, 151; Nelson, *First and Second Kings*, 49. "The dedication of the temple becomes the moment in sacred time located at the center of sacred space that orients Israel's history as a sacred people." Mann, *The Book of the Former Prophets*, 260, where he also suggests that 1 Kgs 8 is the liturgical counterpart to 2 Sam 7.

26. Knoppers, "Prayer and Propaganda," 233. After 1 Kgs 8:21, the ark is not mentioned again (Knoppers, "Prayer and Propaganda," 242).

27. Keel, *The Symbolism of the Biblical World*, 113–20.

which any of God's people or a foreigner, may have their petitions heard in heaven (1 Kgs 8:35, 38, 42, 44, 48).

The bloody petitions of Baal's priests on Carmel illustrate that merely offering prayer at or toward another altar is a religious *cul-de-sac*; Baal could not produce a drop of rain. Deuteronomy's instructions to destroy the altars of other gods are not so much intended to remove rival altars, but places of prayer that give false hope, that invite those who walk on the way of the LORD to enter Lady Folly's house of death (Prov 9:13-18). At the dedication of the temple Solomon's petitions direct God's people to pray toward the LORD's house in Jerusalem, and entreats the LORD to listen to the pleas of his people (1 Kgs 8:29-30) in his heavenly dwelling place (1 Kgs 8:30, 32, 34, 36, 39, 43, 45, 49). Solomon's introduction to the petitions links them to the LORD's commitment to David and his descendants, compliance with covenant polity, thereby showing that what is truly at stake is securing David's throne. Praying toward or at other altars will bring the LORD's house of prayer to ruin (1 Kgs 9:6-8a) and convert Israel into a byword among the nations (1 Kgs 9:8b-9; Deut 28:64-68). No matter the distress that petitions address, they all concern the future of the house of David as an aspect of the sovereignty of the house of the LORD God, the Jerusalem temple. The prayer, then, is a hermeneutical lens through which the audience discerns the narrator's subsequent summary evaluations and amplified depictions of the kings' worship of the LORD God at his or of other gods at their altars.

The Petitions and the Promised Land

Solomon's prayer is composed of seven petitions. The first asks that God affirm an oath made at the altar (8:21-32); the second, defeat of the enemy and a plea for return to the land (8:33-34); the third, a plea for rain (8:35-36); the fourth entreats an end to famine (8:37-40); the fifth, the prayer of a foreigner who has heard of the LORD's name (8:41-43); the sixth, a plea for success in battle (8:44-45); and, the seventh, a plea that their captors treat the exiles with compassion (8:46-53). Kings provides examples of these petitions. Elijah's prayer for rain at the LORD's altar on Mt. Carmel illustrates the third petition (1 Kgs 18:36-37); Naaman's cleansing by calling on the *name* of the LORD, the fifth petition (2 Kgs 5:11, 14); and, Hezekiah's prayer in the temple for deliverance[28] from Assyria, the sixth

---

28. The Chronicler's review of Jehoshaphat's reign teaches the returned exiles the function of such prayer by reminding them that the Lord gave Judah rest (*nwḥ*, 2 Chr 20:30) from the enemy (Ammon and Moab) because he sought the Lord by offering prayer in the house of God (2 Chr 20:3-22).

petition (2 Kgs 19:14–19). Josiah does not pray in the temple, but reads the Book of the Covenant there before destroying and defiling the altars to other gods (2 Kgs 23:2–3).

The prayer maintains the particularity of the promised land from the first through the sixth petition, including a specific plea that God return the petitioner to the land in the second petition (*šwb*, 8:34). The seventh petition maintains the directional character of the prayer—toward the land, the city, and God's house (8:48)—but foregoes a request to be returned to the land. Rather, the emphasis falls on the exiles' turning to the LORD in repentance in the land of their captors (*šwb*, 8:47–48).

Repentance Far Away from Home

The climactic seventh petition confronts its exilic and diasporic audience with an alarming new reality: the new era that dawned with Solomon now lies in ruins and all Israel finds itself far away from home. Some would return with Ezra, but the geographic particulars of Israel's identity—the land promised to the patriarchs, the city God had chosen, the house that Solomon built—remain only in the petitions towards that place. This petition uses the verb "to turn" not to depict a return to the land, but a returning to the LORD, that is, repentance.

The second petition's plea that the LORD bring them back to the land uses a causative form of the verb "to turn" (*šwb*): "cause to return them to the land of their fathers." The seventh petition uses the same verb three times, but in the sense of repent "in the land of their enemies," where they arrived because "God caused to return them" (*whšybk*, Deut 28:68) in ships to Egypt. Having scattered them all over the earth, the LORD's people will serve the other gods and not "find a *resting place* for the sole of your foot" (*mnwḥ*, Deut 28:65). Failing to find a resting place, Noah's dove returned (*šwb*, Gen 8:9) to the ark, safe from the threatening waters. God's exiled people, however, will remain among the "flood" of nations that threaten their covenant polity with strange altars. The seventh petition does not speak of a return to a secure place, but of a return to the LORD. Rather, the petitioner implores God to pardon his people, and to be merciful to them so that their captors treat them with compassion. This petition identifies Israel in terms of their captors, not their ancestors Abraham, Isaac and Jacob; the landed particulars of Israel's identity are gone, all that remains is prayer toward heaven, for the sake of David's throne.

The earthly particulars, however, were never the goal for the people God separated from the nations (1 Kgs 8:53). Rather, it was to love the LORD your God with "all your heart and with all your soul and with all your might" (Deut 6:5), to be completely dependent on the LORD in the land as they were in the desert (Deut 8:2-6), to destroy the other gods' altars and lift their eyes to heaven only at the place where God made his name to dwell. Surrounded by strange altars in the lands of their captors God's people can only ask for compassion, for they have no power to destroy those altars. And the altar to the LORD at Jerusalem lies in ruins. Nevertheless, neither the temple ruins nor the distance from Jerusalem precludes prayer towards the house of the LORD (Dan 6:10), for the LORD's true dwelling place is in heaven. Moreover, the ruins have a purpose. Like the piles of stone in the book of Joshua, they are memorials, in this case of God's judgment on Israel's disloyalty. Still, they are the only place towards which the repentant petitioner can ask heaven to maintain the promise to maintain David's throne (1 Kgs 8:26). No matter how far from home in the "wilderness of the nations" (Ezek 20:35), no matter the distress, prayer towards the LORD's Jerusalem throne acknowledges God's people is secure under the wings of the Almighty. Not Jerusalem, but the LORD himself is their dwelling place (Ps 91:1, 9).[29]

Prayer towards God's house publicly demonstrates utter dependence on the LORD's heavenly rule and faith in God's covenant with David. The ruins of Jerusalem, the directional character of the prayer, and the new reality of life far away from "home," urge a reflection on the future of the earthly location of the divine presence (Ezek 1, 40–48; John 1:14; 2:21). This brings us to the question, "Who, does what?" in the prayer.

Who Does What in Solomon's Dedicatory Prayer?

The narrator locates the building of God's house and its dedication at the center of the Solomon episode. Solomon's wise dealing with the prostitutes and his witty answers to the queen of Sheba's questions frame the building and dedication of God's house, a literary arrangement that links the building of God's house with wisdom (Prov 9:1). The queen exalts Solomon by declaring "*happy* are your servants who continually stand before you and hear your wisdom" ('*šry*, 10:9), and praises "the LORD your God" who set Solomon on Israel's throne "to do justice and righteousness" (10:9). The queen's reference to justice and righteous recalls David (2 Sam 8:15); her "happy are those"

---

29. "As a ruin the Jerusalem temple did not become obsolete. Rather, it became 'an integrating element, which enabled the exiles who fled to Egypt and those who remained in Judah to maintain their religious identity.' The people focused their prayers on these temple ruins, as did the theological reflection of Ezekiel and the Deuteronomist" (translation mine). Janowski, "Ich will in eurer Mitte wohnen," 190–91, citing Otto Weippert.

evokes a state of forgiveness of sins at Zion, of fearing God by obeying covenant instructions and refusing the counsel of the wicked (Ps 1), observing justice and doing righteousness (Ps 106:3). Wisdom depicts similar happiness (Prov 3:13; 16:20; 20:7; 29:18).[30] This incomparably wise and righteous Solomon offers prayer at the altar of God's house.

The introduction hints at and the conclusion to Solomon's reign depicts a king whose love for other women (*nkryh*, 1 Kgs 11:1, 8) compromised his wisdom: for their sake he built and worshiped at other altars. Canonical Solomon ignored his own warnings about liaisons with a strange woman (*nkryh*, Prov 5:20; 6:24; 7:5; cf. 23:27 and Jer 2:21): worshiping at the altars of his wives is tantamount to adultery, for by covenant the LORD is Israel's husband (Hos 2:16–17).[31] This foolish Solomon offers the dedicatory prayer.

This wise and foolish son of David pleads with the LORD on the basis of God's covenant with David, not his own righteousness or wisdom, and asks that God hear his and others' pleas in heaven, a court governed by divine wisdom, unsullied by human folly. That answers the question who does what with respect to the prayer from an earthly point of view. The LORD's response to Solomon's pleas at Gibeon, reminds the audience that God will attend to Solomon's petitions for David's sake, that even the sin that caused the exile is not beyond heaven's hearing. God will hear the prayer of his disobedient people, wherever they are, when they repentantly pray towards the only efficacious altar, for the sake of his servant David. That answers the same question from heaven's point of view.

Together these two answers constitute the hope this prayer offers to Kings' exilic and diasporic audience: God's covenant commitment to David's throne.

What Is Solomon's Dedicatory Prayer about Today?

The historical distance between Solomon's prayer and the contemporary reader may generate reflection on God's immanence and transcendence ("But will God indeed dwell on the earth?," 8:27), or sin, prayer, and repentance ("for there is no one who does not sin," 8:46). Focusing on the general aspects of prayer to the divine by sinful human beings may solve the problem of an ancient prayer's relevance for the contemporary audience, but it ignores the salvation historical particularities of the prayer—the Jerusalem

---

30. Cazelles, "ʾšry," 445–46. On translating ʾšry as "how honorable," see Hanson, "How Honorable! How Shameful."

31. As in Judg 2:17; 8:27, 33; and Hos 4:10,18, where the verb *znh* ("to prostitute") describes such worship.

temple, kingship, the covenant commitment to David, the promised land, deportation from the Jerusalem presence of God—and their thematic continuity in the NT: the body of Christ as the temple of the Holy Spirit, Christ the son of David who is God with us who rules from the heavenly throne, to name a few. Even the questions of divine transcendence and immanence, and the universal character of sin, are caught up in these particularities: the first petition reflects on the nature of God's dwelling with Israel, since Sinai; the second, especially the phrase "for there is no one who does not sin," refers to Israel, the antecedent of "they" (8:46). The prayer itself offers a general level, but within salvation historical particulars, the petitioner: "anyone" of God's OT people or "a foreigner" who prays at or toward Jerusalem, no other altar-city. Moreover, it is not "anyone" who offers this dedicatory prayer, but Solomon, son of David with whom God made a covenant, references to which frame Solomon's prayer. And then there is the Solomon who, having dedicated the temple, is also the fool who worshiped at the altars of other gods. Finally, because the prayer's seventh petition locates it within the consequences of worshiping at other altars, this particular sin defines the nature of the petitioner's repentance.

Hearing Solomon's Dedicatory Prayer Today: The NT

The NT opens with the son of David, Jesus Christ who is "God with us," whose incarnation concludes his people's exile from the earthly presence of God (Matt 1:17c, 23; 28:20b), and who "will save his people from their sins" (Matt 1:21). Because Matthew's incarnation account is juxtaposed to the exilic ending of Jesus Christ's genealogy, the worship of other gods, which provoked the deportation from God's Jerusalem presence, may be thought of as the sin from which Jesus Christ saves his people. Both Matthew and Luke have Jesus rejecting Satan's temptation when he declares "You shall worship the LORD your God and him only shall your serve" (Matt 4:10; Luke 4:8), that is, he rejected serving the supreme "other god," Satan himself.[32]

  The fourth gospel depicts Christ as the Word dwelling "among us" who would rebuild temple in three days (John 1:14; 2:21), thus answering the burning question of God's presence in and for the world: not Jerusalem, but the body of Christ. John's discussion of prayer links its efficacy to petitions in Jesus' name (14:13, 14; 16:23, 26) and the Father's name to Jesus' ministry

---

32. Commentators, for example, Marshall, *Commentary on Luke*, 172, tend to take Jesus' words to be a reference to Deut 6:5 LXX, "with slight variations." Matthew's use of the verb "to serve" instead of "to love," however, is a major variation. It evokes Deuteronomy's concerns about serving other gods (e.g., 7:4; 8:19), rather than the Shema.

(17:6, 11, 26). The question of divine absence, spurred by Jesus' announcing his departure to prepare a place for them with the Father (14:5, 8; 16:18), introduces the Holy Spirit as heaven's gift in Jesus' name (14:25) to dwell among his disciples, not the world (14:17).

To Solomon's question, "Will God really dwell on the earth?" Matthew and John respond: Yes. In Jesus Christ, the perfectly righteous son of David, through the Holy Spirit whose indwelling strengthens the body of Christ in the world, so that the world does not overcome it (John 16:31–33). To Solomon's seventh petition that God grant his people compassion in their captors' eyes, John adds Christ's intercessory prayer "for those whom you have given me," that "they may be one even as we are one" (17:9, 22), for the world has no compassion, only hatred for Jesus' disciples (17:14).

Hearing Solomon's Prayer through Jesus' High Priestly Prayer

The OT background of Jesus prayer are thought to be OT farewell speeches and later Jewish writings,[33] seldom to Solomon's dedicatory prayer.[34] There are arresting parallels between the two prayers. Solomon offers prayer at the altar (1 Kgs 8:22, 54); Christ's prayer occurs before John's shift to Christ as the paschal lamb (John 18–19). Both prayers are intercessory: Solomon for God's people (and the foreigner) and the seventh petition for those in exile (1 Kgs 8:41, 46), Christ for those whom the Father has given him, those who are in the world but not of it (John 17:14). Solomon pleads for compassion in exile, not removal from it (1 Kgs 8:50); Christ that the Father keep his disciples from the evil one, not to be taken from the world (17:15–16).

There are important differences. Solomon pleads on the basis of God's covenant with David (1 Kgs 8:25–26); Christ on the basis of his accomplished work and of having made known the Father's name (John 17:4, 6[35]). Unlike Solomon, Christ himself is the basis for the prayer. Furthermore, where Solomon asks that prayers directed to Jerusalem be heard in heaven, Christ's glorification in the Father's presence is the context of his prayer for his disciples (John 17:5). For John the earthly Jerusalem lies in ruins; prayer towards it

---

33. Ridderbos, *The Gospel According to John*, 546, refers to farewell discourses; Brown, *The Gospel According to John*, 744, refers to Moses' speeches in Deuteronomy; Beasley-Murray, *John*, 293. Dillard, *2 Chronicles*, 52–53, briefly discusses similarities between Solomon's dedicatory prayer in Chronicles and John 17.

34. Kerr, *The Temple of Jesus' Body*, 332n50, links John 17's discussion of the name with Solomon's dedicatory prayer.

35. Kerr, *The Temple of Jesus' Body*, 322–23, calls attention to the alternation of retrospect (as in vv. 6 and 22) and petition (11, 13; 21–23), where he also concludes that this prayer is consistent with other high priestly prayers.

has lost its efficacy. Christ's body is the only temple/altar that provides access to the Father (John 14:6) for those who are in but not of the world. As the entry of the ark into Solomon's temple opened a new era, so Christ's dwelling "among us" opens a new epoch of God's dwelling with his people, now in a spiritual house of prayer built up of living stones, helped by the Holy Spirit "to bring holiness to completion" (2 Cor 6:14—7:1), and "to offer spiritual sacrifices acceptable to God through Jesus Christ" (1 Pet 2:5).

Heard through Christ's intercessory prayer, Solomon's prayer encourages God's people everywhere to plead for shelter from earthly distress in some sense consequent upon its own foolish stewardship of covenant polity: judging the truth of an oath, defeat by an enemy, drought, famine, a foreigner's plea, battle against an enemy, living in but not being of the world (the NT equivalent of not returning to the land), but remaining exiles and strangers (1 Pet 1:1; 2:11; 5:13; Jas 1:1). Where Solomon asks for compassion from Israel's captors by prayer towards the ruins of the temple, Christ's pleas rise to the Father from the new, incarnate house of prayer (John 2:21) that "they may be one, even as we are one" (17:11). Union with Christ and the Father, enabled by the Holy Spirit, allows the disciples to bear the burden of the world's hatred and the power of the evil one. That same union, however, when defiled by the self-inflicted suffering consequent upon God's people praying to or at the altars of other gods, obliges repentance and confession of sin "in the land of their captors"—in the world but not of the world—: "We have sinned and have acted perversely and wickedly (1 Kgs 8:47). To those so burdened and repentant, the Son of David says, "Come to me, . . . and I will give you rest" (*anapauō*, Matt 11:28).

Awaiting the Rest That Still Remains: Nowhere to Place Their Feet

With the ark's entry into the Most Holy Place its seeking rest for God's people (Num 10:33) had come to an end. The internal enemy all around had been defeated, Judah and Israel were "as many as the sand by the sea. They ate and drank and were happy," the nations around Israel brought Solomon tribute (Kgs 3:20–21), and the LORD dwelled in his holy temple. The promised future had arrived: "Blessed be the LORD who has given rest to his people Israel" in his Jerusalem presence (1 Kgs 8:56). But then Solomon built altars to other gods and God raised up adversaries, including Jeroboam who built altars at Dan and Bethel to prevent his subjects from going to Jerusalem, and when Manasseh defiled the temple, Nebuchadnezzar destroyed it. What happened to the rest God had bestowed on Judah and Israel?

Even as the future of LORD's covenant with David does not depend on David's earthly descendants, so the divinely promised rest does not depend on the faithfulness of God's people. Both are anchored in the LORD's covenanted commitments to his people. Since the conquest of Canaan, rest was bound up with a specific geography: rest from the enemy all around in the promised land (Josh 21:43–44).[36] There is no evidence of divine retraction of this rest in the PH, nevertheless, Joshua–Kings shows that the benefits of rest in the land were conferred only on those who faithfully exercised the covenant polity (Josh 23; 1 Kgs 9:1–9).[37] Divine anger at covenant disloyalty depicted in Judges and Kings effects the covenant curses, whose purpose it is to bring Israel to cry to the LORD (as in Judges) and to repentance in exile (Solomon's seventh petition). The gift of rest still remains, but by the end of Kings neither it nor the enemy that tempts Israel to violate that rest are bound to the promised land. Rather, the exile becomes a time of dwelling in the wilderness of the nations, the world in Johannine terms, where the ancient enemy emerges to destroy God's people in Esther because they are not of the world: "Their laws are different from those of any other people, and they do not keep the king's laws, so that it is not to the king's profit to tolerate them" (Esther 3:8 ESV), argued Haman, the enemy of the Jews. The translation "to tolerate," however, while plausible, fails because the underlying verb is the Hebrew verb *nwḥ* "to rest." Haman is arguing that Ahasuerus terminate God's gift of rest that Israel is enjoying (analogous to the compassion by captors in the seventh petition of Solomon's prayer) in the exile become diaspora. That is, to let the Jews enjoy the gift of rest from their enemies is not in Ahasuerus' interest.

Post-exilic "wilderness" wandering evokes the dove that found no rest for its feet (Gen 8:9) and the curse of Deut 28:65: "Among these nations you will no respite, and there shall be no resting place for the sole of your foot." The dove returned to the ark; Israel remains in the wilderness (Lam 1:3; 5:5; Jer 45:3), awaiting the revelation of that resting place that still remains, the LORD himself (Matt 1:18–25; 11:28–29).

36. The phrase "just as he had sworn to their fathers" (Josh 21:44), usually interpreted as referring to the promise of land, here modifies the Lord's giving Israel rest. There is no divine promise of rest (*nwḥ*) to the fathers, i.e., the patriarchs. Jacob envisions Issachar seeing a place of rest (Gen 49:15).

37. On the historical relationship between the Davidic and ancient royal grants, see Knoppers, "A Parallel?," 670–97.

10

The Burden of Waiting for the Rest
That Still Remains Today

Fecisti nos ad te
et inquietum est cor nostrum
donec requiescat in te.[1]

Introduction

FROM BEGINNING TO END of Scripture rest coincides with a place: the garden, the ark, the land, the temple, the temple of Christ's body, the heavenly sanctuary, and the new Jerusalem. The earth is meant to be such a place, that is the import of God's restful placing of the man in the garden with the vocation to till and keep it. East of Eden post-lapsarian earth is bereft of such a place, but the descendants of the man and the woman are constrained to seek it; they cannot avoid their divinely created identity, placement, and vocation. Absent such a place, Cain, Nimrod, and those gathered on the plain of Shinar cannot but create their own restful places, altar-cities. But no earthly city, not even Solomon's Jerusalem, can satisfy humanity's earthly quest for rest. East of Eden, God himself defined such a place for pre-diluvian humanity: the ark. Noah's descendants could not find rest, neither at nor beyond Babel. Humanity, as Augustine confessed, will not find rest until it finds it in God.

The pre-patriarchal narrative's depiction of humanity's city building provides an arresting contrast with that of the patriarchs, who build altars, not cities. Not only that, they and their descendants build altars only where the Lord appears to them (Abraham, Isaac, Jacob), where the Lord instructs them to do so, or how to build and consecrate them (Exod

---

1. "You have made us for yourself, O Lord, and our hearts are restless until they rest in you." Augustine, *Confessions*, I. i (1). Augustine's vocabulary for rest (*inquietum*, *requiescat*) reflects the Vulgate, which translates the Hebrew "rest" (*nwḥ* and *mnwḥh*) thusly in the texts commonly cited in our discussion of "rest," except for Josh 21:42 (44 MT) and 23:1 where it uses *pax* and *pacem* respectively. Josh 22:4 uses *quietum ec pacem*.

27:1–8; 29:36–37).[2] It is at the Jerusalem altar that Solomon announces that God has given his people rest; altars to other gods, built at the behest of others or those built to compete with the Jerusalem altar, proclaim an alternative and competing place of promised rest. The Former Prophets, especially Judges and Kings, illustrate how counter-altars destroyed Israel's divinely created places of rest: the land and temple. It's always about the altars where God's people worship. To this very day the fullness of promised rest depends on an altar built according to divine instruction.

Five features of the biblical theology of rest shape the following discussion. First, rest is an irrevocable divine gift to and constitutive of humanity, and therefore will be sought after. East of Eden, God frustrates this search. Second, east of Eden the divine gift of rest is only enjoyed in divinely designed places that evoke the garden: the ark, the land, the body of Christ, the heavenly Jerusalem. Even as return to the LORD's garden presence requires passing by the well-armed cherubim, so recipients of rest enter those places by virtue of a graciously provided sacrifice. Third, the recipients of rest do not enjoy the full benefits of the divinely appointed place of rest because they ceaselessly succumb to seductive alternative places of rest offered by the enemy all around. Fourth, the recipients of rest await its fulness in exile, the diaspora, or the world, a waiting burdened by their sinful inclination to seek rest elsewhere and the constant pressure of the enemy all around to abandon or modify the gift of rest. Fifth, because the gift of rest is irrevocably tied to a sacrifice on an altar, that of Jerusalem or Golgotha, the enemy all around encourages consideration of other viable sacrifices, especially because awaiting the fulness of rest seems endless.

Given these features, this chapter will discuss the altars of the other gods which tempt God's contemporary people to exchange "the glory of the immortal God for images resembling mortal man and birds and animals and reptiles" (Rom 1:23), then move to a illustrate the contemporary identity of "the enemy all around" that promotes such a conversion.

The Altars of the Other Gods in the NT

The NT refers to gods (Acts 7:40; 14:11; 19:26; 1 Cor 8:5; Gal 4:8) and goddesses (Acts 19:27, 35, 37), but not with the OT phrase "other gods" with the LXX *heteros*. The NT applies *heteros* to name spirits (Matt 12:45; Luke 11:26) and other creatures (Rom 8:39) as obstacles to Christ and the love of God. Luke and Paul speak of Christ's incomparability with the phrase "no other name" (Acts 4:12; 1 Cor 8:4), easily understood as "no other god" in

2. Leder, "City and Altar Building in Genesis," 58–83, 77–8 on Noah's altar.

the light of Solomon's and Christ's prayers. Paul and John warn against sacrifices to idols (*eidōlothuton*, 1 Cor 8:4; 10:19, 28; Rev 2:14, 20). References to altars using the Greek *thusiastērion* are positive; a reference to an altar to the unknow God uses *bōmos* (Acts 17:23). NT literature refers to sacrifices in *bonam partem* (Rom 12:1; Eph 5:2; Phil 4:18 [2:17]; 1 Pet 2:5; Heb 13:16 plus fourteen times; and to the golden calf in Acts 7:41, 42). Finally, the verb to sacrifice (*thuō*, Acts 14:13, 18) refers to the people of Lystra taking Paul and Barnabas being gods, to Christ as the Paschal lamb (1 Cor 5:7), and sacrifices offered to demons (1 Cor 10:19).

The NT acknowledges other gods and their altars, but defines them in terms of creaturely things elevated to the divine, to demons, powers and principalities, the elements of this world, the spiritual forces of evil in the heavenly realms, and things elevated to divine status (Rom 1:21–25; Eph 6:12). These powers oppose the bodily sacrifices of Christ and his disciples, both holy and pleasing to God (Rom 8:1–4; 12:1; cf. Lev 1:9, 13, 17; 2:2, 9, 12; 3:5, 16).

The Challenge of the Enemy All Around Today: The Spirit and the Altar

A post-Enlightenment, disenchanted, and physicalist culture seeks material solutions to social disorders; it denies the transcendent, at least in the West. Whatever transcendent realm there may be is inaccessible to the human mind; there is no scientific proof for a world of spirits and demons. What happens accords with known natural laws. None of this has erased the word "spirit" from the contemporary vocabulary, however, not even in a metaphysical sense. Since the sixteenth century, argues Ephraim Radner, "spirit" has been modern pneumatology's concern. Modern pneumatology seeks to make sense of the relationship among levels of beings or things, their harmony and the challenges to this harmony from unexpected sources: exploration of the oceans, meeting new peoples whose names do not appear in Gen 1–11. "During the early modern era, the category of 'spirit'—*spiritus*—significantly shifted in its referential reach away from its earlier focus on a purely divine sphere where the word referred mostly to God's being." Instead, "spirit's reference was relocated within a functionally created sphere, where people act to accomplish things, and these things are not only divinely sanctioned but end up constituting God's own now happily coherent being." This relocation was not a rejection of God or theology, but "renders theology—talk of God—something now determined primarily by human needs and their resolution."[3] Emerging from British naturalistic pneumatology, "American Naturalism—such as that provided in the late eighteenth century by Elihu Palmer's mixture of Deism, vitalism, and quasi-occultism—represented the successful entry of modern pneumatology into the democratic mainstream," illustrated by Emerson and Whitman's notions of Spirit.[4]

Radner's study of contemporary modern pneumatology's redefinition of God and the Spirit—Emerson, Whitman, Moltmann—[5]represent pneumatological other gods, including combination with theologies of the Holy Spirit.[6] And, as in Judges, Kings and Isaiah, these other gods were human confections: "As the Spirit became the world, at least ideologically, the Church disappeared, a consistent dynamic from sixteenth-century 'spiritual' religion, through Quakerism, and into the American dissolution of ecclesiastical loyalties." This poses a question for those awaiting rest: Are the coherences attributed to the spirit, a new ordering force of the divine—progressive notions of sexual identity and other aspects of remaking a merely material human body, from the role of martyrs to the veiling of Christ's corporeality[7]—authored by the Holy Spirit or another spirit? This restless spiritual search seeks to understand humanity's created east of Eden environment, but is forced to do so amidst unanticipated irruptions that challenge the received order. It is also a search for a safe place, a utopia, in a world that cannot sustain this manufacture place of rest. Radner writes,

> The Spirit of utopia is a myth born of those same human desires that shape today's less benign encounters. Yet neither is the Holy Spirit simply constrained by the "world as it is," precisely because it cannot be identified with these same human desires. What the Word shows is neither "this place" nor our construal of that "good place" that must always be "no place" at all. Instead the Word presents us with a God who is ever in "another place," a "heterotopia" in relation to all the givens of both human work and human desire. That divine place is, as

3. Radner, *Modern Pneumatology*, 52. The word "pneumatology" referring to the study of the Holy Spirit does not occur in this sense until the mid to late nineteenth century. John Owen's five-volume 1674 *Pneumatologia* is an exception (Radner, *Modern Pneumatology*, 59–60).

4. Radner, *Modern Pneumatology*, 139 and 139–153.

5. Radner, *Modern Pneumatology*, 79–81; Cooper, *The Other God*, 237–58.

6. "Pentecostalism . . . is, experientially and historically, an outgrowth of those movements whose search for divine efficacy within pneumatically identified individuals marked one aspect of the early of the early modern search for an ordering spiritual force in the world." Radner, *Modern Pneumatology*, 79.

7. Radner, *Modern Pneumatology*, 155–202, 190.

Paul expresses it, always the Cross of Jesus, a place that is both real and really apart at once.[8]

Graced members of the body of Christ remain east of Eden, seeking to perfect there the wholeness of that rest having experienced its foretaste as temple of the Holy Spirit (2 Cor 6:14—7:1). There also, individually and corporately, the body of Christ encounters alternative offers of rest as it struggles to complete the sufferings of Christ in the flesh, for the sake of Christ's body (Col 1:24). Under the Holy Spirit's guidance, they seek to make sense of their scatteredness in the world and of the persistent offers from alternative spirits and their altars that beckon as places of rest.

Scripture's First and Last Altar

Humanity cannot do without altars. Their shape and location may change, but expressing gratitude, seeking reconciliation, and affirming a sense of coherence are indispensable. The ancient world took altars for granted: Cain and Abel offered sacrifices of tribute and Noah one of thanksgiving for rescue from the flood. The post-modern world cannot escape complicity in this human need east of Eden. The pre-patriarchal sacrificial events also disclose a disturbing reality: a sacrifice is only as good as the deity's acceptance, as Baal's priest's learned on Mt. Carmel; the sincerity of the sacrificand is not in play. Thus, the LORD's looking on Abel and Noah's sacrifices with favor, but not Cain's, is not unexpected: the creature may not decide such cosmic matters, it's tantamount to rebellion. God is transcendent and sovereign. No questions asked. Nevertheless, that is the new normal east of Eden; the various shapes of post-Enlightenment modernity have deep roots.

Among the patriarchal altars and sacrifices, the sacrifice of Isaac stands out as the first one with an identifiable victim. Heretofore, Abraham does not offer a victim at the altars he built, he only calls on the name of the LORD (Gen. 12:8; 13:4, 18; 8:20), as do Isaac and Jacob (Gen 26:25; 35:7). The initial sin and burnt offerings to the Lord by a consecrated Aaron were offered at the desert tabernacle. The LORD responded with favor (Lev 9:22–24), but, shades of Cain, he rejected Nadab and Abihu's sacrifice.[9] Because the sacrifices of Cain, Abel, and Noah mention the sacrificial gifts in typical Israelite cultic terms, their absence in the canonical form of the patriarchal narratives highlights the sacrifice of Isaac. It stands out as the

8. Radner, *Modern Pneumatology*, 46.

9. The history of interpretation is as unsettled on the strange fire as it is on the reason for the LORD rejection of Cain's sacrifice. See, Anderson, "Apophatic Theology," 3–22.

first and governing sacrifice for God's people: in obeying the Lord's instructions Abraham learns that Isaac is the Lord's by sacrifice, forever. Isaac does not return from Moriah with Abraham, he remains bound to the altar, with the substitute.[10] In Isaac's sacrifice, Abraham and Isaac's descendants (*zr ͨ*) know they belong, body and soul, to the LORD; if you are Christ's, then you are Abraham's descendants (*sperma*) and heirs according to the promise (Gal 3:29). That is, if you have been sacrificed with Christ on his cross-altar you daily present "your bodies as living sacrifice, holy and acceptable to God" (Rom 12:1). For Christians, Isaac's altar receives its full significance at the cross, it is the only altar that provides coherence to the restless wandering, because it restfully places the sacrificand in the presence of God (Heb 9:24). Hebrews exhorts God's people: "Let us therefore strive to enter that rest, so that no one may fall by the same sort of disobedience [i.e., of Israel in the desert]" (Heb 4:12), for, as they await the Sabbath rest that still remains, they will be tempted by other spiritual altars.

The Alternative Spiritual Altar

Modern pneumatology's desire for a good place, a utopia, is bound to fail because "just such a place is never, *in fact* given, at least in the sense of resolving those realities that make a search compelling, Christian pneumatology can—or at least *should*—only speak of God as "elsewhere," who is not in the place I strive after." Where the "Spirit of utopia is a myth born of those same human desires, . . . the Holy Spirit is simply [not] constrained by the 'world as it is,' precisely because it cannot be identified with these same human desires."[11]

Understanding altar as the place that lends coherence to experienced reality, I suggest that the greatest alternative spiritual alternative altar is the human body. This for three reasons. First of all, Scripture holds a high view of the human body, created male and female. It received the breath of life as did other creatures (*npš ḥyh*, Gen 1:30; 2:8), but only of the human being is it said that God "breathed into his nostrils the breath of life" and that he made the male and female in his own image. The received human body is unique among all creatures. The LORD God restfully placed this human creature in his garden presence to till and keep it with this received body. Failure to comply with divine instruction reduces the bodily outworking of this

10. See, Leder "Bound to the Altar," 283–96. In a sense, Israel's cult presents the detailed explanation of Isaac's sacrifice: all of life in the camp and the land belongs to the LORD.

11. Radner, *Modern Pneumatology*, 46.

vocation to painful toil (*ʿṣbwn*), the woman in child-bearing and the man in working the soil (Gen 3:16–17). Second, because God has separated Israel from the nations he dispossessed from the land (*hbdyl*, Lev 20:26), Scripture prohibits certain sexual practices to maintain his people's bodily purity (Lev 18, 20). The Corinthian correspondence maintains these strictures, but now in terms of believers as members of the body of Christ whose bodies are temples of the Holy Spirit, who therefore ought to "cleanse [y]ourselves from every defilement of body and spirit, bringing holiness to completion in the fear of God" (2 Cor 7:1; 1 Cor 3:16–17). Third, the post-lapsarian human body in Christ dies twice, once as a result of the curse and once in baptism with Christ. Having died with Christ the Christian believer will, like him, arise: what is sown a corruptible body will be raised incorruptible (1 Cor 15:42–49). Finally, the Christian theological tradition has maintained this Scriptural view of the human body, until recently, with ecclesiastical bodies debating alternative views of the received identity of female and male with respect to human sexuality and marriage. For example, of the United Methodist Church's debates on this matter, Kevin Watson writes, "As American cultural elites began to embrace gay rights and same-sex marriage, United Methodist leaders in the U.S. began to fall in line. Tellingly, the church has become more liberal first in the places where the dominant culture had already become more politically and socially liberal."[12] For them and other ecclesial communions the Scriptural injunction that the body is meant "for the Lord, and the Lord for the body" (1 Cor 6:13) has taken on a whole other meaning and theological justification, especially in the light of these dominant cultural values.[13] The body thus becomes an alternative place to seek coherence in humanity's restless wandering: my body, my altar.

12. On the United Method Church's struggles on this matter, see Watson, "Methodism Dividing," 24. The United Methodist Church's General Conference includes churches from other parts of the world, who oppose such positions. See above, chapter 6 97n15. See also "Christian Proponents of Same-Sex Marriage," 1–142, January 2016, a communication to the 2016 Synod of the Christian Reformed Church, the communion to which I belong. The Synod formed a committee to study the biblical view of human sexuality; the committee was bound to the church's earlier decision on the distinction between homosexuality as a condition and as active. Slated to report to Synod of 2021.

13. See, for example, Carruthers, *Unapologetic*, 16, understands "Queer" to represent "a continuum of possibilities outside of what are considered to be normal sexual or gender identities and behaviors. Affirmation of queerness creates possibilities outside the *norm*." (Emphasis added.)

The Restless Body

"Its *desire* shall be for you," God tells Cain about his sinful anger, "but you must overcome it" (*tšwqh*, Gen 4:7), he must master it. There is no evidence he did. Before that God told Eve, "your *desire* will be for your husband," in the context of her bearing children in pain (Gen 3:16). Westermann writes, "Just where the woman finds her fulfillment in life, namely in relationship to her husband and as a mother of her children, there too she finds that it is not pure bliss, but pain, burden, humiliations and subordination."[14] Whatever else it may mean in Gen 3 and 4, "desire" as part of the human condition must be mastered. To rule over (*mšl*) occurs in both contexts. In the only other appearance of the noun, the Song of Solomon, notes desire's positive side when the bride says, "I am my beloved's, and his *desire* is for me" (Song 7:10). But, the daughters of Jerusalem are adjured to "not stir up or awaken love until it pleases" (Song 2:7; 3:5; 8:4); love may not be forced.

After describing various dualistic views of the human body, especially Gnosticism and Docetism's negative views of human corporeality, Mary Timothy Prokes concludes with the twentieth century's viewing the body as object and artifact: "The ever-expanding ability to objectivize, analyze and rearrange material reality has opened the material universe and *the human body* to enormous restructuring."[15] Put in I what I take to be modern pneumatological terms: "The technological, audio-visual immediacy of people to one another is evoking theological reflection on body-centered issues as diverse as male-female relations, genetic experimentation, societal violence, and the fabrication of 'model' human beings."[16] The material human body has become the locus of a post-modern search for bodily rest, in which the major difference between it and the Christian tradition is the latter's view of human fertility based on female-male family units. The altars to the other

14. Westermann, *Genesis 1–11*, 263.

15. Prokes, *Theology of the Body*, 20. Emphasis in the original.

16. Prokes, *Theology of the Body*, 22. The "Christian Proponents of Same-Sex Marriage," 41, states that "Theologians of disability offer helpful perspectives for this discussion. They caution against authoritative declarations of what constitutes birth defects or disorders resulting from the Fall, reminding us that disorders have historically been defined by those in the majority and comprise those attributes most people consider undesirable. Similarly, many Christian sexual minorities embrace those aspects of their identities that others consider a result of the Fall. The stigmatization experienced by those whom society has devalued, marginalized, and oppressed identifies them with the 'despised and rejected' Christ who, on his resurrected body, carries the physical marks of that stigmatization: the stigmata by which we know our Savior. How does the Church respond to persons who believe their sexual orientation, gender identity, intersex condition, or physical disability is central to their God-given identity rather than a disorder that will be corrected in heaven?"

gods that seduced Israel to seek its fertility—human, animal, agricultural, city-building[17]—from the Baals and the Astheroth,[18] contradicted the fertility proceeding from compliance with covenant polity (Deut 28:1–14). Wasting human seed or offering it to Molech (zr^c, Gen 38:9–10; Lev 20:2–3) undermines that polity and is subject to divine judgment. Moreover, where the pre-patriarchal nations were naturally fertile, Israel's mothers—Sarah, Rebekah, Rachel[19]—were barren; the available human technology, surrogacy and homeopathy (mandrakes), was helpless; the LORD opened their wombs. Comparing old world taboos and contemporary practices concerning fertility, Prokes writes: "In earlier times, taboo rituals were practiced in order to *enhance* fertility for humans, animals and the earth and to placate fertility goddesses so that they would be favorable. In contradistinction, most contraceptives and surgical interventions are now sought to *thwart* fertility. In either case, there is a common fear that fertility requires external intervention."[20] Or enable it in the case of same-sex partnerships.

The United Methodist Church debates and the report "Christian Proponents of Same-Sex Marriage" seek to manage new possibilities of sexuality, both depending on post-modern theological anthropologies, anecdotal evidence of various forms of human sexuality, and advances in scientific understandings of sex and gender, intersex and transgender identities. If fulfilling these desires is possible within the bounds love and charity who can be against it, especially if and when the church decides this liberation is being nudged by the Holy Spirit?[21] But whence such desires and what is their origin?

Angela Franks points to the modern view of desire rooted in Marx's belief that "desires are produced socially," a view that Félix Guattari and Gilles DeLeuze develop to mean that "the body becomes a kind of prime matter, "a surface for the recording of the entire process of production of desire." She continues, "this explains the tattoo phenomenon. If the body is a surface on which desire writes, then desire is free to form it as it wishes. These days, this formation of the body by desire does not stop at sex." "In 'body

17. On the association of mother goddess and branch goddess figurines with fertility, see Keel and Uehlinger, *Gods, Goddesses, and Images of God*, 28, 131.

18. Hiel's sacrificing his sons to rebuild Jericho fulfills Joshua's curse (1 Kgs 16:34; Josh 6:26), and reminds the reader of the covenant polity of offering their seed to other gods (Lev. 20:1–5).

19. This includes Leah. The text does not state that she was barren, but that the Lord opened her womb "because she was hated" (Gen 31:31).

20. Prokes, *A Theology of the Body*, 92. Emphasis in original.

21. "Christian Proponents of Same-Sex Marriage," 12–20, opens with a section on the Holy Spirit and reinterpretation of Scripture.

modification,' people may have horns implanted in their foreheads, and worse—because the body has no innate intelligibility before desire begins to inscribe it with its blind purposes."[22] The resultant ontology of technocracy, Franks argues, "replaces 'a meaning that is not of our own' with 'gods of one's own—idols according to Ratzinger's definition."[23] Desires there are, but east of Eden they are compromised, no longer tending toward pleasing God but the autonomous self. Like unruly steeds their power must be steered toward a transcendent good, but our Western post-Christian culture does not offer the disciplines to do so. It is no accident, writes Frank,

> that the Old Testament connects idolatry with adultery: Both are marked by faithlessness, because both goddess and mistress are means to self-referential ends, not ends in themselves. When another idol seems to provide the end more readily, the worshiper moves on. And there is no end to moving on. So we are weary. Restlessness is baked into idolatry, because finite 'gods of one's own' cannot satisfy the infinite desires implanted in us.[24]

As in Israel and the NT church the tension between a vowed covenant commitment to the received body in Christ and the seductive appeals to an autonomous self that it transform that body according to desire, is palpable and devastating. "Who will rescue us from this body of death?" (Rom 7:24). Paul points to the Spirit of life, who ceaselessly intercedes for the saints with "groanings too deep for words" (Rom 8:26). East of Eden only one altar can transform desire for a truly transformed body, the cross of Christ.

Desire in the Desert

In Willa Cather's *O Pioneers!* Alexandra's maid Signa asks Ivar—an old man the community wants to institutionalize for his unusual ability to heal animals and habit of walking barefoot—why he goes barefoot, "Is it for penance, or what?" He replies,

> No, sister. It is for the indulgence of the body. From my youth up I have had a strong, rebellious body, and have been subject to every kind of temptation. Even in age my temptations are prolonged. It was necessary to make some allowances; and the feet, as I understand it, are free members. There is no divine prohibition for them in the Ten Commandments. The hands,

---

22. Franks, "DeLeuze on Desire," 40.

23. Franks, "DeLeuze on Desire," 41.

24. Franks, "DeLeuze on Desire," 41.

the tongue, the eyes, the heart, all the bodily desires we are commanded to subdue; but the feet are free members. I indulge them without harm to anyone, even to trampling in filth when my desires are low. They are quickly cleaned again.[25]

Like a desert monk, Ivar disciplines his body according to Scripture (he regularly reads it in his native Norwegian), but acknowledges the body's destructive desires. Ivar's version of living in the world but not of it reflects Scripture's injunction that God's people live in the land of promise as if it were the desert (Deut 8), where God fully provided her bodily needs and shaped them by covenant polity (food, body, sexuality, e.g., Lev 11–15, 18, 19). Israel must eschew Egyptian and Canaanite technopolity (Lev 18:1–5). Judges and Kings accuses God's exilic and diasporic people of surrendering to prohibited technopolities. Ezekiel 20:35 proclaims that the exiles are now suffering the consequences of surrendering body's desires to worldly well-being in the wilderness of the nations. If God's people won't live in the land as if it were in the desert, God will bring them back to the desert, there to learn dependence on him and to reshape their desire for God on the way to the rest that still remains. As between Egypt and Canaan, they only survive in that desert because God's presence does not abandon them to it (Ezek 1).

The Location of the Desert

Deuteronomy 8, Jesus' desert temptations, his prayer for his disciples-in-but-not-of-the-world, and Rev 12:13–17 together posit the truth that east of Eden life in God's presence is shaped by the desert. Israel's first desert experience took place between Egypt and the Land; Ezekiel's wilderness in that of the nations.[26]

---

25. Cather, *O Pioneers!*, 136.

26. The desert, "like the sea, was not a place of romantic association, but rather a region of danger and death." Keel, *Symbolism of the Bible*, 76. Humanity has not tamed the sea nor the desert, it can survive them only within the limits of its technology. For that reason, the symbolism of the desert remains true: it's a dangerous place where no one survives, except with some form of outside help. Scripture points to the Lord God: Jesus Christ silenced the waves and survived the desert by the Word. Significantly, Rev 21:1 declares that "the sea was no more" on the new earth. Babylon has been conquered, the enemy of rest in God's presence defeated.

The Sinai Desert

Like a rite of passage, the Sinai experience depicts an unruly, untutored Israel, newly led out of Egyptian slavery under the guidance of Moses who instructs them for life as an adult, i.e., a community committed to its normal way of life. The Sinai instruction permeates Israel's entire experience in the presence of God. They are a "threshold people,"[27] a catechumenate in covenant polity.

Three altars define this desert experience: the altar at the entrance to the tent of meeting where daily burnt offerings sanctify the place of God's meeting with his people, reminds them that the LORD God delivered then from Egypt; the anti-covenantal golden calf altar at which the people adored other gods; and, that of the Baal of Peor. The Sinai desert experience discloses the uncomfortable reality that Israel's impatience with the God of her salvation and his servant Moses moved her to seek another altar of salvation. Israel herself is the greatest enemy of rest in the presence of God. God offered Moses rest (*nwḥ*, Exod 33:14), but this mediator refused. The desert itself does not kill; failure to comply with covenant polity causes death in this desert (Num 11–25).

The Wilderness of the Nations

At the end of Kings God's people finds itself in a pre-patriarchal location: the land of the Chaldeans, abandoned by Abraham and Sarah, where great altar-cities dominate, where Babel-like authorities demand everyone seek heaven as instructed, where those who maintain covenant polity face death (Dan 3:4–12; Esth 3:7–11). This wilderness is composed of the nations who cling to the old ways of Adam and Eve's descendants, who, like Cain, cannot escape their restless wandering but seek it in the comfort of altar-cities. This is the wilderness from which God's people direct their prayer to the now-destroyed Jerusalem altar, so that God in heaven may hear their plea for compassion from their captors, in accordance with the seventh plea of Solomon son of David. This wilderness is the world into which the Father sent Christ to receive his own, for whom he prays for protection from the world. In this wilderness the eternal Haman seeks the destruction of Abraham's descendants (Exod 1:8–22; Rev 12:17). Escape from the ancient adversary comes by divine revelation (Mat 2:13); relief (*nwḥ*, Esth 9:16, 22) from the

---

27. Leder, *Waiting for the Land*, 103–10, on the desert transition from Egypt to Sinai.

enemy for Abraham's diasporic descendants (zr^c, Esth 6:13; 9:27, 28, 31; 10:3) by shrewd discernment of the enemy.

This is a wilderness of two altars: the imitations of Babel's altar-city and the rebuilt temple of its great counter-altar at Jerusalem, Christ's consecrated body. All members of that body enjoy the first-fruits of the rest that still remains, but like Isaac on Mt Moriah, they are bound to Christ's cross, body and soul. This body of Christ, the church, is a desert people.[28]

The Church, a Desert People

The desert is an inconvenient identity for a world or body-affirming Christianity. Nevertheless, it is the Scripturally defined place where God's people strive with body and soul to enter the rest that still remains, and where the adversary's "Did God really say?" pursues the body of Christ. First Peter and James further identify the church as an exilic or diasporic community, and John 17 as the body of Christ in the world but not of it. To this identity 1 Peter's emphasis on suffering as Christians adds self-abandonment, denial of the short-term benefits of technocratic bodily rest. Surrender to covenant polity in the desert is manna for body and soul, the self's abandonment to bodily desire leaves one anorexic. John Moses writes, "The spirituality of the desert challenges the prevailing assumption that life can only be lived through self-revelation and self-fulfillment."[29] This self-fulfillment is authorized by identifying scientific and technological progress with the uncovering of heretofore unknown truths under the guidance of the Holy Spirit,[30]

28. Leder, *Waiting for the Land*, 195–12, esp. 195–209.

29. Moses, *The Desert*, 18. On page 57 he quotes Derek Webster: "The desert cell is Hell's cockpit, no less than a royal palace or a trader's bazaar, a maiden's thigh or the scholar's desk. But what is played out there takes its costume from the hidden thought of each actor, Shape and symbols are invested with power from conjoined dread and desire, both drawn from the soul's deepest wells."

30. As does the report "Christian Proponents of Same-Sex Marriage." On the intellectual roots of the identification of the S/spirit with contemporary events, Radner, *Modern Pneumatology*, writes: "The mostly metaphysical and scientific concerns that joined Spirit to the investigation of natural ontology helped shape the fundamental categories according to which modern pneumatology developed. These ideas helped facilitate the instrumental manipulation of creation for, to put it bluntly, the resolution of pain and conflict" (Radner, *Modern Pneumatology*, 90). "As the eighteenth century wore on, the final destiny of bodies (death) . . . was confronted by increasingly intricate strategies of attempted circumvention . . . English followers of Boehme . . . were among the most radical and creative in rethinking the nature of sexuality itself . . . once the body's spiritual origins and constitution are reframed even in sexual terms, pneumatology becomes an explicit form of self-understanding and hope" (Radner, *Modern Pneumatology*, 118). According to Radner, the British theologian Geoffrey A. Studdert-Kennedy illustrates a classic pneumatological move. His focus on the "corporeal suffering which could not be squared with divine omnipotence," shifted to "the pneumatic

who along with the rest of the godhead is no longer considered objective but subjectively[31] and thus agreeably united to the notion of a human spirit. As a desert people experiencing constant challenges to the altar of Christ, the church requires continuing self-discipline. Among many others, this discipline includes a non-worldly sacrifice of the body (Rom 12:1-2): the fleshly body consecrated to God through the Holy Spirit may not be sacrificed to sexual immorality, idolatry, or the like (Rom 6:9-10, 13).

In the post-Ascension Pentecostal era maturation in holiness includes the Holy Spirit's illumination of our spirit and our not quenching or grieving the Spirit in our bodies. How do we adjudicate claims of the Holy Spirit's leading into newly revealed truths about our bodies? There is no easy answer, for such claims are also made by Christian believers who seek to discern the spirit, they know that not every spirit is of God (1 John 4:1). Profoundly influenced by the spiritual underworld (fortune-telling, omens, mediums, wizards) Manasseh, a son of David, ruled like a king of the nations, subverting covenant polity (Deut 17:14-15). Without discerning the spirit, both people and its king suffered the sanctions of the covenant polity: exile from God's Jerusalem presence to restlessness among the nations (Deut 28:65).

Towards a Theology of the Body as Temple of the Holy Spirit

From its beginning modern pneumatology studied the metaphysics of being, including the spiritual beings of Scripture, but it became consciously naturalistic with respect to the pneumatic human being's self-understanding. "By the middle of the nineteenth century," Radner writes, "*Esprit* and *Geist* more or less replace the doctrinal structures of the Church, which had already begun to recede in force as serviceable religious and metaphysical frameworks."[32] Along with modernity's turn to the subject, the hermeneutic of suspicion, and the cacophony of hermeneutico-exegetical methods applied to Scripture[33] in a variety of forms, these developments produce

---

plane, positing what would later be called a 'process understanding of God,' evolving and unfolding with time and our own experience, and thus worth our faith and trust precisely in the ongoing character of a divine development that leaves behind the bodies of our tears as yet-undeveloped stages of history" (Radner, *Modern Pneumatology*, 182–83).

31. Bavinck, *Reformed Dogmatics*, 486–95. Bavinck acknowledges the religious subject, but this subject does not come to the truth on his own; rather the truth finds the subject, enters into the human spirit, becomes its witness. Knowledge of this, however, comes not from general revelation, but the special revelation of God in Jesus Christ. Bavinck, *Reformed Dogmatics*, 133–34.

32. Radner, *Modern Pneumatology*, 77.

33. Gale Yee's presidential address to the annual meeting of the SBL in San Diego, November 23, 2019: "Thinking Intersectionally: Gender, Race, Class, and the Etceteras of Our Discipline," 3–26.

a variety of arguments for detecting the leading of the S/spirit. And then perhaps only for smaller groups, determined by gender, race, or class, in their struggle against dominant group in so-called communities of faith. It all depends on who can corral the S/spirit for the cause.

But that is the problem! In Judges and Samuel, the Spirit falls on the good, the bad, and the indifferent; for the reborn in Christ he goes where he wills (John 3:8). Scripture forbids attempts to control events by means of false spirits; but Jesus, like Samuel earlier, controlled the spirits (Matt 8:28–34; Mark 5:12-14; 1 Sam 28:8-19). Simon the magician repented of profiting from the Spirit's power, a sin Peter defined as being "in the gall of bitterness and in the bond of iniquity" (Acts 8:23 ESV). Jesus says the Spirit will testify of him, the truth, and no other, for there is no other truth.[34] Uncontrollable by humans, the Spirit can only speak the truth concerning the Christ of Scripture, he is bound to and therefore can lead to only one altar: the body of Christ as Scripturally depicted and deeply reflected on by the church of all ages. Redefining the altar of God's choosing, as did Jeroboam, may be technopolitically expedient but it is spiritually enervating.

The sanctifying work of the Holy Spirit touches body and soul, a being that belongs to the Lord not to any one individual being or community. That body is the locus of the Holy Spirit's illumination to assure believers of their status as God's children, especially as female or male. When Christians struggle with these received identities, or consider their bodies to be machines for pleasing the self (sexual pleasures, reproductive rights, tattooing/piercing, eternal youth, by surgery or the gladiatorial gym; concern with eating the "right" food, veganism or a diet *du jour*[35]) the question of the Spirit's illumination arises. Who decides what is true, what is irrelevant, or even trivial? Who knows how the Spirit moves to illuminate the Church? Scientific studies of sexual orientation and gender warrant a reinterpretation of Scriptural teaching on these matters, some Christians argue, because these studies provide a deeper awareness of general revelation. The Copernican revolution is often cited as an example: the church reinterpreted Scripture in the light of new insight into general revelation. This revolution, however, was not merely one of biblical interpretation as such but with an interpretation irrevocably bound to the cosmologies of the day, Ptolemaic or Aristotelian or mix thereof. The conflict centered on which cosmological theories would now be applied to Scripture,[36] and so

34. In a deflection worthy of post-modernity, Pilate answers Jesus' declaration that he came to bear witness to the truth with "What is truth?" (John 18:38). There are many truths, not one.

35. See Greif, *Essays Against Everything*, 3–56, for a critique of the hedonic bodies: in the gym, the phantasy reshaping an aging body into one of youthful sexuality, the body sacrificed to food.

36. Jaki (*Genesis 1: Through the Ages*) shows how no age escapes reading Scripture

to authorize traditional social hierarchies, especially that of the Roman church against the state. Both Rome and the earth lost their cosmological centrality, but Scripture never taught either. Progress in scientific understanding of creation has occasioned the reinterpretation of Scripture with respect to the phenomena that form the object of scientific study. The objects of scientific study, however, are creaturely things whose meaning is dependent, one way or another, on a defining narrative—Mother Earth, Gaia, naturalism, romanticism, veganism—which defines approved human behavior. In the age of Covid19 it is said that scientific knowledge will save us, but conflicts rage about its technopolitical employment. There's always a defining over-arching narrative.

The human body is a creaturely thing, but its corporeal character and its relationship to science differs from one narrative to another (Christianity, Hinduism, Islam, Buddhism, Taoism, New age animism, Feminism, LGBTQ). Scripture has no particular view about science. On revelation it's specific: God's speech through the prophets, in Scripture or Incarnate as testified by Scripture. General revelation is about available knowledge of God's eternal nature and power. The Gentiles, who do not have the law, may do things according to the inescapable creation order structures which Paul negatively identifies with homosexual and gay behavior as contrary to nature (Rom 1:24, 26–7). General revelation is not about material reality as such, but about how that creaturely reality conforms to the Creator's will. Being plain to all, that revelation is sufficient to accuse the descendants of Adam and Eve of denying the Creator, who gives them up (Rom 1:24, 26, 28) to all manner of bodily dis-ease. General revelation is not, however, the lens to clarify the contemporary culture's difficulties with special revelation. Rather, special revelation of God is the lens that gives insight to the creation's publication of God's being, for "our very being is nothing but subsistence in the one God."[37] This is the very essence of the promised rest: conformity to God, in body and soul, according to the nature of man's being as disclosed in special revelation.

The Holy Spirit testifies to the truth in Christ—special revelation—to the sacrifice of his body. In this role he groans on behalf of the saints' denying their bodily desires in order to main the purity of the temple of Christ's body, brings to the heavenly throne the daily confessions of sin that defile that temple so that the Almighty may hear our repentance in Christ's name. He also brings the groans rising from denial of a hedonically reimagined body, from repeated unwanted surrenders to it, from bodies that do not experientially conform to the revealed and received identity to the heavenly throne. No one member of the body of Christ is exempt from the discipline

in the light of its scientific understanding.

37. Calvin, *Institutes*, I.1.i.

of self-denial of bodily desire. In a pluralistic democratically organized society, it is the culturally blessed bodily desires that increase the burden of that self-discipline, not Scripture.

The Burden of Waiting for the Rest That Still Remains

The burden of waiting for the rest that still remains is the waiting, the incompleteness, the brokenness, the temptation to surrender to the pain of bodily incoherence, and the never ending discerning the spirit behind the conflict. The origin of a brokenness may even be the adversary's meddling into God's affairs: "a thorn *was given*[38] in the flesh, a messenger of Satan to harass me" (2 Cor 12:7 ESV). On his altar, hung between heaven and earth, Christ's "My God, my God, why have you forsaken me?" spoke towards the heavenly throne for all who cried in pain and conflict: "Why are you so far from saving me, from the words of my groaning. O my God, I cry by day, but you do not answer, and by night, but I find no rest" (Ps 22:1b–2). From under the heavenly altar souls of the martyrs cry: "How long?" (Rev 6:9–10). Even the faithful departed are burdened as they await their redemptive wholeness.

As we wait, we thankfully receive the gifts of medical and technological wisdom. None of these, however, have the competence to remove the burden of waiting or to restfully place whole bodies of the descendants of Adam and Eve in God's presence. Waiting for God to transform our earthly bodies while denying their sinful desires is a burden to which the culture adds by applauding free reign to such desires. In the wilderness of nations, the burden of waiting can only be dealt with by prayer addressed to the heavenly throne. Solomon's prayer teaches self-denial by confessing our sin of worshiping at other altars and, if heaven will, mercy and compassion from their captors. Christ prays for the disciples' life in the world that hates them, that their strength in resisting the evil one come from their unity with Christ and the Father. These prayers sustain the desert disciplines of separation from the world and self-denial and the knowledge that "I am not my own, but belong, in body and soul, in life and in death, to my faithful Savior Jesus Christ."[39] Our hearts are restless until they find their rest in the LORD alone, there is no other place.

38. The passive suggests a situation similar to that of Job 1:12; 2:6.
39. Opening line of the *Heidelberg Catechism*'s answer to its first question: "What is your only comfort in life and in death?"

Appendix

A Brief Study of nwḥ/mnwḥh in Genesis

Introduction

IN HIS ESSAY ON the theme of rest from the enemy, Gerhard von Rad writes that although the deuteronomic literature often speaks of this rest "as something which was accomplished in the past . . . it is significant that in this great work the *beginning* of the divinely given rest is not uniformly represented, i.e. there is no single starting point for it."[1] Von Rad concludes that "the idea of 'rest' . . . is by its very nature firmly bound up with the Old Testament of the 'way.'[2] It is a message addressed to the whole human situation, viz., the hardship of human life and the problem of man's relationship to God." [3] These statements raise questions: Where is this "message" and this "problem of man's relationship to God" first defined?

When he discusses God's sabbath rest[4] in connection with the NT's (Heb 3–4) reception of Psalms 95 and 132, von Rad understands it as "a 'rest'

1. Von Rad, "There Remains Still a Rest," 96, emphasis added.

2. The noun *drk* is closely associated with *nwḥ* in Exod 33:14. Zehnder, *Wegmetaphorik*, 625–56, does not list *nwḥ* as a parallel to *drk*. But he lists *drk* as subject of the verb *nsᶜ* in Num 10:33 where *nwḥ* is its parallel (*Wegmetaphorik*, 632).

3. Rad, "There Remains Still a Rest," 101. Von Rad refers to "that massive historical work to which we apply the designation 'deuteronomic' (from *Genesis* to *II Kings*)" ("There Remains Still a Rest," 101). See also, Braulik, "Gottes Ruhe," 41–44.

4. Here von Rad cites Gen 2:2. The fourth commandment in Exod 20:11 and Deut. 5 use *nwḥ* with God and "your servants" as subject. Von Rad does not discuss the two traditions of rest (*nwḥ* and *šbt*) describe both God's and the servants' rest on the sabbath day, given that the former has the sense of rest from an obstacle, the enemy, in deuteronomic texts and the latter the rest of completion? Von Rad does not sort out the issues involved. See Westermann, *Genesis 1–11*, 173. Houtman, *Exodus*, 39–50, acknowledges the use of *nwḥ* in the fourth commandment, but provides no further comment. For a recent discussion of *šbt*, see Waschke, "Das Sabbatgebot und die Gottebenbildlichkeit

which has no immediate bearing whatever upon human life," unlike the no-tion of rest (*nwḥ*) which is "part of the promise of redemption."[5] That is, the Deuteronomist view of *nwḥ* is redemptive, it looks forward to the end of the journey towards this redemption, "the altogether tangible peace granted to a nation plagued by enemies and weary of wandering."[6] But Israel's wandering begins with Abraham's abandoning of Ur upon divine instruction, its post-Egypt encounter of enemies is only another phase of the patriarchal journey to the land. That being the case, who is the pre-exodus enemy from whom God seeks to grant his people this "altogether tangible peace," that is, "rest"? And, what is this pre-rest state? Is restlessness the normal state of human affairs to which the God of Israel brings order, redemption, for his people? Is restlessness an intrusion into an orderly state of affairs? Does the Primary History's (PH) account of the beginning depict humanity at rest alongside God's *šbt* rest, or is human rest something different?

Scholarship continues to think of rest (*nwḥ*) from the enemy as a Deuteronomistic theme located in Deuteronomy 3:20; 12:10; 25:19 and Joshua 1:13, 15; 21:44; 22:4; 23:1.[7] From the point of view of the larger historical work in its received shape, however, the theme of rest does not begin in Deuteronomy. Moses warns the second generation of the conse-quences of disobedience: "Among those nations you shall find no ease, no resting place (*mnwḥ*) for your feet (*lkp rglk*)" (Deut 28:65 NRSV), a conse-quence which echoes the restlessness of Noah's dove: "But the dove found no place (*mnwḥ*) to set its foot (*lkp rglh*), and it returned to him to the ark, for the waters were still on the face of the whole earth." (Gen 8:9 NRSV) Both exile from the land as depicted in Deuteronomy 28, and the creatures without the ark, lack rest or security: the waters of chaos threaten the one and the tumult of nations the other. The last chapters of the PH depict the reality of Deuteronomy 28:65: among the nations the rest received in God's temple presence is no longer available. They also evoke the exile from the garden-presence of God, a garden where God placed the man restfully (*nwḥ*, Gen 2:15). East of Eden and east of the land of promise, rest from the enemy seems impossible (Lam 1:3), but worth fighting for, as

---

des Menschen," 13–24.

5. Von Rad, "There Remains Still a Rest," 101.

6. Von Rad, "There Remains Still a Rest," 95. This is the basic sense of the noun according to Hulst, "De betekenis van het woord *menūḥā*," 63, 65.

7. Roth, "The Deuteronomic Rest Theology," 7. Roth argues for two Deuterono-mists: the first characterized by the phrase "from the enemy," (DtrG); this is a landed rest; the second "rest for obedience," (DtrN), a rest possible wherever and whenever Israel turns to the Lord. Nelson, *Joshua*, 31; Laansma, *The Rest Motif in the New Testa-ment*, 18–22, limits his study of the OT theme of rest to the Deuteronomistic tradition.

did Esther and Mordecai. In the meantime, a certain restlessness (*n^c wnd*, Gen 4:12, 14) obtains among Adam and Eve's descendants. This hoped for rest among the nations coincides with von Rad's understanding that rest from the enemy is "an eschatological expectation, . . . an entering into that rest which there has always been, from the beginning, with God."[8] If the Enneateuch in its received form begins and ends with depictions of serious restlessness, is it the case that waiting for the eschatological rest is a theme that shapes not only the DH and the Hexateuch, but also the Enneateuch or PH?

From the point of view of the PH, Genesis responds to the first two questions above when it depicts the "problem of man's relationship to God" in its opening chapters, and locates the beginning of that journey which ends in rest from the enemy in Genesis 12:1–4, in the context of Genesis 2:4—11:26. That the journey towards rest begins with Israel's ancestor Abraham is not disputed; that the theme of rest (*nwḥ*) begins its narrative journey in Genesis requires comment. It is noteworthy, therefore, that *nwḥ/mnwḥh* in Genesis 2:15; 8:4, 9; 8:21;[9] 19:16; 39:16; 42:33; 49:15, five of which occurrences are usually translated as "to place" or "to set down," or "to be left."

Translating *nwḥ* in Genesis 2:15

Lexical studies define the basic meaning *nwḥ* as "the idea of roosting or landing upon," or, "for the most part, in reference to both bodily and psychic states of rest."[10] According to Stolz, "the two chief meanings of the qal 'to rest' and 'to settle down' correspond to two formally distinct forms in the hiphil (and hophal): hiphil I, 'to cause to rest' and hiphil II, 'to lay down"; the nominal derivatives *mnwḥ* and *mnwḥh*, "resting places."[11]

Genesis utilizes forms of *nwḥ* seven times 2:15 [hiphil II II]; 8:4 [qal], 9 (*mnwḥ*); 19:16 [hiphil II]; 39:16 [hiphil II]; 42:33 [hiphil II]; 49:15 (*mnwḥ*). In their contexts the various translations make sense: 2:15, "put" (NRSV, NIV, NOAB), "placed" (JPS); 8:4, "rest" (NRSV), "came to rest" (JPS, NIV, NOAB); 8:9, "no place to set its foot" (NRSV, NIV, NOAB), "not find a resting place" (JPS); 19:16, "left him outside the city" (NRSV, JPS, NOAB), "led them safely outside the city" (NIV); 39:16, "she kept" (NRSV, NOAB, NIV, JPS); 42:33,

8. Von Rad, "There Remains Still a Rest," 97, 101–102.

9. "Gott roch der Geruch der *Beruhigung*," Dillmann, *Die Genesis*, 149 (emphasis added); and, "soothing sacrifices" have a "restful (*nwḥ*) soothing," Wenham, *Genesis 1–15*, 189.

10. Oswalt, "*nwḥ*," 56–9; Stolz, "*nwḥ*," 722–24.

11. Stolz, "*nwḥ*," 722.

"leave one of your brothers" (JPS, NRSV, NIV); 49:15, "resting place" (NRSV, NOAB, NIV), "security" (JPS). These translations also suggest that the root idea of "rest" or "security" shapes the understanding of 8:4 and 49:15 (realized sense) and 8:9 and 19:16 (not realized); in its context the use *nwḥ* in 39:16 suggests insecurity, and 42:33 the security of a hostage.

Applied to Genesis 2:15, the root idea of "rest" would suggest that God's "placing" or "putting" the man secures him in a uniquely designed space, the Garden. Similarly, Genesis 49:15 speaks of a secure place (*mnwḥ*), but now with reference to Abraham's descendants in the land of promise. It is to these texts we now turn.

The Verb *nwḥ* in Genesis 2:15

The verb *nwḥ* first appears in a nuanced resumptive repetition of the phrase "he put (*śym*) the man" in Genesis 2:8, after an insertion which describes the garden.[12] According to Jürgen Ebach, by using *nwḥ* in Genesis 2:15 and not repeating the expected verb *śym* the narrative transforms the action as follows: "Immediately before any word about humanity's role, the text describes God's placement of humanity with a word whose root meaning is 'rest. . . . which means 'to bring into a position of rest, to put down, to leave at rest, to lower.'"[13] That is, although the common translation "to place" or "to put" is not in itself incorrect, the shift from *śym* to *nwḥ* characterizes this placing in some sense as restful: The man is not merely placed in the garden, but restfully placed. This character and location of *nwḥ* continues Ebach, "does not mean that humanity is destined to rest, but that God's creation is complete, that a particular *Lebensraum* has been fully prepared for humanity."[14] This first use of *nwḥ* in Genesis, and thus the PH, is not about rest from fatigue, but denotes God's restfully placing *nwḥ* humanity in the divine presence, a secure and fertile space. That is, the Garden itself is a place where such restfulness obtains; it is divinely secured, restful place,[15] man's normal place of embodied being.

12. Noted by Westermann, *Genesis 1–11*, 219–20, but 2:15 is another voice from that of 2:8. No comment on *nwḥ*; and, Wenham, *Genesis 1–15*, 67, translates *nwḥ* as "put," but acknowledges the root meaning as "rest"; Croatto, *Crear y Amar en Libertad*, 71, provides the translation "placed at rest," without further comment.

13. Ebach, "Arbeit und Ruhe," 93–94. Translation mine. See also Stolz, "*nwḥ*," 17.

14. Ebach uses *Heimat* to describe humanity's being "rested" in this Garden presence: Ebach, "Arbeit und Ruhe," 94; so also, Waschke, "Zum Verhätnis von Ruhe und Arbeit," 75. This and subsequent translations mine. The sense of completion Ebach attributes to *nwḥ* is also the sense of *šbt*, but here in the sense of completing work.

15 Ebach, "Über 'Freiheit' und 'Heimat'," 495–518.

Expulsion from this original resting place casts the man's descendants into a restless wandering (n^c *wnd*), Gen 4:12; l^3 *mṣ³h mnwḥ*, Lam. 1:3), an enforced drifting on the periphery during which humanity seeks rest in heaven's presence (Gen 11:1–9). It is an impossible quest because divinely placed cherubim guard (*šmr*, Gen 3:24) the entry-way. Genesis locates post-exilic humanity "east of Eden," where restless wandering is humanity's new normal way of being. The restlessness of dislocation also affects humanity's vocation.

From a Restful ^{c}*bd* and *šmr,* to a Restless ^{c}*bd* without *šmr*

After God restfully places the man in Eden he instructs humanity in its complementary, embodied vocation:[16] to ^{c}*bd* and *šmr* this restful *Lebensraum*. The verb ^{c}*bd*, also used in Genesis 2:5 and subsequently in 3:23; 4:2, 12, often has the sense of "cultivating," but can also have the religious sense of serving God, often with reference to the tabernacle (Num 3–4). Its partner *šmr* often means simply "to guard," or "to keep," but more commonly with respect to observing religious instruction.[17] Commenting on these verbs, Ebach paraphrases the divine instruction of Genesis 2:15 as follows:

> Secure the garden and protect it from ruin, but remain within the provided *Lebensraum*, maintain its boundaries! You are not required constantly to extend its boundaries; the product does not require constant growth. In short: Against increase of production, preserve and cultivate.[18]

Genesis 2:15, then, defines humanity by its restful placement (*nwḥ*) in a prepared space, indwelt by the divine, there to execute the divine instruction to realize its complementary task of ^{c}*bd* and *šmr*.[19] This is humanity's normal, because created, state of vocational being.

According to Ebach, expulsion from this divinely created resting place transforms humanity's complementary vocation,

16. Westermann, *Genesis 1–11*, 221, citing Benno Jacob.

17. Wenham, *Genesis 1–11*, 67.

18. Ebach, "Arbeit und Ruhe," 96. Ebach's discussion of *nwḥ* arises in the context of Greek classical thought that "Ruhe *statt* Arbeit bezeichnet das Ideal"; that work is the province of slaves and rest that of the elite. "Arbeit und Ruhe," 90. The Old Testament depicts humanity as a working being from the beginning: the phrase "to work the ground" (2:5, *l°bd ³t °dmh* and 3:23, *l°bd ³t ³dmh* [exiled humanity]) describes the work of expelled humanity, especially Cain (4:2, 12, *l°bd ³t ³dmh*). But this is not the way it was supposed to be.

19. So understood by Westermann and Wenham, but neither links it to *nwḥ*.

first with Adam, who, after being expelled from the Garden only does *ʿabad* while the *šomer*, the cherubim, separates him from his former orderly way of life; and then . . . with Cain, driven away even further: The *ʿobed* is not a *šomer*. Both cases experience similar consequences. Humanity, driven from the Garden, must now work under pain and affliction, against an unruly and contrary nature; Cain, who killed his brother, now lives without brothers, a restless runaway.[20]

Exiled from its resting place humanity begins to wander restlessly (Gen. 4:12). In its new way of being humanity's vocation is reduced to *ʿbd* but now supplemented by an alien element in parasitic symbiosis. East of Eden, humanity's *ʿbd* is complicated by *ʿṣbwn*: Eve in her way (Gen 3:16, including the noun *ʿṣb*), and Adam in his (3:17). It is hoped that Noah will bring relief or rest from this "painful toil" (Gen 5:29).[21] Such a relief would require the end of painful toil and a re-joining of *šmr* and *ʿbd*, but even Noah's compliance with God's instructions is described with *ʿśh* not *šmr* (Gen 6:22; 7:5). And, although the ark continues to provide security when it rests on Ararat (*nwḥ*, 8:4), there is no resting place for God's post-diluvian creatures (*mnwḥ*, 8:9) on the earth. Even the rest evoked by Jacob's blessing on Issachar (*mnwḥ*, 49:15) is understood in the context of painful toil (*lms ʿbd*, Gen 49:15).

After the verb *šmr* is torn from *ʿbd* and left to the cherubim to perform, it[22] does not appear again in Genesis until God instructs Abraham "you must keep my covenant, . . . the covenant you are to keep" (17:9, 10). Later, just before the destruction of Sodom and Gomorrah, God muses: "For I have chosen [Abraham] . . . to keep the way[23] of the Lord by doing right

20. Ebach, "Arbeit und Ruhe," 95.

21. MT: *ynḥmnw*. The Greek reads *ynḥnw*, which provides a better explanation of the name Noah, especially in the context of painful toil which describes the loss of *nwḥ*. Contra Westermann, *Genesis 1–11*, 360, who finds the reference to Gen 3:16–17 awkward. The verb *ynḥmnw* need not be emended, for it rhymes with the following *mmśnw*. Consonants within the verb echo the notion of rest provided by the name Noah. So Wenham, *Genesis 1–15*, 128. "The importance of this event is emphasized . . . by a pun on the verb *nûaḥ*, 'rest,' which is the root of Noah's name." Rad, *Genesis*, 128. In the light of the text's use of *nwḥ* and *ʿṣbwn*. Antonioz ("Noé ou le repos du guerrier," 185–199) argues for a proto-midrashic technique for understanding the name Noah, especially against the background of mythological ANE sources. Understanding Noah as a warrior resting from combat, especially in his vineyard, is not convincing.

22. Cain's refusal to be his brother's keeper (*šmr*, Gen 4:9) illustrates humanity's refusal to keep the law of brotherly love (Lev 19:18). Cain's analogue Esau expresses the same desire (*wᵉhrgh ᵓt yᶜqb*, 27:41), but the younger brother averts this tragedy. Because a human is the object of *šmr*, Swenson, "Care and Keeping East of Eden," 378, argues it underscores Cain's unique position in the opening depiction of humanity East of Eden.

23. This is also the first appearance of the noun "way" East of Eden (cf. *drk* in Gen

and just" (Gen 18:19). Abraham is the first to be depicted on the way to a restoration of humanity's complementary vocation by reuniting *šmr* to its east-of-Eden *ᶜbd*,[24] a painful toil that includes servitude to others (Gen 14:4; 15:14; Jacob: 29:18, 20, 25, 27, 30; 30:26bis; 29; 31:6, 41; Esau: 27:40; the Lord's speech to Rebekah, 25:23; Isaac's blessing of Jacob, 27:29; and Jacob's blessing on Issachar, 49:15).

Von Rad's "problem of man's relationship to God," and "the beginning of restlessness," can be located in the narrative depiction of humanity's exile from the place where the Creator "rested" or "placed" the man (Gen 2:15), especially Cain's restless wandering. Humanity's subsequent restlessness begins to be addressed when Abraham and Sarah abandon their "east of Eden" location to begin their journey to the land Genesis later characterizes by *mnwḥ* in Jacob's blessing of Issachar (Gen 49:15).

The Noun *mnwḥ* in Genesis 49:15

At the narrative time of Jacob's blessing, Abraham's journey (*drk*, Gen 18:19) towards the land is generations long. In Egypt his descendant Jacob blesses his sons with a view to their being in the land of promise. Genesis 49 has proleptic force,[25] but it also recalls past narrative events. Wenham, for example, points to the following: the order of the blessings are roughly the same as their order of birth; Jacob's condemnation of Reuben, Simeon and Levi; and only Reuben, Simeon, Judah and Joseph have their names explained at birth by reference to the divine name.[26] To these should be added the words and phrases in Genesis 49:15 which recall earlier chapters: *ky ṭwb* (cf. Gen 1:4, 7, 12, 16, 21, 25, 27; 3:6); *mnwḥ* for the second time in Genesis (cf. 8:9)

3:24), and in conjunction with the verb *šmr*.

24. This unification is massively described in Exodus-Deuteronomy where Abraham's descendants are instructed to *šmr* in Exod 19:5; 34:11 and Lev 19:19, 30. In Deuteronomy Moses instructs Israel to be careful (*šmr*) not to *ᶜbd* the other gods by destroying their altars and to offer sacrifices only at the place the Lord himself chooses (12:13–14, the initial clause begins with *hšmr*). Doing this will bring Israel into its promised *nwḥ/mnwḥh* (Deut 12:9–10). Forms of *ᶜbd* occur twice in Deut. 12:2, 30; *šmr* five times (12:1, 32 [*yqtl*]; 13, 19, 30 [imv]). The placement of these verbs in vv. 1and 2, 30 and 32 forms an inclusion to this unit with *nwḥ/mnwḥh*, closely associated with the place of divine presence, located almost in the middle. Deut 28:64's speech about rest (28:65) also links *ᶜbd* and *šmr* (28:58, 64). By the end of the PH, Israel finds itself exiled from the presence of God for failure to *ᶜbd* and *šmr* (*šmr*, 2 Kgs 17, 37; 21:8; *ᶜbd*, 2 Kgs 17:12, 16; 21:3, 21).

25. *bᵊḥryt hymym*, Gen 49:1b. Watts, *Psalm and Story*, 70, 171. Of Watts' two synchronic criteria in his study of inset hymns, participation in plot and the sharing of vocabulary with the narrative (*Psalm and Story*, 17), Gen 49:1–28 clearly fits the second.

26. Wenham, *Genesis 16–50*, 468.

in concert with ᶜbd (cf. Gen 2:15, etc.); hᵓrṣ, evoking "the land which I will show you" (12:1, ᵓrᵓk).

> **a** When he saw (rᵓh) how good (ky ṭwb) was security (mnwḥ),
> **b** And how pleasant was the country (hᵓrṣ),
> **c** He bent his shoulder to the burden (lsbl),
> **d** And became a toiling serf (lms ᶜbd). (Gen 49:15, JPS)

By repeating crucial vocabulary from Genesis 1–12, Gen 49:15ab creates a link that recalls the beginning; the vocabulary in 49:15cd anticipates the subsequent enunciation of the theme nwḥ/mnwḥ in Exodus (33:14), Numbers (10:32, 36), Deuteronomy (3:20, 10:12; 25:19; 28:65) and beyond (e.g., Josh 1:13, 15; 21:44; 1 Kgs 8:56).

The theme nwḥ/mnwḥ in Genesis 49:15 is notable for several reasons. First, by parallelism the text links mnwḥ with a particular place, hᵓrṣ, the land promised to Abraham and his descendants. Second, it describes this "landed rest" as good (ky ṭwb), thereby recalling the creation narrative of Genesis 1 and the temptation scene in which Eve sees the prohibited tree and sees that it is good (wtrᵓ hᵓšh ky ṭwb hᶜṣ, Gen 3:6; wyrᵓ mnwḥ ky ṭwb, Gen 49:15). Third, the phrase lms ᶜbd is the last time Genesis uses a form of ᶜbd and the first time in connection with nwḥ/mnwḥh after Genesis 2:15. Below follows a brief comment on each.

Genesis 49:15ab, mnwḥ and hᵓrs.

Issachar's entering its mnwḥ seems to depict the end of the journey begun by the nations and Abraham. But what was impossible in the post-diluvian world (Gen 8:9) now describes a potential reality among Abraham's descendant Issachar. This is not so because humanity finally found its way past the cherubim into the Garden presence, but because God led Abraham's descendants to the land and gave it rest (Josh 21:44), also according to the Dtr tradition (Deut 12:9–10). When rest and the divinely gifted land come together, they depict a place unlike any other in all the earth, unlike any of the places where east of Eden humanity had always lived. East of Eden each nation possessed land, defined that land in terms of long settlement and history, and of the blood, sweat and tears of the ancestors that soaked the soil. In other words, a land "where we've always lived." But Abraham's descendants do not have such a place; beginning with Abraham they no longer own land east of Eden. Writes Ebach:

> As Heimat, mnwḥh is that land into which one will enter and
> has entered, never that land in which one always lived, settling

speaks to the end of the journey, . . . *mnwḥh* is not the result of human action. To the contrary, it is and remains God's gift (*ntn*). Humanity cannot restore this *mnwḥh*, only find it; it cannot possess it, only enter it, be in it.[27]

Although this is the nature of *Heimat* and properly the end of restlessness, a question remains: What does it mean that Issachar sees (*rʾh*) this good and secure land?

Genesis 49:15a, *mnwḥ rʾh* and *ky ṭwb*.

Not only do land and rest come together in Genesis 49:15, this landed rest is modified by the approval phrase *wyrʾ* . . . *ky ṭwb*, problematic because it modifies the feminine noun *mnwḥ* and thus should read *ky ṭwbh*. Following Westermann, Ebach argues for a formulaic use of the approval phrase, which thereby evokes Genesis 1 and 3 exactly. [28] Genesis 49:15's evocation of Genesis 1 in the context of *mnwḥ* and land argues for understanding the Promised Land as a place as special as that which God brought into being in Genesis 1. The *wyrʾ* . . . *ky ṭwb* of Genesis 3, however, links the land to the Garden in the context of Eve's seeing the forbidden fruit, precursor to humanity's exile from its resting place and the severing of *šmr* from *ʿbd*.[29] Thus, *wyrʾ* . . . *ky ṭwb* is used in a positive and a negative sense of viewing an object.

Like Eve's seeing the tree that led to a severing of *ʿbd* from *šmr*, so Issachar's seeing the good and secure land leads textually to the depiction of his becoming a toiling serf (*lms ʿbd*, JPS). Bringing Genesis 1 and 3 together Ebach writes:

> The "approval formula" *wyrʾ*. . . *ky ṭwb* in Genesis 1 depicts the completion of work. Read from the point of view of Genesis 1, Issachar's *wyrʾ*. . . *ky ṭwb* includes a twofold change: one of the subject and one of time. That is, Issachar, as if he were God, decides his journey has come to an end; he approves, as if he were God, a too early and because of that a too costly bought *menuḥah*.
>
> For Issachar *menuḥah* and *ʾrṣ nʾmh* become objects of greed; that is how the relationship to Gen 3:6 must be understood. The woman in the Garden of Eden also sees what is "good" in her eyes and grasps it without thinking of the consequences. With

27. Ebach, "Über 'Freiheit' und 'Heimat,'" 507–8.

28. Ebach, "Über 'Freiheit' und 'Heimat,'" 501.

29. As did Lot: *wyrʾ ʾt-kl-kkr-hyrdn ky klh mšqh . . . kgn yhwh kʾrṣ mṣrym* (Gen 13:10).

the forfeiture of a theonomically grounded freedom, "autonomous" decisions come to an end in Gen 49:14f and Gen 3.[30]

Jacob's blessing depicts Issachar as receiving landed rest, but only at the terrible cost of becoming a toiling serf. At the end of a journey he himself defined, Issachar still awaits the rest that remains.

Genesis 49:15ad, *mnwḥ* and *lms ᶜbd*

The translations of *lms ᶜbd* —"toiling serf" (JPS), "willing serf,"[31] "labouring drudge,"[32] "forced labor,"[33] "forced to toil as a slave,"[34]—all depict Issachar negatively: in "a shameful reversal of the normal relations between Israel and the Canaanites (Josh 16:10, 17:13 [=Judg 1:28], Ju. 1:30, 33, 35)," according to Skinner.[35] Joel D. Heck contests this majority translation by suggesting "a laborer who tills." This translation would understand 49:14–15 in the same positive terms as the surrounding verses and include these verses among other positive animal comparisons. LXX's understanding of *ᶜbd* as tilling also supports it. Furthermore, the noun *ms* is likely an Egyptian verb understood to mean "bringing an offering, bringing taxes, dragging prisoners, . . . certainly not a technical phrase for slave labor, but its use in certain contexts to refer to dragging prisoners lends itself well to a later technical meaning in the OT."[36]

Vocabulary in 49:15c, however, places Issachar's activity in a negative light. The infinitive *lsbl*, "to [shoulder] the burden," anticipates *sblh* in Exodus (1:11; 2:11; 5:4, 5; 6:6, 7) burdens which were part of Israel's enforced vassalage as depicted by the *ᶜbd/ᶜbdh* complex. And while it is true that *ᶜbd* can mean "to till," and has that meaning in Gen 2:15 and 4:2, by Gen 4:12 it has the negative meaning, to be in the service of another, it has elsewhere

30. Ebach, "Über 'Freiheit' und 'Heimat'," 504.

31. Speiser, *Genesis*, 362.

32. Skinner, *Genesis*, 525.

33. Westermann, *Genesis 37–50*, 218.

34. Wenham, *Genesis 16–50*, 454.

35. Skinner, *Genesis*, 526.

36. Heck, 394–396. Heck does not provide evidence of a "later technical meaning in the OT." By "later" he can only mean "in the subsequent narrative," such as Josh 16:10 and 1 Kgs 5:27. Heck's appreciation for Egypt as the narrative location of Jacob's blessing seems to be convincing of its "early" Egyptian understanding when he says, "What is more natural than for Jacob, a resident of Egypt at the time these words were spoken, to make use of a native word to convey the idea he has in mind?" ("Issachar: Slave or Freeman?", 395).

in Genesis. Within Genesis, then, the participle ᶜbd can hardly have a positive character, especially when at the outset it is separated from its normal partner šmr. With that in mind, translating the noun sm negatively makes sense. Jacob's blessing of Issachar describes his future with words closely associated with Israel's enforced vassalage in Egypt. Thus, his resting place is anything but the expected end of the journey. To the contrary, the use of lms ᶜbd here is similar to the Israelite foremen describing themselves to Pharaoh as "your vassals"; Issachar's rest is no better than Israel's "surrendered" servitude (Exod 5:15, 16 [ᶜbdyk], cf. 6:9; 16:3).

For the sake of what is good in his own eyes, Issachar defines the end of the journey himself: he has become a willing slave to others. By the end of the PH Israel's kings have become unwilling vassals (2 Kgs 17:3; 24:1), having neglected to comply (šmr, Deut 28:58) with divine instruction.

Conclusion to mnwḥ/nwḥh in Genesis

Von Rad's "problem of man's relationship to God," and the resultant restlessness begins to be addressed with the journey of Abraham toward the land understood to be the resting place (mnwḥ) in Gen 49:15 (cf. 8:9), Deut 12:9 (cf. 28:65) and 1 Kgs 8:56. From PH's point of view of the PH this suggests that the theme of rest, so clearly enunciated in Deuteronomy and developed subsequently in Joshua–Kings, is anchored in the narrative problem defined in the opening chapters of Genesis.

Jacob's blessing on Issachar is suggestive of the narrative problem: his arrival in the land is not restful because humanity's painful toil—the ᶜbd that is not yet united to šmr—has not been resolved. Beginning with Exodus, the relationship between these two verbs takes on a major role: Israel must keep (šmr) the instructions of Sinai and not serve (ᶜbd) other gods (Exod 23:20–33, esp. 20–21, 24–25, 33).[37] At the conclusion of Exodus, Abraham and Sarah's descendants, like Adam and Eve, find themselves in the close presence of God (Exod 40:34–38; cf. Gen 1:31; 2:1–3 and Exod 39:42–43). This generation and the descendants of the second generation in the land, defined in Numbers 26–35 and Deuteronomy, will refuse divine instruction and ultimately be expelled from God's presence in the land.

---

37. In what may evoke Gen 3:24, Israel must heed (šmr) the angel's voice in the way (drk) to the place God has set apart for it (Exod 23:20–21).

Bibliography

Albertz, Rainer. "Religionsgeschichte Israels statt Theologie des Alten Testaments: Plädoyer für eine forschungsgeschichtliche Umorientierung." *Jahrbuch für Biblische Theologie* 10 (2001) 3–24.

Alter, Robert. *The Art of Biblical Narrative.* New York: Basic, 1981.

———. *The Art of Biblical Poetry.* New York: Basic, 1985.

Anderson, Gary A. "Apophatic Theology: The Transcendence of God and the Story of Nadab and Abihu." In *Christian Doctrine and the Old Testament: Theology in the Service of Biblical Exegesis,* 3–22. Grand Rapids: Baker Academic, 2017.

———. "Creation: *Creatio ex nihilo* and the Bible." In *Christian Doctrine and the Old Testament: Theology in the Service of Biblical Exegesis,* 41–58. Grand Rapids: Baker Academic, 2017.

Antonioz, Stéphanie. "Noé ou le repos du guerrier." *Revue Biblique* 117 (2010) 185–199.

Attridge, Harold W. "How Priestly Is the 'High Priestly Prayer' of John 17?" *CBQ* 75 (2013) 1–14.

Auzou, Georges. *De la servitude au service: Étude du livre de L'Exode.* Connaissance de la Bible 3. Paris: L'Orant, 1961.

Bach, Alice, ed. *The Pleasure of Her Text: Feminist Readings of Biblical and Historical Texts.* Philadelphia: Trinity, 1990.

Baker, David L. *Two Testaments, One Bible: A Study of the Theological Relationship between the Old & New Testaments.* Downers Grove, IL: InterVarsity, 1991.

Bavinck, Herman. *Reformed Dogmatics: Abridged in One Volume.* Edited by John Bolt. Grand Rapids: Baker Academic, 2011.

Beasley-Murray, George R. *John.* WBC 36. Waco, TX: Word, 1991.

Beattie, D. R. G. *Jewish Exegesis of the Book of Ruth.* JSOTSup 2. Sheffield: JSOT, 1977.

Bolsinger, Tod. *Canoeing the Mountains: Christian Leadership in Uncharted Territory.* Downers Grove, IL: InterVarsity, 2015.

Brandt, Richard B. "Hedonism." In *The Encyclopedia of Philosophy,* edited by Paul Edwards, 3:432–35. New York: Macmillan, 1967.

Braulik, Georg. "Gottes Ruhe: Das Land oder der Temple? Zu Psalm 95,11." In *Freude an der Weisung des Herrn: Beiträge zur Theologie der Psalmen. Festgabe zum 70. Geburtstag von Heinrich Gross,* edited by Ernst Haas and Frank-Lothar Hossfeld, 41–44. Stuttgarter biblische Beiträge 13. Stuttgart: Katholisches Bibelwerk, 1986.

Brenner, Athalya, ed. *A Feminist Companion to Ruth.* Feminist Companion to the Bible 3. Sheffield: Sheffield Academic, 1993.

————, ed. *A Feminist Companion to Samuel and Kings.* Feminist Companion to the Bible 5. Sheffield: Sheffield Academic, 1994.

————, ed. *Ruth and Esther.* Feminist Companion to the Bible 2/3. Sheffield: Sheffield Academic, 1999.

Brenner, Athalyah, and Gale A. Yee, eds. *Joshua and Judges.* Texts @ Contexts. Minneapolis: Fortress, 2013.

Bright, John. *The Authority of the Old Testament.* Grand Rapids: Baker, 1975.

Brown, Raymond E. *The Gospel according to John XIII–XXI.* AB 29A. Garden City, NY: Doubleday, 1970.

Brueggemann, Walter. *The Land.* Overtures to Biblical Theology. Philadelphia: Fortress, 1977.

Butler, Trent C. *Joshua 1–12.* 2nd ed. WBC 14A. Grand Rapids: Zondervan, 2014.

————. *Judges.* WBC 9. Nashville: Nelson, 2009.

Calvin, John. *Institutes of the Christian Religion.* Library of Christian Classics 20. Translated by Ford Lewis Battles. Edited by John T. McNeil. Philadelphia: Westminster, 1960.

Carruthers, Charlene A. *Unapologetic: A Black, Queer, and Feminist Mandate for Radical Movements.* Boston: Beacon, 2018.

Cather, Willa. *O Pioneers!* (E-book). New York: Bantam Classics, 2008.

Cazelles, Henri. "ʾśry." In *TDOT* 1:445–448.

Childs, Brevard S. *Biblical Theology in Crisis.* Philadelphia: Westminster, 1970.

————. *The Book of Exodus: A Critical, Theological Commentary.* OTL. Philadelphia: Westminster, 1974.

————. *Introduction to the Old Testament as Scripture.* Philadelphia: Fortress, 1979.

————. *Old Testament Theology in a Canonical Context.* Philadelphia: Fortress, 1985.

Christ, Carol P. *The Laughter of Aphrodite: Reflections on a Journey to the Goddess.* San Francisco: HarperOne, 1987.

Classis Grand Rapids East. "Study Report on Same-Sex Marriage." Grand Rapids, 2016.

Clifford, Richard J. *Proverbs: A Commentary.* OTL. Louisville: West-minster John Knox, 1999.

Clines, David J. A. *The Bible and the Modern World.* Sheffield: Sheffield Academic, 1997.

————. *Ezra, Nehemiah, Esther.* New Century Biblical Commentary. Grand Rapids: Eerdmans, 1984.

————. *What Does Eve Do to Help? and Other Readerly Questions to the Old Testament.* JSOTSup 94. Sheffield: Sheffield Academic, 1990.

Coloe, Mary L. *God Dwells with Us: Temple Symbolism in the Fourth Gospel.* Collegeville, MN: Liturgical, 2001.

Cooper, John W. *Panentheism: The Other God of the Philosophers: From Plato to the Present.* Grand Rapids: Baker, 2006.

Crenshaw, James L. "Method in Determining Wisdom Influence upon 'Historical' Literature." *JBL* 88 (1969) 129–42.

Croatto, J. Severino. *Crear y Amar en Libertad: Estudio de Génesis 2:4—3:24.* Buenos Aires: Aurora, 1986.

————. *Exodus: A Hermeneutics of Freedom.* Translated by Salvator Attanasio. Maryknoll, NY: Orbis, 1978.

Cross, Frank M. "The Themes of the Book of Kings and the Structure of the Deuteronomistic History." In *Canaanite Myth and Hebrew Epic. Essays in the*

History of the Religion of Israel, 274–89. Cambridge: Harvard University Press, 1973.

Davis, Tamie S. "The Condemnation of Jephthah." *Tyndale Bulletin* 64 (2013) 1–16.

Day, John. "Whatever Happened to the Ark of the Covenant?" In *Temple and Worship in Biblical Israel*, edited by John Day, 250–70. Library of Hebrew Bible/Old Testament Studies 422. London: T. & T. Clark, 2005.

Dearman, J. Andrew, and Sabelyn A. Pussman. "Putting Ruth in Her Place: Some Observations on Canonical Ordering and the History of the Book's Interpretation." *Horizons in Biblical Theology* 27 (2005) 59–86.

dePury, A. et al., ed. *Israel Constructs Its History: Deuteronomistic Historiography in Recent Research*. JSOTSup 306. Sheffield: Sheffield Academic, 2000.

Dillard, Raymond B. *2 Chronicles*. WBC 25. Waco, TX: Word, 1987.

Dillmann, August. *Die Genesis*. 5th ed. Kurzgefasstes exegetisches Handbuch. Leipzig: Hirzel, 1886.

Dozeman, Thomas B. *Joshua 1–12*. Anchor Bible 6B. New Haven: Yale University Press, 2015.

Dozeman, Thomas B. et al., eds. *Pentateuch, Hexateuch or Enneateuch? Identifying Literary Works in Genesis through Kings*. Ancient Israel and Its Literature 8. Atlanta: SBL, 2011.

Driver, S. R. *An Introduction to the Literature of the Old Testament*. 1913. Reprint, Gloucester, MA: Smith, 1972.

Earl, Douglas S. *Reading Joshua as Christian Scripture*. Journal of Theological Interpretation Supplement 2. Winona Lake, IN: Eisenbrauns, 2010.

———. *Reading Old Testament Narrative as Christian Scripture*. Journal of Theological Interpretation Supplement 17. Winona Lake, IN: Eisenbrauns, 2017.

Ebach, Jürgen. "Arbeit und Ruhe: Eine utopische Errinerung." In *Ursprung und Ziel: Errinerte Zukunft und erhoffte Vergangenheit. Biblische Exegesen, Reflexionen, Geschichten*, 90–110. Neukirchen-Vluyn: Neukirchener, 1986.

———. "Über 'Freiheit' und 'Heimat': Aspekten und Tendenzen der *menûhâ*." In *Ernten, was man sät: Festschrift für Klaus Koch zu seinem 65. Geburtstag*, edited by Dwight R. Daniles et al., 495–518. Neukirchen-Vluyn: Neukirchener, 1991.

Exum, J. Cheryl. "On Judges 11." In *A Feminist Companion to Judges*, edited by Athalyah Brenner, 131–44. Feminist Companion to the Bible 4. Sheffield: Sheffield Academic, 1993.

Fishbane, Michael. *Biblical Interpretation in Ancient Israel*. Oxford: Clarendon, 1985.

———. "Israel and the 'Mothers.'" In *The Garments of Torah: Essays in Biblical Hermeneutics*, by Michael A. Fishbane, 49–63. Bloomington: Indiana University Press, 1992.

Fokkelman, Jan P. *Narrative Art in Genesis: Specimens of Stylistic and Structural Analysis*. Assen: Van Gorcum, 1975.

Franks, Angela. "DeLeuze on Desire." *First Things* (April 2010) 37–42.

Fretheim, Terence E. *Deuteronomic History*. Interpreting Biblical Texts. Nashville: Abingdon, 1983.

———. "'I was only a little angry': Divine Violence in the Prophets." *Int* 58 (2004) 365–75.

Fuchs, Esther. "Marginalization, Ambiguity, Silencing: The Story of Jephthah's Daughter." In *A Feminist Companion to Judges*, edited by Athalya Brenner, 116–30. Feminist Companion to the Bible 4. Sheffield: Sheffield Academic, 1993.

Gane, Roy. *God's Faulty Heroes*. Hagerstown, MD: Review & Herald, 1996

———. *Old Testament Law for Christians: Original Context and Enduring Application*. Grand Rapids: Baker Academic, 2017.

Gnuse, Robert. *Heilsgeschichte as a Model for Biblical Theology: The Debate Concerning the Uniqueness and Significance of Israel's Worldview*. College Theology Society Studies in Religion 4. Lanham, MD: University Press of America, 1989.

Goering, Greg Schmidt. "Honey and Wormwood: Taste and the Embodiment of Wisdom in the Book of Proverbs." *Hebrew Bible and Ancient Israel* 5 (2016) 23–41.

Goswell, Gregory. "What's in a Name? Book Titles in the Torah and the Former Prophets." *Pacifica* 20 (2007) 262–77.

Gottwald, Norman K. *Tribes of Yahweh: A Sociology of the Religion of Liberated Israel, 1250–1050 BCE*. Maryknoll, NY: Orbis, 1979.

Greif, Mark. *Essays against Everything*. New York: Vintage, 2017.

Hanson, K. C. "How Honorable! How Shameful! A Cultural Analysis of Matthew's Makarisms and Reproaches." *Semeia* 68 (1994[96]) 81–111.

Hawk, Daniel L. *Every Promise Fulfilled: Contesting Plots in Joshua*. Louisville: Westminster John Knox, 1991.

Heck, Joel D. "Issachar: Slave or Freeman? (Gen 49:14–15)." *Journal of the Evangelical Theological Society* 29 (1986) 385–96.

Henry, Matthew. *Matthew Henry's Commentary on the Whole Bible*. 6 vols. New York: Revell, n.d.

Holwerda, David E. *Jesus & Israel: One Covenant or Two?* Grand Rapids: Eerdmans, 1995.

Horowitz, Elliott. "Amalek: The Memory of Violence and the Violence of Memory." In *Reckless Rites: Purim and the Legacy of Jewish Violence*, 107–46. Jews, Christians, and Muslims from the Ancient to the Modern World. Princeton: Princeton University Press, 2006.

Houtman, Cornelis. *Exodus*. Translated by Sierd Woudstra. Historical Commentary on the Old Testament 3. Louvain: Peeters, 2000.

———. "Rewriting a Dramatic Old Testament Story: The Story of Jephthah and His Daughter in Some Examples of Christian Devotional Literature." *Biblical Interpretation* 13 (2005) 167–90.

Hubbard, Robert L., Jr. *The Book of Ruth*. New International Commentary on the Old Testament. Grand Rapids: Eerdmans, 1988.

Hulst, R. A. "De betekenis van het woord *menūḥā*." In *Schrift en Uitleg*, edited by Dirk S. Attema, 62–78. Kampen: Kok, 1970.

Hurowitz, Victor. *I Have Built You an Exalted House: Temple Building in the Bible in the Light of Mesopotamian and Northwest Semitic Writings*. JSOTSup 15. Sheffield: Sheffield Academic, 1992.

Hutton, Rodney R. *Charisma and Authority in Israelite Society*. Minneapolis: Fortress, 1994.

Jacob, Benno. *Exodus: The Second Book of the Bible*. Translated by Walter Jacob. Hoboken, NJ: Ktav, 1992.

Jaki, Stanley L. *Genesis 1: Through the Ages*. London: Thomas More, 1992.

James, Fleming. *Personalities of the Old Testament*. Hale Lectures, 1938. New York: Scribner, 1951.

Janowski, Bernd. "Ich will in Eurer Mitte wohnen: Struktur und Genese der exilischen Schekina-Theologie." *Jahrbuch für Biblische Theologie* 2 (1987) 165–93.

Jobling, David. "Ruth Finds a Home: Canon, Politics, Method." In *The New Literary Criticism and the Hebrew Bible*, edited by J. Cheryl Exum and David J. A. Clines, 125–39. JSOTSup 143. Sheffield: Sheffield Academic, 1993.

———. *1 Samuel: Studies in Hebrew Narrative & Poetry*. Berit Olam. Colleville, MN: Liturgical, 1998.

Josipovici, Gabriel. *The Book of God: A Response to the Bible*. New Haven: Yale University Press, 1988.

Keel, Othmar. *The Symbolism of the Biblical World: Ancient Near Eastern Iconography and the Book of Psalms*. Translated by Timothy J. Hallett. New York: Seabury, 1978.

Keel, Othmar, and Christoph Uehlinger. *Gods, Goddesses, and Images of God in Ancient Israel*. Translated by Thomas H. Trapp. Minneapolis: Fortress, 1998.

Keil, Carl F., and Franz Delitzsch. *Joshua, Judges, Ruth*. Translated by James Martin. Commentary on the Old Testament. 1868. Reprint, Grand Rapids: Eerdmans, 1971.

Kerr, Allan R. *The Temple of Jesus' Body: The Temple Theme in the Gospel of John*. Journal for the Study of the New Testament Supplement 220. Sheffield: Sheffield Academic, 2002.

Kittel, Rudolf. *Great Men and Movements in Israel*. Translated by Charlotte A. Knoch and C. D. Wright. Library of Biblical Studies. New York: Ktav, 1968.

Klein, Lillian. *The Triumph of Irony in the Book of Judges*. JSOTSup 68. Sheffield: Almond, 1988.

Knapp, Henry M. "Jephthah's Daughter in English Post-Reformation Exegesis." *Westminster Theological Journal* 80 (2018) 279–97.

Knierim, Rolf P. "On Gabler." In *The Task of Old Testament Theology: Method and Cases*, 495–56. Grand Rapids: Eerdmans, 1995.

Knoppers, Gary N. "Ancient Near Eastern Royal Grants and the Davidic Covenant: A Parallel?" *Journal of the American Oriental Society* 116 (1996) 670–97.

———. "Prayer and Propaganda: Solomon's Dedication of the Temple and the Deuteronomist's Program." *CBQ* 57 (1995) 229–54.

———. "'There Was None Like Him': Incomparability in the Books of Kings." *CBQ* 54 (1992) 411–31.

Laansma, John. *"I Will Give you Rest": The Rest Motif in the New Testament with Special Reference to Mt 11 and Heb 3–4*. Wissenschaftliche Untersuchungen zum Neuen Testament 2/98. Tübingen: Mohr/Siebeck, 1997.

Leder, Arie C. "Bound to the Altar: The Isaac of Genesis 22:1–19." *CTJ* 51 (2016) 283–96.

———. "Celebrating Relief from the Enemy: Discerning and Preaching Esther's Post-canonical Enemy." *CTJ* 50 (2015) 230–46.

———. "From the Mountain of YHWH to Israel's מנוחה: The Desert Itinerary of Numbers 10:11–36." *Old Testament Essays* 29 (2016) 513–34.

———. "Hearing Esther after Joshua: Rest in the Exile and the Diaspora." In *The Book of Joshua*, edited by Ed Noort, 267–79. Bibliotheca Ephemeridum theologicarum Lovaniensium 250. Louvain: Peeters, 2012.

———. "Presence, then the Covenants: An Essay on Narrative and Theological Precedence. Part One." *Nederduitse gereformeerde teologiese tydskrif* 53 (2012) 179–93. https://ngtt.journals.ac.za/pub/article/view/126.

———. *Waiting for the Land: The Storyline of the Pentateuch*. Phillipsburg, NJ: P & R, 2010.

———. "Who Builds the House of Israel?" *Revue Biblique* (2020), forthcoming.

Legaspi, Michael C. *The Death of Scripture and the Rise of Biblical Studies.* New York: Oxford University Press, 2010.

Levenson, John D. *Death and the Resurrection of the Beloved Son: The Transformation of Child Sacrifice in Judaism and Christianity.* New Haven: Yale University Press, 1993.

———. *Esther: A Commentary.* OTL. Louisville: Westminster John Knox, 1997.

———. *The Hebrew Bible, The Old Testament, and Historical Criticism.* Louisville: Westminster John Knox, 1993.

———. *Sinai & Zion: An Entry into the Jewish Bible.* San Francisco: Harper & Row, 1985.

Lohfink, Norbert. "*ḥrm.*" In *TDOT*, 5:180–99. 1986.

Lubac, Henri de. *Medieval Exegesis: The Four Senses of Scripture.* 2 vols. Grand Rapids: Eerdmans, 1998, 2000.

Mann, Thomas W. *The Book of the Former Prophets.* Eugene, OR: Cascade, 2011.

Marsden, George. *Understanding Fundamentalism and Evangelicalism.* Grand Rapids: Eerdmans, 1991.

Marshall, I. Howard. *Commentary on Luke.* New International Greek Testament Commentary. Grand Rapids: Eerdmans, 1978.

McConville, J. Gordon, and Stephen N. Williams. *Joshua.* Two Horizons Old Testament Commentary. Grand Rapids: Eerdmans, 2010.

McEntire, Mark. "Recent Books on Violence and the Bible: A Review Essay." *Perspectives in Religious Studies* 42 (2015) 319–24.

Meyers, Carol. *Rediscovering Eve: Ancient Israelite Women in Context.* New York: Oxford University Press, 2012.

Miller, Patrick M. "Cosmology and World Order in the Old Testament." *Horizons in Biblical Theology* 9 (1987) 53–78.

Milton, John. *English Minor Poems, Paradise Lost, Samson Agonistes, Areopagitica.* Edited by Robert Maynard Hutchins. Chicago: Encyclopeadia Britannica, 1952.

Moberly, R. W. L. *The Bible in a Disenchanted Age: The Enduring Possibility of Christian Faith.* Grand Rapids: Baker, 2018.

Moore, Stephen D., and Yvonne Sherwood. "Biblical Studies 'after' Theory: Onwards Towards the Past. Part Two: The Secret Vices of the Biblical God." *Biblical Interpretation* 18 (2010) 87–113.

Moses, John. *The Desert: An Anthology for Lent.* Harrisburg, PA: Morehouse, 1997.

Muilenburg, James. "Form Criticism and Beyond." *JBL* 88 (1969) 1–18.

Muller, Richard A. "The Study of Theology: From Biblical Interpretation to Contemporary Formulation." In *Foundations of Contemporary Interpretation*, edited by Moisés Silva, 539–664. Grand Rapids: Zondervan, 1996.

Nelson, Richard D. *The Double Redaction of the Deuteronomistic History.* JSOTSup 18. Sheffield JSOT, 1981.

———. *First and Second Kings.* Interpretation. Louisville: John Knox, 1987.

———. *The Historical Books.* Interpreting Biblical Texts. Nashville: Abingdon, 1998.

———. *Joshua.* Interpretation. Louisville: Westminster John Knox, 1997.

Nemet-Nejat, Karen Rhea. *Daily Life in Ancient Mesopotamia.* Peabody, MA: Hendrickson, 1998.

Noort, Ed. "Josua und Amalek: Exodus 17:8–16." In *The Interpretation of Exodus: Studies in Honour of Cornelis Houtman*, edited by Riemer Roukema, et al., 155–70. Contributions to Biblical Exegesis and Theology 44. Louvain: Peeters, 2006.

Noth, Martin. *The Deuteronomistic History*. JSOTSup 15. Sheffield: JSOT, 1981.

Oeming, Manfred. *Contemporary Biblical Hermeneutics: An Introduction*. Translated by Joachim Vette. Aldershot, UK: Ashgate, 2006.

Oswalt, John N. "Nwḥ." In *NIDOTT* 3:56–9.

Palmer, Richard E. *Hermeneutics: Interpretation Theory in Schleiermacher, Dilthey, Heidegger, and Gadamer*. Evanston, IL: Northwestern University Press, 1969.

Peacore, Linda D. "An Evangelical Feminist Perspective on Traditional Atonement Models." *Ex Auditu* 26 (2010) 145–63.

Perdue, Leo G. *Wisdom & Creation: The Theology of Wisdom Literature*. Nashville: Abingdon, 1994.

Plantinga, Alvin. "Two (or More) Kinds of Scripture Scholarship." In *Warranted Christian Belief*, 374–421. New York: Oxford University Press, 2000.

Prokes, Mary Timothy. *Toward a Theology of the Body*. Grand Rapids: Eerdmans, 1996.

Propp, William H. C. *Exodus 1–18*. AB 2. New York: Doubleday, 1999.

Provan, Iain, et al. "The Death of Biblical History?" In *A Biblical History of Israel*, 3–35. Louisville: Westminster John Knox, 2003.

Rad, Gerhard von. "The Deuteronomic Theology of History in I and II Kings." In *The Problem of the Hexateuch and Other Essays*, 205–21. Translated by E. W. Trueman Dicken, London: SCM, 1966.

———. "The Form-Critical Problem of the Hexateuch." In *The Problem of the Hexateauch and Other Essays*, 1–78. Translated by E. W. Trueman Dicken. London: SCM, 1966.

———. *Genesis: A Commentary*. Rev. ed. Translated by John H. Marks. OTL. Philadelphia: Westminster, 1972.

———. "There Remains Still a Rest for the People of God: An Investigation of a Biblical Conception." In *The Problem of the Hexateuch and Other Essays*, 94–102. Translated by E. W. Trueman Dicken. London: SCM, 1966.

———. *Wisdom in Israel*. Translated by James D. Martin. Nashville: Abingdon, 1972.

Radner, Ephraim. *A Profound Ignorance: Modern Pneumatology and its Anti-modern Redemption*. Waco, TX: Baylor University Press, 2019.

Rendtorff, Rolff. *The Canonical Hebrew Bible: A Theology of the Old Testament*. Translated by David E. Orton. Tools for Biblical Studies 7. Leiden: Deo, 2005.

———. "Die Hermeneutik einer kanonischen Theologie des Alten Testaments." In *Der Text in seiner Endgestalt: Schritte auf dem Weg zu einer Theologie des Alten Testaments*, 61–70. Neukirchen-Vluyn: Neukirchener, 2001.

Ridderbos, Herman. *The Coming of the Kingdom*. Translated by H. de Jongste. Edited by Raymond O. Zorn. Philadelphia: P&R, 1962.

———. *The Gospel according to John: A Theological Commentary*. Translated by John Vriend. Grand Rapids: Eerdmans, 1997.

Ritt, Hubert. *Das Gebet zum Vater: Zur Interpretation von Joh 17*. Forschung zur Bibel 36. Würzburg: Echter, 1979.

Roskop, Angela R. *The Wilderness Itineraries: Genre, Geography and the Growth of the Torah*. Winona Lake, IN: Eisenbrauns, 2011.

Roth, Wolfgang. "The Deuteronomic Rest Theology: A Redaction-Critical Study." *Biblical Research* 21 (1976) 5–14.

Russell, Jeffrey Burton. *Paradise Mislaid: How We Lost Heaven and How We Can Regain It*. Oxford: Oxford University Press, 2006.

Rutledge, Fleming. *The Crucifixion: Understanding the Death of Christ*. Grand Rapids: Eerdmans, 2015.

Sæbo, M. "*Ywm*." In *TDOT* 6:7–32.

Sakenfeld, Katharine Doob. *Ruth*. Interpretation. Louisville: John Knox, 1999.

———. "Whose Text Is It?" *JBL* 127 (2008) 5–18.

Satterthwaite, Philip E., and J. Gordon McConville. *Exploring the Old Testament: A Guide to Historical Books*. Downers Grove, IL: InterVarsity, 2007.

Selzer, Richard. *Mortal Lessons: Notes on the Art of Surgery*. San Diego: Harcourt Brace, 1987.

Senior, Donald, and Carroll Stuhlmueller. *The Biblical Foundations for Mission*. Maryknoll, NY: Orbis, 1984.

Sheppard, Gerald T. "Hearing the Voice of the Same God through Historically Dissimilar Traditions." *Int* 36 (1982) 21–33.

Silva, Moisés. "Has the Church Misread the Bible?" In *Foundations of Contemporary Interpretation*, edited by Moisés Silva, 15–87. Grand Rapids: Zondervan, 1996.

Skinner, John. *Genesis*. 2nd ed. International Critical Commentary. Edinburgh: T. & T. Clark, 1930.

Smart, James D. *The Strange Silence of the Bible in the Church: A Study in Hermeneutics*. Philadelphia: Westminster, 1970.

Smit, Laura A., and Stephen E. Fowl. *Judges & Ruth*. Brazos Theological Commentary on the Bible. Grand Rapids: Brazos, 2018.

Speiser, E. A. *Genesis*. AB 1. Garden City: Doubleday, 1964.

Steinmetz, David C. "John Calvin on Isaiah 6: A Problem in the History of Exegesis." *Int* 36 (1982) 156–70.

———. "The Superiority of Pre-Critical Exegesis." *Theology Today* 37 (1980) 27–38.

Stek, John H. "Rahab of Canaan and Israel." *CTJ* 37 (2002) 28–48.

Stendahl, Krister. "Biblical Theology, Contemporary." In *IDB*, 1:418–32.

Stolz, F. "*nwḥ*." In *TLOT* 2:722–24.

Sturcke, Henry. *Encountering the Rest of God: How Jesus Came to Personify the Sabbath*. TVZ Dissertationen. Zurich: TVZ, 2005.

Sugirtharajah, R. S. *Voices from the Margin: Interpreting the Bible in the Third World*. Maryknoll, NY: Orbis, 1991.

Swenson, Kristin M. "Care and Keeping East of Eden: Gen 4:1–16 in Light of Gen 2–3." *Int* 60 (2006) 373–84.

Talbot, Elizabeth. "Rest, Eschatology and Sabbath in Matthew 11:28–30: An Investigation of Jesus' Offer of Rest in the Light of the the Septeuagnit's Use of Anapausis." In *"What Does Scripture Say?": Studies in the Function of Scripture in Early Judaism and Christianity*. Vol. 1, *The Synoptic Gospels*, edited by Craig A. Evans and H. Daniel Zacharias, 57–69. Studies in Scripture in Early Judaism and Christianity 17. London: T. & T. Clark, 2012.

Thistleton, Anthony C. *New Horizons in Hermeneutics: The Theory and Practice of Transforming Biblical Reading*. Grand Rapids: Zondervan, 1992.

Thompson, John L. "Reading Sex and Violence." In *Reading the Bible with the Dead: What You Can Learn from the History of Exegesis That You Can't Learn from Exegesis Alone*, 185–214. Grand Rapids: Eerdmans, 2007.

———. "Sacrificing Jephthah's Daughter." In *Reading the Bible with the Dead: What You Can Learn from the History of Exegesis That You Can't Learn from Exegesis Alone*, 33–47. Grand Rapids: Eerdmans, 2007.

Tolbert, Mary Ann. "Protestant Feminists and the Bible: On the Horns of a Dilemma." In *The Pleasure of Her Text: Feminist Readings of Biblical and Historical Texts*, edited by Alice Bach, 5–32. Philadelphia: Trinity, 1991.

Treier, Daniel J. "The Superiority of Pre-Critical Exegesis? Sic et Non." *Trinity Journal* 24 NS (2003) 77–103.

Trible, Phyllis. *God and the Rhetoric of Sexuality*. Overtures to Biblical Theology. Philadelphia: Fortress, 1978.

———. *Texts of Terror: Literary-Feminist Readings of Biblical Narratives*. Overtures to Biblical Theology. Philadelphia: Fortress, 1984.

Tsumura, David Toshio. *The First Book of Samuel*. New International Commentary on the Old Testament. Grand Rapids: Eerdmans, 2007.

Van Dyk, Leanne. "Vision and Imagination in Atonement Doctrine." *Theology Today* 50 (1993) 4–12.

VanGemeren, Willem A. *The Progress of Redemption: The Story of Salvation from Creation to the New Jerusalem*. Grand Rapids: Academie Books, 1988.

———. *Interpreting the Prophetic Word*. Grand Rapids: Academie Books, 1990.

Van Reken, Calvin P. "Christians in This World: Pilgrims or Settlers?" *CTJ* 43 (2008) 234–56.

Vos, Geerhardus. *Biblical Theology: Old and New Testaments*. Grand Rapids: Eerdmans, 1983.

———. "The Idea of Biblical Theology as a Science and as a Theological Discipline." In *Redemptive History and Biblical Interpretation: The Shorter Writings of Geerhardus Vos*, edited by Richard B. Gaffin Jr., 3–24. Phillipsburg, NJ: P&R, 1980.

Walsh, Jerome T. *1 Kings*. Berit Olam. Collegeville, MN: Liturgical, 1996.

Walters, Stanley D. "Twain Heights: Spirit and Word in Biblical Prophesying." *Journal of Inductive Biblical Studies* 1 (2014) 60–79. DOI: 10.7252/JOURNAL.02.2014S.04

Warrior, Robert Allen. "A Native American Perspective: Canaanites, Cowboys, and Indians." In *Voices from the Margin: Interpreting the Bible in the Third World*, edited by R. S. Sugirtharajah, 287–95. Maryknoll, NY: Orbis, 1991.

Waschke, Ernst-Joachim. "Das Sabbatgebot und die Gottebenbildlichkeit des Menschen: Überlegungen zu zwei verschiedenen Traditionen." In *Mensch und König: Studien zur Anthropologie des Alten Testaments*, edited by Angelika Berlejung and R. Heckl, 13–24. Herders biblische Studien 53. Freiburg: Herder, 2008.

———. "Zum Verhältnis von Ruhe und Arbeit in den biblischen Schöpfungsgeschichten Genesis 1–3." In *"Gerechtigkeit und Recht zu üben" (Gen 18,19): Festschrift für Eckart Otto zum 65. Geburtstag*, edited by Reinhard Achenbach et al., 69–80. Wiesbaden: Harrasowitz, 2009.

Watson, Kevin. "Methodism Dividing." *First Things* (May 2020) 21–25.

Watts, James W. *Psalm and Story: Inset Hymns in Hebrew Narrative*. JSOTSup 39. Sheffield: JSOT Press, 1992.

Weaver, J. Denny. *God without Violence: Following a Nonviolent God in a Violent World*. Eugene, OR: Cascade, 2016.

Webb, Barry G. *The Book of Judges: An Integral Reading*. JSOTSup 46. Sheffield: Sheffield Academic, 1987.

———. "Judges as Christian Scripture." In *The Book of Judges*, by Barry G. Webb, 55–67. Grand Rapids: Eerdmans, 2012.

Wenham, Gordon J. *Genesis 1–15*. WBC 1. Waco: Word, 1987.

———. *Genesis 16–50*. WBC 2. Dallas: Word, 1994.

———. "Sanctuary Symbolism in the Garden of Eden Story." *Proceedings of the World Congress of Jewish Studies* 9 (1986) 19–25. Reprinted in *I Studies Inscriptions from before the Flood: Ancient Near Eastern, Literary, and Linguistic Approaches to Genesis 1–11*, edited by Richard S. Hess and David Toshio Tsumura, 399–404. Sources for Biblical and Theological Study 4. Winona Lake, IN: Eisenbrauns, 1994.

West, Gerald O. "Indigenous Exegesis: Exploring the Interface between Missionary Methods and the Rhetorical Rhythms of Africa." *Neotestamentica* 36 (2002) 147–62.

West, Gerald O., and Beverley G. Haddad. "Boaz as 'Sugar Daddy': Re-Reading Ruth in the Context of HIV." *Journal of Theology for Southern Africa* 155 (2016) 137–56.

Westermann, Claus. *Genesis 1–11*. Translated by John J. Scullion. Continental Commentaries. Minneapolis: Augsburg, 1984.

———. *Genesis 37–50*. Translated by John J. Scullion. Continental Commentaries. Minneapolis: Augsburg, 1986.

Wharton, James A. "Secret of Yahweh: Story and Affirmation in Judges 13–16." *Int* 27 (1973) 48–66.

Whitekettle, Richard. "Levitical Thought and the Female Reproductive Cycle: Wombs, Wellsprings, and the Primeval World." *Vetus Testamentum* 46 (1996) 376–91.

———. "Leviticus 15.18 Reconsidered: Chiasm, Spatial Structure and the Body." *Journal for the Study of the Old Testament* 49 (1991) 31–45.

Wolfenson, L. B. "Implications of the Place of the Book of Ruth in Editions, Manuscripts, and Canon of the Old Testament." *Hebrew Union College Annual* 1 (1924) 151–78.

Wolff Hans Walter. "The Kerygma of the Deuteronomic Historical Work." In *The Vitality of Old Testament Traditions*, edited by Walter Brueggemann and Hans Walter Wolff, 89–99. Atlanta: John Knox, 1984.

Yee, Gale A. "Thinking Intersectionally: Gender, Race, Class, and the Etceteras of Our Discipline." *JBL* 139 (2020) 3–26.

Zehnder, Markus Philipp. *Wegmetaphorik im Alten Testament: Eine semantische Untersuchung der alttestamentlichen und altorientalischen Weg-Lexeme mit besonderer Berücksichtigung ihrer metaphorischen Verwendung*. Beihefte zur Zeitschrift für die alttestamentliche Wissenschaft 268. Berlin: Walter de Gruyter, 1999.

Zenger, Erich, et al. *Einleitung in das Alte Testament*. 6th ed. Kohlhammer Studienbücher Theologie 1/1. Stuttgart: Kohlhammer, 2006.

Author Index

Subject Index

Scripture Index

Genesis

1–11	168
1:1—2:3	20, 35, 82
1:4	25, 27, 89
1:7	25, 27, 89
1:16	25, 27, 89
1:21	25, 27, 89
1:28	23, 112
1:26–28	36
1:30	171
2–3	109
2:4—11:26	38, 185
2:4—4:26	20
2:4—3:24	9
2:7	36
2:8–17	36, 155
2:8	36, 171
2:15–17	4, 9, 19, 61, 82, 83, 129
2:15	36, 42, 184
3:1	111
3:6	129, 189, 190
3:8	41
3:14	23, 129, 188
3:15	19
3:16	37, 172, 173
3:17	23, 37, 129, 172, 173, 188
3:23	37
3:24	187
4:1—11:26	20, 130
4:1–24	20
4:7	173
4:9	37, 188n22
4:10	38
4:11	23, 129
4:12	4, 35, 38, 40, 43, 185, 187
4:14	38
4:15	20
4:16	38
5: 1–32, esp. 29	23, 129, 188, 188n21
6:1–7	38, 129, 156
6:5	32, 38, 70, 94
6:8	119
6:11–13	20, 40, 112
6:14	20, 40, 112
6:22	38
7:5	38
7:11	80
7:17	38
8:4	20, 35, 38, 125, 159, 165, 184, 186, 188
8:9	20, 35, 38, 125, 159, 165, 184, 186, 188
8:20	170
9:8–17	61
9:25	23, 129
10:9–10	130
10:32	112
11:1–9	187
11:10–26	23, 112

Deuteronomy (cont.)

18:16	134
18:18	128
20:10–15	82
22:30	111
23:3–6	56, 108, 124
23:21–23	59, 89, 91
24:19–22	54, 121
25:5	111
25:7–19	41
25:19	28, 29, 40, 41, 85, 184, 190
26:5–9	15
27:20	111
28:1–14	54, 69
28:1–11	41, 174
28:15–68	69
28:37	102
28:38–42	108, 115
28:56	58, 104
28:61	69
28:64	58, 104
28:65	28, 38, 41–42, 43, 45, 158, 159, 165, 179, 184, 190
28:68	31, 159
30:10	69
31:7	41
31:16	69
31:23–29	41
34:4	23

Joshua

1	16, 156
1:1—5:21	74
1:5	121
1:7–8	11, 28, 54, 69, 75, 153
1:1–9	12, 79, 129, 133
1:10–15	79
1:13	30, 42, 69, 121, 184, 190
1:14	24
1:15	30, 42, 69, 121, 184, 190

1:16–18	51, 59, 74, 77, 79
1:18	75
2–6	73
2	57
2:8–11	57, 83, 121
2:13	59
2:17	59
2:20	59
3:1—4:24	12, 28
3:1	28
3:3	28
3:5	41
3:7–9	76
3:11	28, 42
3:13	28, 42
3:14	28
4:1–8a	76
4:3	29, 30, 42, 74
4:5–9	29, 30, 42, 74
4:12	24
4:15–17	76
4:18	41, 41
4:19–24	76n17
4:20	29, 30, 42, 74
4:21	29, 30, 42, 74
4:21–23	86
4:23–25	28
5:1	121
5:2–9	77
5:2	74, 76, 77
5:7	74, 76, 77
5:10–12	28
5:13—12:24	74
5:13	78
6	73, 82, 83
6:2–8	76, 79
6:3	29, 31
6:4	29, 31, 81
6:5	81
6:6	81
6:7	29, 31
6:8	74, 81
6:9	81
6:11	29, 31, 81
6:12–21	79
6:13	29, 81
6:14	29, 31
6:15	29, 31

Judges

Hebrew Index

www.ingramcontent.com/pod-product-compliance
Lightning Source LLC
Chambersburg PA
CBHW060334100426
42812CB00003B/989